W9-BYF-298

"Andy has put so much passion into his book that it is impossible to read before bed: the book incites a disturbing concoction of adrenaline and hormones that rages against that good night. Not only does Andy not go gently there, he refuses to go, period. This book is heartfelt and honest."

—Bernie Rath, former executive director,
American Booksellers Association

"Everything you always wanted to know about the book business but were afraid to ask. Even I, after 40 years writing, found this an eye-opener. Publishing, bookselling, 'should I open my own bookstore'—it's all in this entertaining, biting book."

—Eric Carle, author of *The Very Hungry Caterpillar*

"This is a phenomenal book. Laties has been in the trenches of bookselling and community organizing for the last 20 years. Herein you'll find part autobiography/memoir of the bookselling years (he's still doing it today), part history of the book industry, and part how-to guide to start, and succeed, in your own bookselling business

comp

Laties

nently

sell

strip

mac

the

REBEL
BOOKSELLER

WHY INDIE BUSINESSES REPRESENT EVERYTHING
YOU WANT TO FIGHT FOR—FROM FREE SPEECH TO
BUYING LOCAL TO BUILDING COMMUNITIES

REVISED AND UPDATED EDITION

ANDREW LATIES

Foreword by Edward Morrow
Afterword by Bill Ayers

7

SEVEN STORIES PRESS
New York

First Seven Stories Press edition, July 2011
Revised and updated edition

Originally published as *Rebel Bookseller: How to Improvise Your Own Indie Store and Beat Back the Chains* by Vox Pop, June 2005

Seven Stories Press
140 Watts Street
New York, NY 10013
www.sevenstories.com

College professors may order examination copies of Seven Stories Press titles for a free six-month trial period. To order, visit http://www.sevenstories.com/textbook or send a fax on school letterhead to (212) 226-1411.

Front Cover: Nolen Strals & Stewart Cauley
Interior Design: David Seager & Jon Gilbert

Library of Congress Cataloging-in-Publication Data
Laties, Andrew.
 Rebel bookseller : why indie bookstores represent everything you want to fight for from free speech to buying local to building communities / Andrew Laties ; foreword by Ed Morrow ; afterword by Bill Ayers. -- Rev. and updated ed., 1st Seven Stories Press ed.
    p. cm.
 ISBN 978-1-60980-139-7 (pbk.)
 1. Booksellers and bookselling--United States. 2. Independent bookstores--United States. 3. Laties, Andrew. I. Title.
 Z471.L38 2011
 381'.450020973--dc23

                              2011017038

Printed in the United States

9 8 7 6 5 4 3 2 1

For my mother, father, daughter, and son

Books are not absolutely dead things, but do contain a potency of life in them to be as active as that soul was whose progeny they are; nay, they do preserve as in a vial the purest efficacy and extraction of that living intellect that bred them. I know they are as lively, and as vigorously productive, as those fabulous dragon's teeth; and being sown up and down, may chance to spring up armed men.

—*Areopagitica*: A Speech by John Milton for the Liberty of Unlicensed Printing to the Parliament of England

Insane generosity is the generosity of rebellion, which unhesitatingly gives the strength of its love and without a moment's delay refuses injustice. Its merit lies in making no calculations, distributing everything it possesses to life and to living men. It is thus that it is prodigal in its gifts to men to come. Real generosity toward the future lies in giving all to the present.

—Albert Camus, *The Rebel: An Essay on Man in Revolt*

CONTENTS

REBEL BOOKSELLERS

by Edward Morrow

In these *interesting times*, *change* is widely recognized as a permanent condition, and new skill sets are required to successfully deal with the challenges perpetually altering conditions. In *Rebel Bookseller*, Andy Laties offers a perceptive and engaging historical tutorial on acquiring these essential skills.

The book's subtitle, *Why Indie Businesses Represent Everything You Want to Fight For—From Free Speech to Buying Local to Building Communities*, accurately describes its admirable leitmotif but sells short the book's full offering. While the context of his advice is set in the world of books, much of it has more universal applicability, certainly for other independent retailers but also for other endeavors—how to approach any job or task, dealing with the systemic problems of large organizations or ingrained industry practices, etc. Beyond its practical, informational attributes, *Rebel Bookseller* is good reading for anyone interested in the book and its future, or in how nimble, small businesses can swim with the sharks.

The bookselling community's infatuation with the creative mind and its warm collegiality—a spirit Andy captures so well—was so overwhelmingly apparent upon my first exposure to it at an American Booksellers Association four-day school in New York in 1974, that I immediately decided to become a bookseller. I first crossed paths with Andy when he and his partner, Chris, attended a class I was giving on financial management at an ABA school held in Boston. This was ten years after the bookstore my wife and I opened in Vermont had outgrown its original building and we had decided to bid on a large, vacant, more-than-one-hundred-year-old inn being auctioned off. As it happened, it was during that lecture that I received word we were the highest bidder and now owners of a twelve-thousand-square-foot building in need of repair and transformation.

So began the second of four evolutionary leaps in the Northshire Bookstore's incessantly evolutionary thirty-five-year existence. The need for continual innovation—never being able to rest on your laurels—and constant improvement is a thread that Andy adroitly weaves through his chapters. We recognized the persistent need for experimentation and adaptation upon opening in the late seventies, and Andy experienced it in the late eighties. The imperative to change only intensified and accelerated since. The rebel bookseller's descriptive anecdotes and engaging rants illustrate the need to respond to impermanence with more vividness than the Red Queen's classic complaint that "it takes all the running you can do to stay in the same place. If you want to get somewhere else, you must run at least twice as fast as that."

But Andy's passionate advocacy for sparking individual creativity, and the concrete examples he lays out, illustrate how to rig the mental block and tackle that makes it possible. Active and disciplined expression of *individuality* is a mainstay of this rigging. Nurturing and exposing one's uniqueness—showing one's personality—is a key to differentiation, to getting noticed. This point is made in a multiplicity of ways throughout the book, but one felicitous quote from British biologist P. B. Medawar does it masterfully in an appropriate coupling with the need for continuing evolution: "If . . . individuality were to be extinguished . . . then selection would have nothing to act on, and the species would be left without evolutionary resource."

The worldwide glut of insipid sameness—corporate stores replicated cookie-cutter fashion, clustered in Disneylike, retail golden ghettos—fosters a hunger for, and appreciation of, individuality, personality, idiosyncrasy, discovering the unique. *Rebel Bookseller* focuses on ways to take advantage of this phenomenon by exploring the parameters of three "Rough Rules of Rebel Bookselling." While it is important to acquire a solid understanding of established "conventional wisdom," with the financial ratios, operational benchmarks, and recognized "best practices," it is even more important to know when to go your own way, to get creative and follow your gut, applying the preeminent rule: *Adapt, Don't Adopt.* The practical application of this rule is illustrated through scores of examples drawn from Andy's own experiences and his exposure to booksellers worldwide.

This new edition is updated throughout where appropriate, but most importantly it encompasses the hot issues generated by the latest fire-breathing dragon in the neighborhood—Amazon.com—as well as a look at the significance of a current renaissance in entrepreneurial indie bookstore openings. I see these two developments as manifestations of the *high tech vs. high touch* dichotomy, having subscribed to the perception developed by John Naisbitt in 1982 upon publication of *Megatrends*. He fleshed out the concept in his 1999 book, *High Tech/High Touch: Technology and Our Search for*

Meaning. His premise is straightforward: "The two biggest markets in the United States are consumer technology and escape from consumer technology." . . . and our instinct is to both embrace it and escape from it. Books and the indies' approach to bookselling offer a desired high touch respite from the high tech world of dot-coms and e-books.

Amazon's revolution in the retail distribution of physical product is now sixteen years old. It started with books, added recorded music, and gradually every "sideline" under the sun. As Andy makes clear, booksellers have long understood the profit in non-book items. But, with a focus on their book-oriented mission, all non-book items, while appreciated for helping subsidize the mission, are thought of as merely "sidelines." Unfortunately, Amazon's founder, Jeff Bezos, focuses maniacally on market share over profits, which has caused havoc in bookselling. But even the titanic impact of this burgeoning new channel for retail book distribution has been dwarfed by Bezos's successful market development of e-reader/e-book technology (the e-book here defined as an electronic file of content formatted to simulate a book to be read on an electronic device using specialized software). The book as we have known it up through the twentieth century, the codex, as modified by print technology, is now often being referred to as the *p-book*; I will continue to call it a *book* and refer to the bits-and-bytes version as an *e-book*.

Over the last four years Amazon has driven the first mass wave of early-adopters to the high-tech leisure reading experience. The accelerating speed and scope of e-book acceptance is seen by the publisher/bookseller community with dread and awe as *the writing on the wall*, er . . . uh, screen? Some see an *e-pocalypse*. But the only consensus about its meaning is that e-books will capture some percentage of the book market. The guesses about how much and how fast cover the ballpark.

Andy Laties's assumptions about the unassailable core position of books within our culture is so ingrained that the Chimera of books themselves disappearing is not only not taken seriously in *Rebel Bookseller*, but the rebel, quite in character, sees it as a benefit, not a threat. I stand on the same outlook with Andy cautioning the reader against taking the *book vs. e-books* brouhaha too seriously.

On one extreme, doomsayers proclaim the end of the Gutenberg era. *The book is dead. Long live the*e-book*!* While industry observers have seen independent bookstores on the endangered list for a long time, the warnings are approaching crescendo. I maintain that these extrapolations discount the interplay of three critical factors, 1) the technology of the print codex (multiple signatures—folded sheets, stitched & bound—bound together under a cover), 2) the technology of e-books, and 3) human nature.

First, the book has many practical advantages: compactness, sturdiness, portability, random access ease of reference, economical, self-contained versatility of use . . . without a power source. This technology enabled vast transformations of much of the history of the past half millennium giving the book iconic status in all major cultures.

Beyond practical attributes, the book embodies designs conceived a thousand years before the printing press, developed over the centuries to encompass the arts and crafts of paper making, bindings, font design, cover art/design, content structure/format, page layout, and much more. The book became so powerfully ingrained in the cultural psyche that it branched into its own art form, recognized as a distinct genre. The term "book" has long been understood to cover a spectrum from *pulp* and *mass market*, through *commercial*, *best-seller*, *fine press*, *limited edition*, culminating with *artist's book* and *book art*.

But of greatest significance, the book is inextricably intertwined with its content. Even as content and its book-convention formatting become available digitally (without the book's other attributes), the book—the physical book—will continue to carry the powerful aura of the creative mind, intellectual content, ideas, knowledge, and mind expansion.

Second, the book-is-dead Jeremiahs have been seduced, perhaps understandably in the spotlight of the e-book's burgeoning market acceptance, by the incipient realization of its revolutionary promise. However, there is as yet little discussion of the barely visible counter-reaction to the growing prevalence of e-books.

E-books offer major improvements in access and portability, but they also have major drawbacks. For example, you can't use an e-book to prop open a door or to throw at someone. You can't display them in your library arranged with neighbors by themes or associations with special meaning. You can't even buy one, despite the nomenclature used to make you believe you are buying one. E-books can't be owned. You can pay for a license to access and read the digital content, but that's all. That license can be revoked, as Amazon proved when it electronically repossessed the copies of George Orwell's *1984* that their customers thought they had purchased. In the digital world, possession is no longer nine-tenths of the law—owning is not owning, and possession does not mean you have it. What you do have, however, is loss of privacy; when you read on a Kindle, a big brother is looking over your shoulder. Amazon keeps track of what you highlight and maybe more. They even report on the most highlighted passages in given books.

With time and use, transmissions, electrical surges, and mysterious bugs, data files get lost or corrupted—e-books have their own bookworms, mites, and silverfish. What happens when your e-book vendor goes out of business, or its data center burns down, or is sabotaged or hacked? What happens when you buy new hardware and for whatever reason—no app, poor design, a software glitch—you are unable to access your library of e-books? What happens when the not-yet-thought-of happens?

The blogosphere is rife with speculation about the nature and extent of eventual e-book substitution of the book, cataloging thousands of different reasons, and often passionate statements, about why the book is irreplaceable and will continue to thrive. For instance, an e-book purchase is being likened to a movie ticket—a one-time event. A book then is seen as comparable to a DVD, purchased because of a desire to own the work for repeated viewing and enjoyment, and eventual free choice of disposition.

It is what the book is, does, represents, and how it interacts with human nature that gives great comfort about its future. In short, it is *real.* You can hold it, as Garrison Keillor expressed it, "the spine lies easily in the hand." It offers access to intellectual content (as do e-books) and it accommodates marginalia, multiple bookmarking, dogearing. It will patiently sit on a shelf, projecting a comforting sense of permanence, looking pretty or dignified, awaiting perusal, or reference when needed. It can be shared, lent, or given. With its sisters and brothers, it makes statements about your interests, their breadth, how they've changed over time. They keep one company, they are mementoes of life periods, events, intellectual development, shared moments, epiphanies. They decorate your home. Many maintain inseverable umbilical connections to their owners.

The book is a cultural signifier that touches deep human feelings, often garnering almost mystical attachment. Books are so important and influential they are banned, censored, and burned, like witches at the stake. But they are organic objects, subject to damage and decay, and yet astonishingly durable. The book has become a ubiquitous object in daily life, as important a home accessory as a painting or table lamp. Books and book shelving show up in every interior designer's portfolio—one book genre is even named for its display location: the coffee table. The fact is, our notion of the book is deep seated and somewhat amorphous, to the point of being greater than the sum of its defining parts. Garrison Keillor expressed it as well as I've seen in his 1989 book *We Are Still Married: Stories & Letters*:

> Slow to hatch, as durable as a turtle, light and shapely as befits a descendant of the tree. Closed, the *objet d'book* resembles a board. Open, its pale wings brush the fingertips, the spore of fresh ink and pulp excites the nose, the spine lies easily in the hand. A handsome useful object begotten by the passion for truth. . . . Ages before the loudspeaker and the camera, came this lovely thing, this portable garden, which survives television, computers, censorship, lousy schools, and rotten authors.

The book's obituaries stem from a belief that the accelerating pace of e-book and e-reader sales will continue until nearly everyone is reading e-books and the book market becomes too small to support brick & mortar bookstores. But I believe the history of innovation teaches us otherwise. The scroll and the codex coexisted for centuries, as did manuscript and print books. Television didn't replace radio or the movies, they all coexist nicely. Movie theaters continue to thrive next to streaming Internet and DVDs. VCRs haven't done in TV. Velcro hasn't done in zippers, just as zippers didn't kill buttons. A host of "miracle" synthetic fabrics can't overcome the demand for wool and cotton. Examples such as these abound. I am persuaded that a healthy market for both will exist beyond any reasonable prediction period into the future, or for about as long as we continue to use wheels.

Rebel Bookseller champions the importance of the role of the independent bookseller in our society as Johnny Appleseed sowers of cultural, social, political, educational, and ideological diversity, even as they foster the shared emotional connection of healthy community life. Without minimizing the difficulties, this book paints a vivid picture of bookselling, and the quite natural, evolving process of bookseller community involvement, using Andy's and other booksellers' real world problem-solving examples. One comes away with a good understanding of the difference between a bookseller and a corporation that sells books. Andy relates how that difference helped independent bookselling achieve a huge comeback in the eighties. Interestingly, coupling the Introduction's discussion of the incipient renaissance in entrepreneurial indie bookstore openings with the current dire straits of a bookselling mega chain corporation opens up the prospects for a repeat performance by the indies.

The intimacy and personality of independent bookstores provides a high-touch environment complementing the rich experience of the book—an antidote to the relentless technological acceleration in our lives; a counterbalance to the local disconnect felt by the globally connected. *Rebel Book-*

seller brings this home and makes clear *Why Indie Businesses Represent Everything You Want to Fight For.*

Edward Morrow
cofounder, Northshire Bookstore

INTRODUCTION TO THE SECOND EDITION

The smell of sawdust greeted me as I entered Brooklyn's Greenlight Bookstore for the first time in October 2009. One month before opening, hundreds of boxes filled the store-front while a dozen volunteers were at work coloring the bookcases with warm brown woodstain. I'd come in from Western Massachusetts for this day prepping the store; my sixth time helping launch a bookselling company; thirty years since my first bookstore job.

I noticed a big pile of Random House boxes and remembered how in 1979, at age twenty, during my first month as a receiving clerk at a B. Dalton chain store in Chicago, I'd been checking in a box from just such a Random House stack when I came across two copies of Saul Alinsky's 1946 title *Reveille For Radicals.* I browsed the book, bought it, and read it that night. Alinsky was a Chicago labor activist who in the 1930s helped organize the meat-packing plants searingly depicted in Upton Sinclair's 1906 novel, *The Jungle.* Later Alinsky had moved on to community organizing, fighting for civil rights and social justice. I remembered Alinsky's eye-opening book decades after while struggling with the question of how to write about my turbulent life as a bookseller. I'd decided to try to create a book that I would have enjoyed reading back when I was twenty. *Rebel Bookseller: How to Improvise Your Own Indie Store and Beat Back the Chains* was the outcome of my effort to live up to *Reveille For Radicals.*

Rebel Bookseller, however, was not published by a big publishing company. This was impossible since I'd attacked major houses as "sycophantic lackeys" during the expansion of New York indie bookstore Barnes & Noble into a huge national corporation that for fifteen years held the whip hand in the book industry. Rather, *Rebel Bookseller* was put out by Vox Pop, a hybrid company just being launched by controversial publisher Sander Hicks, who had previously founded Soft Skull Press. In 2004 I'd helped Hicks create his new publishing house, bookstore, and performance café in Brooklyn.

In October 2005, a few months after Vox Pop had released *Rebel Bookseller*, during an author event at the New Atlantic Independent Booksellers Association (NAIBA) convention in Atlantic City, I'd addressed two hundred booksellers, encouraging them to assist in the needed resurgence of indie bookstore openings. Most of these booksellers had received free sample copies of *Rebel Bookseller*. I didn't know then that among those present was a twenty-six-year-old employee of Three Lives & Company, of Manhattan, who the previous day had launched a blog announcing that she hoped to eventually open her own bookstore. The blog was called *Written Nerd*, and the blogger was Jessica Stockton.

Exactly four years later, I was standing in Jessica Stockton's almost-open Greenlight Bookstore. And now I knew something I hadn't known when I'd first met Jessica: she hadn't had any money, nor access to any through her family. Her drive, her creativity, and her social skills had been her only assets. Perhaps one of the things that had led her, on her blog, to call *Rebel Bookseller* "awesome," "revolutionary," and "one of my own inspirations" was my assertion that you don't need any money to launch your indie bookstore: a rather unconventional opinion. But by the time Greenlight opened, Jessica's networking skills had led her to partner Rebecca Fitting—the Random House sales representative for the New York City region—and had resulted in the accumulation of nearly $350,000 in start-up funds.

How did a blogger conjure a bookstore? Jessica's approach was to alternate passionate book reviews with essays challenging doomsaying about the prospects for indie bookselling. The quality of her posts attracted an array of commenters (including me), and, by 2006, lively debates about the state of the book industry and the future of indie bookselling were in progress every week at her salon on the web.

On Jessica's blog, I made the point several times that the book industry goes through cycles, alternating between concentration and decentralization, and that these cycles are generated through the actions of individuals. Conditions are always ripe for committed booksellers to make an effort. The only question is whether indie storefront bookstores are a better thing for our culture than competing models such as chain stores or Internet-based distribution. For instance, in May 2006 I commented:

> A situation like back in say 1991 when there were 5,100 indie stores plus 2,000 chainstores is a lot healthier than the current 1,700 indie stores and (STILL only!) 2,000 chainstores. As to why people shop for books on the Internet: in a country that had thousands more storefronts selling books, there'd be many fewer people buying books on the Internet. We lost all those storefronts BEFORE the rise of online bookselling, and with the rise of a new generation of storefront indie booksellers, people will cut back on their Internet bookbuying and spend more time out hobnobbing with neighbors in all the swell new indie bookstores. It doesn't matter at all what the Indie Bookstore

Shopping Experience is like today. Tomorrow's will be a helluva lot better.

I also argued that indie bookstores are an engine for community economic development, and that this offers a fundraising opportunity to prospective bookstore owners. Here's a comment of mine from January 2007:

> What about creating some flavor of Real Estate Investment Trust? The intent is for this entity to buy a building in which to house a bookstore. Potentially, the trust would also plan to buy additional buildings. Because: we know, in advance, that any time a new bookstore is added to ANY neighborhood, real estate values all around that store will rise. . . . And friends, family, future neighbors, community activist types, other real estate investors can be pretty confident that they'll ultimately get their money back out of a real estate investment. So—now—in the context of establishing this REIT—you also do the fundraising to launch the bookstore itself. This entire process by the way gives you an excuse to do wonderful pre-marketing work for the store.

In late 2005, Jessica Stockton left Three Lives & Company and moved to Labyrinth Books (later renamed Book Culture), near Columbia University on the Upper West Side of Manhattan. She developed a specialty in the fast-growing field of graphic novels. Meanwhile, she cofounded the New York City branch of Emerging Leaders, an American Booksellers Association (ABA) initiative that encourages young people to stay committed to their bookselling careers. She was invited to be a graphic novel expert panelist during the ABA's educational program at the June 2006 Book Expo America convention in Washington DC. Then she was invited onto the NAIBA board, and in February 2007 she attended the second ABA Winter Institute, a new educationally oriented industry gathering designed to spark innovation in indie bookselling.

All of this was thoroughly reported in a genial and energetic voice, online. Because of Jessica's blog, her career had shifted into overdrive.

The existence of Labyrinth Books was excellent evidence that indie storefront bookselling success could come from developing an innovative collaborative model. The store had been founded because influential professors and the provost at Columbia University were frustrated with campus bookseller Barnes & Noble's failure to stock a sufficiently intellectual book inventory. The provost had reached out to Jack Cella, manager of Chicago's renowned Seminary Co-op Bookstore—often called the best academic bookstore in the country. Jack declined to open a branch in New York, but his engagement—bolstered by letters of support from the faculty—encouraged the university to facilitate the development of an independent bookselling company created by New York booksellers Chris Doeblin and Cliff Simms. The new bookstore, launched in 1997, benefited from preferential lease and incentive terms from landlord Columbia University.

Jessica worked at Labyrinth for a year then further broadened her bookselling education by moving on to McNally Robinson Booksellers (now McNally Jackson Books), in SoHo. There, in addition to supervising the graphic novel department, she became events coordinator.

Bookstore founder Sarah McNally had launched her company in 2004. New York is a city dominated by Barnes & Noble, and the location Sarah McNally chose—although as far from B&N as she could make it—was still fairly close to a large branch. She was closer to several indie stores, including St. Mark's Bookshop, founded 1977, which in 1989 had been saved from collapse by a loan from independent publisher and bookstore fan Robert Rodale.

The St. Mark's story might have given pause to another prospective bookstore owner assessing a neighborhood for its ability to support an additional indie bookstore. But the fate of specific bookstores is anecdotal, not cautionary; every bookstore has a unique trajectory. And in particular, St. Mark's Bookshop was able to repay the Rodale loan with interest. This happy ending offered an important insight. Just as Columbia University was needed to facilitate the creation of Labyrinth Books, and offered to do so when asked, so it was evident from the providential intervention of Robert Rodale that New York's huge population of book lovers would offer enough support to keep many indie bookstores afloat and viable, if only their owners specifically asked for this support and made careful decisions while accepting it.

Sarah McNally's way of asking for the support of New Yorkers was simply by creating a fabulously beautiful new bookstore, a skill she had learned growing up inside of the McNally bookselling family of Canada. With vigorous outreach via an aggressive special events program, McNally Jackson was welcomed as a marvelous addition to New York literary culture. Similarly, thousands of neighborhoods nationwide could energetically support new bookstores.

Jessica Stockton expanded the literary events series at McNally Jackson, and diligently documented her activity on the *Written Nerd* blog, further extending McNally Jackson's outreach. In turn, Sarah McNally was supportive of Jessica's plans to open her own bookstore. This courage to assist a future competitor is unheard of in many industries, but it is often seen in the bookstore business.

Similarly implementing this collaborative approach, Chris Doeblin of Book Culture reached out to Sarah McNally, to his former employee Jessica Stockton, to St.

Mark's Bookshop cofounder Terry McCoy and, with them, to dozens of other New York bookstore owners. Together, in early 2008, these booksellers founded New York's first city-wide bookstore coalition: Independent Booksellers of New York City (IBNYC). Again, the entire process was narrated on the *Written Nerd* blog.

I attended IBNYC's founding meeting, held on the twelfth floor of Random House corporate headquarters at Fifty-fifth Street and Broadway. Random House's support demonstrated the desire of this major publisher to assist the efforts of indie booksellers to increase their market share and sell more books. Twenty-five bookstore owners were present, and the group identified an array of joint projects, such as creating a bookstore-locator website.

We went around the table introducing ourselves. I said I represented Vox Pop, in Brooklyn, and was the author of *Rebel Bookseller*. It turned out that several of the booksellers had been carrying my book, and one, Peter Soter of Morningside Bookshop, said he always kept a copy on display behind him at the cash register.

I was delighted to meet New York's leading bookselling professionals. One puzzling thing about being a bookseller is the widespread misconception that we are not practicing a profession. But yes, bookselling is a profession, on a par with psychiatrist, librarian, university professor, lawyer, or investment banker (in fact it's a little of each). Unlike these recognized professions, however, in bookselling there is no path to certification; no form of accreditation. Booksellers are autonomous. We pursue opportunities as our capacities permit.

Our mission is to understand the authors and readers we hope to serve, and to bring them together. In so doing we must ensure that our work is financially viable, using either for-profit or nonprofit methodologies, and increasingly a combination of the two.

We stand for freedom of expression. Our sixteenth-century forebears were sometimes burned at the stake, and we may be targeted too, as were the members of Sedition, the Houston bookselling collective whose store was set on fire in 2007 for stocking pro-immigrant and radical literature.

The most brilliant bookstores—Politics & Prose Bookstore, in Washington DC; City Lights Books, in San Francisco; The Tattered Cover Book Store, in Denver—are beacons for the rest of us, encouraging our efforts to stand out in unique ways.

It can be frightening to be out there on our own, but we rarely regret the effort. Even when our bookstores close, we look back with pride.

A few months later at the next IBNYC meeting, ABA's new buy-local initiative, IndieBound, was on the table. IndieBound brought all types of locally owned companies together online to spread the word about how communities benefit when neighbors support independent businesses. Combining social media and e-commerce, the project represented ABA's most innovative Internet-based effort to support indie bookstores in collaborating with their small business colleagues. At the IBNYC meeting, we decided our initial IndieBound production would be a celebratory week of coordinated special events in November.

The buy-local movement is sometimes thought to be a modern-day progressive initiative but it is rooted in the 1920s, when populist Southerners were worried about the invasive cultural impact of chain stores. Their antichain movement's major achievement was the Robinson-Patman

Act of 1936. For decades afterward, federal antitrust regulations provided locally owned stores some protection from short-term monopolistic underpricing by national competitors.

Unfortunately, local stores were not necessarily loved by neighbors. The owners constituted small-town elites with economic power. Many perpetuated racial discrimination. Labor union members preferred the newly unionizing chain stores, with their apparently better-value products.

By the 1960s, the federal government was increasingly focused on protecting the rights of workers, consumers, and minorities, and began to cut back on enforcement of Robinson-Patman rules that protected local stores from national chains.

In our era, federal government control over the local enforcement of human rights laws is more securely established. Meanwhile, labor unions are disenchanted with chain stores like the nonunionized Walmart. Since the 1990s, indie bookstores like Women & Children First, in Chicago's Andersonville neighborhood, have been spearheading the movement to organize small businesses in jointly urging their mutual customers to buy local. Today's buy-local movement cites analyses like *The Andersonville Study of Retail Economics* to prove that when customers spend in locally owned stores, much of the money recirculates in the community, bolstering quality of life. In contrast, most money spent in chains or on the Internet leaves hometowns. Online purchases in particular are usually not subject to sales tax, so states are starved of funds for education, public services, and Medicaid most times someone chooses to buy online. After decades of infatuation with big-box chain stores, community leaders have finally learned that durable economic revitalization hinges on the launch of new businesses owned by local residents. Wall Street investors have tired of paying premium prices for book superstore company shares (Barnes & Noble and Borders having failed to deliver on their 1990s-era promise of unending growth), so national chains have lost access to once seemingly unlimited capital to plunk lavish store build-outs into saturated local markets. The tide has turned in favor of prudently managed, locally owned stores, which are quite cost-effective to launch relative to the benefit to their host communities.

Jessica Stockton Bagnulo (she'd gotten married) wrote a business plan and entered it into a prestigious competition sponsored by the Brooklyn Public Library and Citi Foundation. She won the $15,000 first prize, and shortly after, entered into her quiet collaboration with Random House sales representative Rebecca Fitting.

Since childhood Rebecca had dreamed of having her own bookstore. At age eighteen she joined an Albany, New York, branch of Borders Books & Music, then helped launch Borders stores in Peabody, Massachusetts, and Memphis, Tennessee. She managed an indie store, The Deliberate Literate, for two years before being hired by Random House, spending ten years in publishing working the upstate New York and New England region, then the metro New York territory.

During the months after they established their working relationship, Jessica and Rebecca failed to further advance their project. They knew hundreds of thousands of dollars in start-up funds should be in place prior to launch. Jessica's blog posts documented increasing frustration. I commented that her asset was her social capital and that she needed to find a way to cash it in.

Serendipitously, this was happening on its own. A Brooklyn neighborhood organization had found, through stakeholder analysis, that community members identified *bookstore* as the missing element in their local revitalization efforts. The Fort Greene Association had failed to attract the interest of any existing New York bookstore in opening a branch. Now they learned that a bookstore business plan was the recent winner of the Brooklyn Public Library PowerUp! Competition.

They contacted Jessica Stockton Bagnulo and Rebecca Fitting. In a whirlwind of private and public meetings, parties, negotiating sessions, and fundraising events, a bookstore suddenly became feasible.

A local real estate investor offered below-market rent on a hot Fulton Street location a few blocks west of the Brooklyn Academy of Music. Hundreds of thousands of dollars were gathered through friends-and-family promissory note sales to neighbors, and from the World Trade Center Small Business Recovery Fund. Jessica and Rebecca were thrust headlong into doing what they had promised to do: open a storefront indie bookstore.

My day of bookcase staining in October 2009 was the least of the start-up work, but like the hundreds of other people involved in making Greenlight Bookstore a reality, I feel a proprietary pride and obligation. When I receive Greenlight's e-mailed reminders of author readings, panel discussions, cooking demos, comedy nights, concerts, and children's story hours, I feel joy in this upsurge of activist bookselling. When I'm in Brooklyn and I stop by the store, there are usually dozens of browsers. I always discover great books that I absolutely must buy.

In June 2010, *New York* magazine published an article that announced the surprising resurgence of indie bookselling in New York City. Several of IBNYC's newer members were profiled, among them Idlewild in Union Square, WORD in Greenpoint, and Greenlight Bookstore in Fort Greene. Financial data provided by Jessica and Rebecca were eye-popping; the store was tracking close to a million dollars of revenue in its first year in business, meeting its financial targets and obligations, including debt repayment.

The marketplace changes every day, and the early success of Greenlight Bookstore does not provide a roadmap. Rather it demonstrates that an innovative approach can work even when naysayers abound.

As I write this introduction, the hot question of the day is what impact electronic books will have on physical books and storefront bookstores. As with any market transformation, the e-book revolution provides myriad business opportunities for creative people. Far from imperiling the indie storefront bookstore paradigm, this particular change can strengthen it, since more than ever an excursion to a bookstore is driven by a reader's wish to spend time in the presence of physical books and in the company of other readers, not by the need to scan the content of a specific book. And when it comes to creating exciting spaces where community members can gather, indie booksellers are approaching high-end restaurateurs in skill. So indie booksellers should welcome the arrival of plentiful e-books. We can expect to see renewed interest in book reading among the public. Physical books will find more buyers because the pleasure of owning, reading, and sharing these is different from the experience of perusing a restricted-access electronic display on a screen. These media do not compete: they supplement one another. Readers can even support local bookstores by purchasing e-books from ABA IndieCommerce-affiliated websites like Greenlightbookstore.com.

□   □   □

In this book's eleven chapters, I weave tales of the birth, death, and reincarnation of several personal businesses into a behind-the-scenes history of the late twentieth- and early twenty-first-century book industry. I've selected stories that obliquely illustrate strategies explained in the ten interlacing *rants,* which are specifically devoted to the subject of how to improvise an independent store. I allow this whole narrative process to expose and clarify three Rough Rules of Rebel Bookselling: 1) ADA (Adapt, Don't Adopt); 2) SMOWS (Sell More of What's Selling); and 3) BLSH (Buy Low, Sell High). I didn't invent these rules, but I appreciate them, and there aren't many rules I appreciate.

If you'd appreciate *lots* of rules, I apologize. With the exception of the "Showcasing Your Store" articles in the appendix—which were distributed by the American Booksellers Association at dozens of Booksellers Schools—I've steered clear of prescriptions for success. My hope is to provoke originality. Personally, I find that books filled with checklists generally fail to help me determine how best to solve the problem of simply surviving. Checklists can imply that running a business is a matter of building a better mousetrap. But in a marketplace dominated by corporations flush with cash, the real issue may be deciding what to do when ten other mousetraps encircle yours.

I've run a lot of mazes, and been eaten by several fat cats: I'm qualified to offer not checklists but legends, allegories,

fables, parables, ritual incantations, tales from the crypt—
the whole suffused with paranoia, mania, and ingenious
financial advice.

For this second edition I've revised and expanded *Rebel
Bookseller* to reflect industry changes since 2005. Chain-
store companies have, as I defiantly predicted, proven
vulnerable: one thousand of their storefronts have closed,
leaving many towns without a bookstore. Therefore this edition calls out beyond prospective booksellers to all indie
business owners, as well as to community groups, real estate
developers, nonprofit organizations, universities, and urban
planners. A revival of locally controlled indie bookselling
is essential for fostering the creative, locally autonomous
citizenry this nation requires. We all have a role. Now is the
time for action.

And if you are a working bookseller, or one of those laid
off during the recent chainstore closings, please be assured
that a life in indie store ownership is worth striving for.

MEET THE AUTHOR

JUNE 1989

I'm late. Careful not to bump any of the other dealers' packed displays, I maneuver the bookstore van through to my own eight bare tables. Since 5:00 AM I've been piling thirty large boxes full of publishers' overstock and store markdowns. This first bookfair of the summer season is at Printers Row, a street of red brick printing plants renovated to galleries, restaurants, and bookshops. The scene of bustling booksellers arranging their volumes on hundreds of tables is deeply familiar.

When I was growing up, my dad and I ritually hit the garage-sale book hunters' circuit in the spring, the huge charity book sales in the fall, and all the bookstores we could find while traveling on summer holiday. I loved the hunt for the impossible book and always had a list of the ones I needed: Mervyn Peake's *Titus Alone,* Kurt Schwitters's *Ursonate,* Stanislaw Lem's *Memoirs Found in a Bathtub.* They were an excuse for spending hours searching the endlessly suggestive bookshelves hoping for something as good. Discovering a book on the list was usually a thrill tempered with disappointment: the find was rarely as rich as its prospect. Dad would say, "Why don't you open a bookstore?" I'd answer, "I don't want to open a bookstore."

As I unload the boxes, Jennifer, Donna, and Kate arrive to work the booth. We sort the titles by baby book and picture book, middle reader and nonfiction, and when the table display is well under way, I ease the van out from the fair clutter into a lot.

When I'm back, Erminio Pinqué and his life-sized Big Nazo Puppets have arrived. They've come 1,500 miles for the fair, straight from a street performers' festival in Maine. Mild-mannered Pinqué is the secret identity of Quasimodo, a nine-foot-tall, charmingly belligerent hunchback with yard-long face and bulbous nose. He travels with Hog, a grotesque, child-chomping mouth. They and two other monsters will infiltrate the browsing crowd, improvising scenes of deranged proof readers and offended authors, penny-pinching publishers and bombastic booksellers. I go with them to change into my own costume.

Soon I'm dressed all in green, dancing through the thousands of book buyers, playing the garden hose like a jazz trombone: laying down a walking bassline and punctuating with riffs of melody. I buttonhole six-year-old hot dog munchers and their frazzled parents, insisting they join the Marvelous Monster Story Hour beginning in five minutes. When I've got a parade of kids in tow, we jostle through the crowd to the church opposite our bookstall.

In the spacious blue-carpeted assembly room, the puppets and I read monster books, finishing with *Jabberwocky*. The new Graeme Base version has lots of extra pictures, leaving plenty of time for the kids to sop up the words. As a child, home from school sick, I'd listen to Cyril Ritchard's 16-record reading of *Alice in Wonderland* and *Through the Looking Glass*, curled up on the kitchen couch among pillows and blankets. Following along in Martin Gardner's *Annotated Alice*, I'd sort through the notes in the margins, steeping in the familiar language.

After the story hour, we act portmanteau words. All mimsy, we gyre and gimble in the wabe—way before, way behind, way beyond.

While detective author Mary Monsell runs a kids' writing workshop, I thread through the crowd announcing Shanta the Storyteller and nearly knock over our family pediatrician. He seems startled to see me in green playing the hose but asks, "How's Chris, how are the kids?" I'd met Dr. Weissbluth several years before when he'd stopped by the store and asked for a copy of *Crybabies: Coping with Colic.* I'd led him to a far corner and pulled one out. He was pleased: he'd written it. His second book, *Healthy Sleep Habits, Happy Child,* sold briskly since he sent his whole practice to the store for it. The book saved our sanity during our son Sam's first year, when he refused to sleep. Sam learned early to brandish Eric Carle's *The Very Hungry Caterpillar* or Ralph Steadman's *That's My Dad* as a defense against bed, knowing we couldn't resist reading to him.

I'm back at the bookstall, helping kids who've just signed up for library cards choose their free books, when I'm interrupted by a studious-looking teenager in wire rims and his dark-haired young mom. They're anxious. "Is Daniel Pinkwater really coming?" the young man asks.

"In an hour. Do you like his stuff?"

"I started writing him when I was nine—he always wrote back, nice letters. I haven't written for a long time."

I recognize myself in him. "He'll remember you."

I grew up too early for Pinkwater but devoured the strange visions of Gogol, Kafka, Nabokov, and Lem. Still, Pinkwater's been on my mind for a few years. First people were asking for his books in hushed voices: *Snarkout Boys and the Avocado of Death; Yobgorgle, Monster of Lake*

Ontario; Fat Men from Space. You couldn't get his work: he was an underground children's author with an adult following. Then came the *Village Voice* article, the National Public Radio commentaries, and suddenly his books were back in print with new ones coming out.

One afternoon when I was browsing at Act One Books, Emily the owner told me her roommate had written Pinkwater a crazy fan letter and he'd phoned at 2:00 AM. He'd grown up in Chicago and was thinking of visiting, but he lived out East and needed an excuse. Could she line up a reading?

I wrote him; we talked by phone; I offered trainfare; he got overbooked. A year passed. Finally I had money: a grant of $3,500 from Chicago Board of Trade for the Printers Row Bookfair Young Readers' Program—part earmarked for an author. I called again. He said Lynda Barry the cartoonist had a show playing at the Live Bait Café. She'd invited him to see it. He'd love to come.

I'm working the crowd, trumpeting the imminent arrival of Daniel Pinkwater, when there he is at our booth, not as tall as I'd expected but as energetically round, in red beret, hieroglyphic-spattered yellow shirt, and tiny John Lennon sunglasses. He looks happy to be surrounded by books but says he shouldn't have come. He's nervous the girl his mom tried to match him with in high school will show. Spiky-red-haired Lynda Barry surprises him from behind, and he's all smiles.

There's a healthy crowd: 150 people. In the church he reads from unpublished work in that quizzical, humorous voice, then emerges to sign books at our booth. He seems to know his fans, and takes time with them—drawing pictures in his books, writing personal notes. When the teen with wire rims reaches the front, there's a spark: they talk like old friends.

Booksellers are catalysts. I regret I'll never meet one of my own early idols—they're voices confined to books and minds. In any case what would I say?

I realize Stanislaw Lem is alive; I should write.

The cable access TV crew's set up. As the crowd drifts away, I grab Quasimodo and Hog, and we head into church to tape *Book Break*. This is the moment I've fantasized: Pinkwater meets Pinqué. Quasimodo could be a character from a Pinkwater book, but now monster is master of ceremonies. When Pinkwater insults Quasimodo—inquiring how long he's been a strange freak—Quasi retaliates, borrowing Pinkwater's red beret and blowing his nose in it noisily. Later when Pinkwater attacks his host's talk-show skills, Quasi cuts things short with "Sic-em, boy!" and Hog the monstrous mouth lurches on camera, devouring Pinkwater whole. Afterward Pinqué emerges from costume, and Pinkwater declares him a genius.

There's a late rush of business, then things wind down. I stroll to the next stall, where two retirees from Minnesota are selling used children's books. Chris hired me into my first bookstore job in '79. Sometimes when we meet an elderly husband-wife team we sense we're meeting ourselves.

Browsing their eclectic collection, I stumble on a beat-up first edition of Ingri and Edgar Parin D'Aulaires' *Leif the Lucky*, a biography of America's Viking discoverer. At seven I read the book over and over during a summer haunting the library. I haven't seen it since: the jacket illustration of a boy with wild hair and fiercely confident expression reminds me of Sam. I buy it for him. I recall it as an optimistic tale of accidental adventure—kind of how Chris and

I felt during our time backpacking the world. In Tokyo, Calcutta, or Katmandu, whenever we were frustrated or disoriented, we knew if we could find a bookstore we'd be okay.

It's getting dark. Packing up, there are eight empty boxes: we've sold lots of books. Tomorrow's Father's Day, the bookman's holiday. Word going round is fair weather. I remind myself to call Dad.

Jennifer's husband and son pick her up. As I'm reviewing the day's shape with Donna and Kate—pulling the van from among the tables—Pinqué stops me, Quasi in bag, wanting to make sure he'll get the Pinkwater tape. I give him my word.

And resolve to write Lem.

DEATH ENERGY

S o you're thinking of opening a bookstore.
Are you crazy?

Back when Chris and I were running The Children's Bookstore, someone would come in every month asking for advice on opening their own. But now the membership in the American Booksellers Association has dropped by two-thirds. It's so obvious to everyone that you can't open a bookstore anymore that no one even bothers to ask how.

Who wants to compete with these huge superstores, with their big inventories, long hours, and in-store coffee shops? Not to mention the Internet, which of course makes every book in print easily available to anyone. Nope, you've got to be insane to open a bookstore.

Well, it's true that we've now been booksellers for over three decades, operating several different stores. And, it's true there are still about two thousand independent bookstores in the US that never closed down but weathered the storm. I'd be irresponsible not to be honest with you though. Now, or ten years ago, or fifty years ago, or fifty years from now, you should never open a bookstore. Nobody who ever opened a bookstore should have done it. Right now, Reason X is the reason why a bookstore won't work. Next time, it'll be Reason Y. So, do yourself a big favor: tell your friends, next time they urge you on, it's easier to lose money than to make it. Forget about this bookstore thing. Put it out of your mind.

Lots of quaint little neighborhoods have nice shops, and if you pay attention to who's in those storefronts over a five- or ten-year period, you notice new stores are going in and old stores are going out every few years. Each time a store disappears, that's someone's $50K or $150K down the tubes. Most of the time.

I don't know if it qualifies as a tragedy or not. So many people delude themselves as to what running a small business is about. In '86 we hosted a party at The Children's Bookstore for people who were attending a Prospective Booksellers School put on by the American Booksellers Association. I had a conversation with a psychologist who had no bookselling experience. She said she was preparing to open a chain of six psychology bookstores in Washington DC, as a sideline to her full-time psychology practice. That sort of idea was typical in the late eighties. People thought of bookstores as something they could do in their spare time. Independent bookselling was invincible: hundreds of new indies were opening every year. The corporate superstore chains blind-sided everyone, using discount pricing to lure hapless customers away from the local stores they treasured. Once we were gone, goodbye to across-the-board discounts. But most of those independent bookstores would have gone out of business anyway—just not so fast and not all at once. They were losing a little money, and they started losing a lot.

The question is, where do you stand at the moment when *you* go out of business? Are you in control? Did you pull money out during the life of the company and park it elsewhere? Has that money grown?

For instance, it's a rarely mentioned truth of the book-store business that the only way to make money is to buy your building. While your operation may be just scraping by, you earn yourself a building with all those occupancy payments. Or, a tactic we managed to pull off may be the way you make money: packaging and leveraging your store's image to do a completely different project. This was how we ended up owning the store at Chicago Children's Museum. That site guaranteed a lot of traffic for our shop, located as it was in a tourist mall without retail footprints that could accommodate a superstore to compete with us.

The point is, you can focus on the fact your independent bookstore is doomed and then let this reality prevent you from launching the thing. Or you can focus on your doom and use this foreknowledge to help you plan for finessing your business's reincarnation.

That's what Buddhists call death energy. Every moment, you think about your possibly imminent death. This gives you the courage to take chances. After all, what's the point in fear or delay? You might not live ten more seconds.

CHAPTER ONE

BREAKING THE ICE

SEPTEMBER 1979

The fall after I dropped out of college to become a jazz musician, Chris Bluhm hired me for a bookstore day job as a receiving clerk. She'd spent eleven years working in bookstores and libraries in Michigan, Minnesota, Wisconsin, and Illinois while going to college and graduate school in art history and library science. At twenty-eight, she was managing the spanking new, high-profile B. Dalton Bookseller across from the fancy Water Tower shopping complex on Chicago's Magnificent Mile. The day before I showed up, she'd had to fire her previous receiving clerk because another employee had discovered a box of books addressed by the receiver to his own apartment: the box was sitting out ready to be picked up by UPS.

A few days after Chris hired me, she took off for a one-week impulsive trip to Israel with her friend Dorit from Minneapolis. When I asked her, on her return, about this sudden departure, she said she was always thinking about her next trip. Which, now, would be next year, to Indonesia: the East Indies. I wasn't clear where Indonesia was.

Our B. Dalton held a couple of author signings that year. In running these now-commonplace programs, this chain bookstore was unusual in '79. Our owner, Dayton-Hudson Corporation, only arranged them to compete with Stuart Brent's decades-old independent bookstore down the block.

Stuart was well known for promoting Chicago authors, and he hated the new B. Dalton, which we who worked there thought was unfair because we were all book lovers. He told his customers not to shop at our store, but Chris was secretly friends with Stuart's store manager, and Stuart knew Chris only as a pleasant customer. Once when I had a conversation with Stuart about my college major—archaeology—he offered me a job. I didn't exactly tell him I was working for B. Dalton.

Our store had photographer Ansel Adams a few weeks after I arrived, and a few months later, after Chris and I had secretly started our scandalous romance and decided I'd join her on her trip to Indonesia, Harrison Salisbury, the legendary *New York Times* reporter, came through to autograph his title *Travels Around America*. Chris told Salisbury we were going to Indonesia. Salisbury was tall, silver-haired, very distinguished looking, but he had a feverish glint in his eye. He said if we were going to Southeast Asia we had to go to Burma. In particular, Pagan. Miles and miles of abandoned Buddhist temples. Our future travels began to blossom outward. Why go only to Indonesia?

We ended up traveling and working overseas for two years before returning to Chicago. In Konarak, India, during a week of wandering conversation, we'd decided to open a bookstore. We figured if we could travel together, we could do anything.

THOUSANDS OF BOSSES

Are you still alive? That's nice.

Let's face it, there's no point in opening a bookstore unless you've completely thought through a strategy for succeeding, lasting a good long time, and getting out on your own terms. This plan will be in tatters inside of a year, but at least you will have gotten moving.

The thing that always drove us nuts back in the days when lots of people were asking us to help them was when prospective booksellers had already signed a lease on a space that had opened up convenient to their lives. They thought to ask us—the established independent booksellers—for advice only after they'd made this huge commitment. Everyone knows the old *location, location, location* mantra, right? Often called the most important element in retail success? And yet, lots of people choose their new store's location on the basis of convenience for their current lives. They must not really want to own their own bookstore, because with that kind of forethought they're not going to own it for long.

So how would you survive and thrive if you were going to open a bookstore, which fortunately you're too smart to do?

By figuring out what someone needs and isn't getting.

It's unfortunate that what you want to do may have nothing to do with what your potential customers might realize they would want you to be doing, if you were already doing it.

People get on a power trip when they start thinking about opening their own store. All that stuff about *be your own boss*. But the truth is, you trade one boss for thousands of bosses. The customers are in charge of your life. And if they're not in charge, you don't have a business. So the first thing to get out of your mind is that you're opening a bookstore. Rather, you're trying to figure out if there's some gap in some real market that corresponds to the territory of *bookstore* in the minds of your potential customers.

If you can't detect the right market, and the right gap, you'd better not open the store.

How do you find that magical gap in the market? It's hard. Everyone already in the book business is constantly discussing gaps in markets. All conversations land there. What chance do you have of finding one if experienced people are searching for exactly this thing?

Well, whatever you have done, whoever you have known, wherever you've lived or traveled, every network you've belonged to, every expertise you've acquired: you'll have to tap them all. Bring every scrap of knowledge to bear. Ask everyone's opinion. Read voraciously. Your special life story contains clues to business opportunities no one else has access to.

Ralph Waldo Emerson says, "Nature arms each man with some faculty which enables him to do easily some feat impossible to any other, and thus makes him necessary to society."

This is why big companies are constantly stealing ideas from innovative independents. Gigantic bureaucracies can't create; they can only manage. Creativity emerges from personal emotion.

You've decided you want to open a bookstore for your own reasons. But everyone has already got places they're buying their books. Clearly there's no reason you can pull them away from those perfectly satisfactory sources and get them to give their book-buying business to you. The solution to this puzzle is in the junction of your individuality with that of your customers. You must feel something is missing from your life. Do your potential customers also feel something is missing from theirs?

Perhaps you've come to a realization they haven't yet arrived at. We live in a culture that makes noise about how every individual is great and terrific and unique, and how every child can grow up to be president. But simultaneously we're checking and being checked to make sure we fit in and are perfectly normal. There's a disconnect here, an outright lie disturbing to everyone. How can a person be both unique and normal?

Mass media stokes our desires, but no one has enough money to buy all the stuff they find themselves wanting. Everyone's discontented and restless.

In thinking about opening your own bookstore, you're trying to address these issues. First, you want to change your own life, to stake out some personal territory where you can help transform the world and make it more human and less plastic. Second, you want to create a little universe where other members of the human family can sense an opening for their own imaginative natures.

Books are an elegantly collaborative bodying forth of

art and wisdom. Surviving improbably into our electronic era, this fifteenth-century technology hasn't been surpassed.

Bookstores are personal, quirky assemblages of the rich artifacts called books. Bookstores inspire the creation of analogous, personal libraries for individuals to use to enrich their lives and relationships and futures.

So, from a practical perspective, what's flawed with book acquisition processes now available to your potential customers?

How can you, in a way impossible for anyone else to accomplish, open up new avenues of personal development to these people?

CHAPTER TWO

OPENING MINDS

Chris felt she needed to learn as much as possible about operating an independent bookstore before we tried one, so she worked in lots of different stores. At one point she worked in three simultaneously: Seminary Co-op, near the University of Chicago; Rizzoli, in the Water Tower; and Guild Books, in Lincoln Park. We landed on the idea of a Third World travel and anthropology bookstore, to be modeled on Asiateque and Harmattan, two Parisian bookstores we'd loved.

I told my parents we were planning to open a bookstore when I was home for Thanksgiving. My uncle was there too; he'd been in business for years, selling banknotes and coins from around the world. He estimated opening a small bookstore would cost us $50K. When I was born, my grandfather had set up a $10K trust fund for me, and this had grown to $125K in the stock market under my dad's careful stewardship. My mom said Grandpa Simon had thought one way I might be able to use my trust fund would be to start a business. While my parents were uneasy with me opening a bookstore, they were hopeful it could prove a reasonable life direction.

After several months of location hunting, Chris and I signed a three-year lease on a small Clark Street space. We put down five months' rent and security deposit up front. Shortly afterward, in the spring of '84, while I was working as an actor with Child's Play Touring Theatre and living in a hotel in Edwardsville during one of our Illinois Arts Council Rural Tours, Chris called with the news she'd shown our great new six-hundred-square-foot location to a successful bookseller: Howard Cohen, the owner of Booksellers Row. Howard had told Chris the location was a terrible mistake because since our space was down a hallway no one would see the store was there. He said we *had* to pull out of the lease and, ideally, wait for a location to come on the market near his own store on Lincoln Avenue, the best street in town for bookselling.

I was irritated. Our deposit was nonrefundable. I couldn't understand why Chris had shown Howard the space. I figured he wanted us on Lincoln so we'd strengthen the street he'd invested in himself. Chris and I had shopped all over town and hadn't found anything better than that Clark Street space in the price range we'd set for ourselves. We'd known we'd be running a destination business. Sure, the space might be invisible, but Clark Street was a major retail neighborhood. Our clients would find us. But Chris and I agreed we'd get together with Howard once I got back to town.

As it turned out, Howard was stunningly sure of himself and alarmingly negative. He was adamant we should walk away from the deposit. I barely knew this guy. We did what he said. What was the point of moving back to Chicago to tap Chris's contacts if we didn't pay attention when the most successful gave us vigorous advice?

Howard put us in touch with his own landlord, Larry Edwards, who owned several buildings on Lincoln, including the legendary Biograph Theater, where thirties gangster John Dillinger had been betrayed to the FBI by the Lady in Red.

We ended up waiting a full year for another tenant to leave one of Larry's storefronts so we could move in.

This gave us time to rethink our plans. We gradually came to the conclusion there weren't enough Third World travel bookstore customers in Chicago to justify taking this larger space on a hot entertainment street. Maybe in New York, San Francisco, or Paris, but not Chicago in '84. We found ourselves back at the drawing board, toying a bit desperately with other specialty concepts. We thought of doing a cooking and travel combination bookstore. We'd heard there was one in San Francisco. We thought of doing an arts, cooking, and travel bookstore.

A friend who'd also worked for Chris at Dalton now owned her own store: Booknook Parnassus. Connie Reuveni told Chris she'd been talking with her aunt about us. Her aunt had had a conversation with the wife of the owner of a foreign language bookstore in Evanston: Europa Books. The wife of the Europa owner was thinking about opening a children's-only bookstore in Evanston that would be similar to a children's bookstore in Glencoe called Children's Reading Corner, owned by a former schoolteacher named Sylvia Rosten.

Connie's aunt suggested that Connie advise Chris we should open a children's bookstore in Chicago like Sylvia Rosten's.

Neither Chris nor I had ever heard of a children's bookstore. We thought the children's niche wasn't strong enough to succeed on its own. How could anyone sell enough *children's books* to make a whole store run on just that category? But since I'd been working in children's theater, I *had* planned to use some of our new bookstore's space to run children's performances as a sideline. So it made sense we should sell children's books as part of our mix. We settled on a travel and children's bookstore.

In June, Chris attended the American Booksellers Association's three-day school in Boston. I wasn't able to go along for the whole program, as I was working a six-week tour with Child's Play in the Catskills, but I sat in for the final day on financial planning, and then that summer practically memorized the ABACUS Financial Profile, a comprehensive analysis of the financial structures and profitability of hundreds of bookstores coast to coast.

For instance, I learned that, with our twelve-hundred-square-foot store, we should shoot for between $250 and $350 in sales per square foot per year, equaling between $300K and $420K gross sales per year.

Then I learned that in order to obtain our target sales level of $400K per year we'd need an average annual on-hand inventory of about one-third that total: $133K, priced at retail. The wholesale cost of this average annual $133K in inventory would be about 60 percent of its retail value, so, $80K. I also learned that these annual averages concealed the seasonal nature of the book business, in which a third of sales take place during November and December. Thus, in truth, an inventory at wholesale cost of as much as $110K might be required in December, versus an inventory at wholesale of as little as $60K for much of the rest of the year.

I learned that average staffing expense, not including the working owners, for our target $400K-per-year store was 15 percent of the gross, or $60K. That meant perhaps two full-timers and two part-timers.

Average advertising and marketing expense should be about 2 percent of the gross: $8K per year.

Although at the time I didn't understand the reasons for the averages, choke points, benchmarks, and trends revealed in ABACUS, I memorized them anyway and relied on them for years. Financial management was our weak point, as neither of us had a business education. The data were invaluable.

A Dalton colleague of Chris's from her Milwaukee days had gone on to manage one of the Harry W. Schwartz bookstores, later marrying Harry's son David. In August of '84, Chris called Carol to see about us coming up to get advice from David Schwartz about our bookstore plans.

David grilled us portabello mushrooms for dinner. Then he told us, with as much energy as Howard Cohen had displayed on the subject of our location, that we could not open a travel and children's bookstore because the two category clienteles were too different from one another. We should open a children's-only bookstore.

This was hard to accept. We'd spent two years living outside the country. We'd seen the US through the world's eyes and had developed our own ideas about what was good and what needed changing. We'd been in dozens of countries, and we had lots of ideas for would-be voyagers, especially young ones like ourselves.

But David was talking from a strong knowledge base; bookselling had been his life. He was treasurer of the American Booksellers Association. He'd recently helped lead a young bookseller revolt, re-energizing the trade group after a period when it had stood by helplessly as chain stores swamped hundreds of independents.

David was especially passionate on the dry subject of shipping costs. Publishers frequently shipped books in small quantities to booksellers, and the mailing expense was tacked onto the bill. A book with a retail price of $10 often arrived in a little envelope with a bill from the publisher that listed $6 as the wholesale cost of the book plus a $4 charge for shipping. It cost the bookseller $10 to get the book, and then he had to sell it for $10! How could you survive and make money if your books were costing you the same as your selling price? Yet no amount of arguing with publishers had been able to eliminate this imbecilic practice despite eighty-five years of organized booksellers complaining to publishers.

After a fun evening talking the ins and outs of the arcane but fascinating vagaries of bookselling, we decided again to take our expert's advice.

Unfortunately we knew practically zilch about children's literature. Working with Child's Play Touring Theatre performing thousands of stories written by children themselves hadn't taught me anything about children's books. Working in a dozen general bookstores had taught Chris a lot, but not enough to competently fill a complete children's bookstore. She started doing research and discovered there was a special library at the University of Chicago associated with their doctoral program in library science, called the Center for Children's Books. This place was operated by someone named Zena Sutherland.

One windy day in October of '84, Chris and I went down to the University of Chicago library and buzzed the intercom of the Center for Children's Books. We hadn't made an appointment.

Someone answered the intercom. We went up the elevator. A short, fierce-looking sixty-something woman with blond-white hair admitted us to the center. She asked why we'd come. We explained we were preparing to open a children's bookstore and hoped to browse this library for ideas about what books to sell.

Zena Sutherland scrutinized us. She began asking questions. I felt like I was back in third grade, but Chris was sturdier. Once Zena had determined that we knew very little about the field of children's literature, she said, "Come into my office."

Seated behind her desk, she announced, "The first thing you should do is read my book."

I asked, "What book?"

Her eyes widened, and she answered, "*Children and Books*," producing a college textbook and handing it to Chris. It was in its sixth edition. At this point I realized we should have called for an appointment.

Chris was undaunted and started asking questions. I was relieved to see Zena understanding Chris wasn't a novice bookseller. Zena said, "You're going to get a lot of support for this project. Many people have been waiting for this a long time. You should join the Children's Reading Round Table right away. There are 1,500 members—authors, librarians, teachers—they'll want to be involved, and they'll provide good advice and send you business. You may even be able to hire some to work for you. When will you open?" I was startled by this shift from challenging to welcoming. Perhaps she wasn't a dragon?

Again we did exactly what our expert told us to. We bought Zena's book and worked our way through it. We'd already requested sales catalogs from two hundred publishers. Over the next several months we compared these publisher lists, author by author, title by title, with the index

of *Children and Books.* Flipping back and forth between catalogs and textbook, we taught ourselves children's literature,
and in the process proceeded with compiling the opening
order for The Children's Bookstore.

We had visited the children's book department of every
Chicago bookstore and noticed that these future competitors were ignoring nonfiction. In *Children and Books* there
were chapters devoted to history, biography, science, and
the arts; we decided the gamut of general bookstore categories should be replicated in our children's bookstore.

We'd been the first paying customers for our neighbor
Jean Fishbeck's Booklog inventory management software,
developed in conjunction with Women & Children First
Bookstore and used today by over a thousand stores. We
created lists of categories and subcategories that one would
expect to find in any general bookstore; as we added titles to
our Booklog database we assigned each to its category. Our
Booklog operating skills improved as our database grew.

We measured our store's interior and drew possible lay-
outs of bookcases. We'd counted the number of books per
shelf-foot on bookcases in bookstores around Chicago; now
we estimated how many books and titles we would be able
to fit into our store. As we added more and more titles to
our database we realized we wouldn't be able to buy all the
books we wanted. We would need help deciding which
titles to cut, ideally from someone with experience selling
children's books. Chris took out an ad in the newsletter of
the Children's Reading Round Table and a librarian
named Karen Rizzo gave us a call. She had recently
moved from Madison, Wisconsin, where she'd worked at
the children's bookstore Pooh Corner. Karen reviewed our

category printouts over a period of months and gave us invaluable advice.

We decided to develop an inventory of science toys that would earn extra profit while calling attention to our nonfiction books. Howard Cohen recommended we go to New York, visit a terrific store called Star Magic, and ask for their vendor list. We phoned. The person who answered said the owner certainly would not give us a vendor list but if we wanted the name of one supplier he might be willing to provide it.

We needed much more information than that. We went to Star Magic and surreptitiously copied down the vendor addresses off toy labels. When we got back to Chicago we called the vendors and requested their catalogs. Many turned out to sell additional interesting products we'd never seen anywhere.

We wanted to establish accounts with lots of publishers so we wouldn't have to lay out much cash, but all required prepayment of initial orders. We came up with the idea of attending the upcoming American Booksellers Association convention in San Francisco with our entire initial order printed out and ready to place. We would visit the booth of each publisher and hand our opening order to the highest-ranking person at each booth, along with printed materials detailing our strategy, credentials, and financial position. In this way we hoped to bypass credit department people who would insist on prepayment.

Most publishers did in fact offer us extended payment terms right away. They were impressed with the work we'd put in and with Chris's résumé. When they looked at our opening orders they noted we'd chosen broadly and intelligently from their lists; several publishers said they took this as a good indicator of future success.

At a number of booths authors were scheduled to auto-graph their books. We placed advance orders for quantities of these, at the same time arranging for some of these authors to visit our store in the future. At the end of each day of the show we collected the books we'd had signed for us, paid with a check, and brought the books to the convention center's mail-out area.

We left the convention having made many new friends who, as it turned out, would assist us for decades.

STEAL THIS TECHNIQUE

You think I'm being evasive. You want me to be specific and get on with explaining exactly how to make this thing work for you, step by step.

Forget it. Sure I can tell anecdotes about what we did. Unfortunately, none of those approaches will work again, because they've been ripped off by chain stores. You'll have to do something completely new. You'll then have the exquisite pleasure and torture of witnessing your creative work replicated and magnified by big corporations.

Or, you can grow your own store into one of the next generation of bookstore chains. (And there *will* be a next generation, distinct from the current crop. All that will remain of the current chain stores will be personal fortunes amassed by their founders and swell new charitable foundations.)

What I *can* tell you specifically though is how to find the breakthrough operational techniques that will make your own independent bookstore successful.

Steal them.

Yes, steal them, but then twist them around, mix them up. Use The First Rough Rule of Rebel Bookselling:

ADA
(Adapt, Don't Adopt)

Where do you steal these great techniques from? Other fields. Don't look at bookstores, look at business models from other industries, other professions, other countries. Look at social models from history. Look at trends in all areas of culture. Brainstorm. This conceptual work is the heart of what your new identity will be.

The idea you'll be happy with your life as a bookstore owner contains an unexplored assumption: that owning a bookstore will make you a new person. But you'll still be your old self unless you've created a bookstore that demands a different you to enact it. So if you want to escape from your current life, you must create a new bookstore reality, and if you do so in a compelling manner, people will be drawn to the work you've done.

Maybe a good analogy would be the restaurant business. Just as an innovative restaurant can be successful despite the existence of many competitors, so can a new bookstore.

Oddly, most people when they imagine launching a bookstore picture a standardized, clichéd operation. You can list the elements fairly easily. You can also find them in your local chain store. That store adapted this assemblage of ideas from us indies of three decades ago. We adapted them from public libraries. I'm sure you're seeing there is no reason to use this model. Your store should have original concepts. Operations, design, procedures, theories, interactive elements, community function, meaning for the public, impact: all must be invented afresh. If you accept conventional wisdom, you'll be out of business fast.

Composer Charles Ives says, "Nature loves analogy and hates repetition. Botany reveals evolution not permanence." Biologist P. B. Medawar says, "If . . . individuality were to be extinguished . . . then selection would have nothing to act on, and the species would be left without evolutionary resource."

Perhaps your customers shouldn't even think of you as a bookstore. These days ours think we're a museum store, whatever that means to them.

There are technical terms for this activity I'm suggesting: positioning, target marketing, specialization. Those terms from the business vocabulary are empty. I say imagining your bookstore is making art, pure and simple. But it has the added dimension that this art has to be profoundly transformative on an ongoing basis for thousands of your future customers.

Can you hack this?

CHAPTER THREE

BECOMING THE BOOKSTORE

July of '85 was hot: we kept lights off in our disastrously messy storefront at 2465 Lincoln. Chris's window displays made us look like a functioning store, but there was no room to move among hundreds of boxes. Nights, the ticket line at the Biograph Theater snaked past. We knew we'd click: when we snuck out for coffee those moviegoers would peer in excitedly at our explosion of books.

One afternoon someone knocked. I threaded through and unlocked the door. A short, white-haired African-American woman in patterned kaftan asked, "Are you going to carry my records?"

"Who are you?"

"Ella Jenkins."

I'd heard Ella lived in town but our paths had never crossed. "Ella!? Of course, yes, we have some already. Come in!"

She stepped through the door but didn't try maneuvering farther. I had an idea. "Would you play a concert for our opening?"

"Love to. When?"

"We're shooting for a month from now."

"Have to ask Bernadelle where I'll be. I think I'm in Europe, don't know when I'm getting back. Give her a call; do you have a pencil?"

I wormed toward the computer, returning with pencil and

paper. She scribbled her phone number and address: a few blocks away! "You'll do well. I play birthday parties for neighbors; they'll all shop here. I'll tell everyone you're opening."

"Thank you! I can't believe you thought to knock."

"I had to make sure you were going to sell my records, didn't I?"

"You know, we bought them last month at the American Booksellers Association convention in San Francisco from an old guy at the Folkways booth."

"So you met Moe?"

"Moe? I didn't get his name."

"Moe Asch. He usually works conventions alone. What did your guy look like?"

"You, but white."

"That's Moe. How's he doing?"

"He seemed tired. But that's ABA. We bought samples at peoples' booths because we'd heard they'd sell us books cheap so they wouldn't have to lug them home. He was happy we took a box of records off his hands."

"Moe's been working shows for us a long time. Well, call Bernadelle and set up that concert." She gestured at our choked store: "Good luck with that."

"Thanks!"

Moe Asch founded Folkways in the forties, and reading his catalog was quite an experience. Blues singers from the South, children performing skip rope rhymes, *Sounds of North American Frogs* recorded live onsite, and of course Pete Seeger, Woody Guthrie, and other pioneers of the forties and fifties folk music revival. Ella's records with Moe started coming out in the fifties too. My mother is a folk music fan, and as a four-year-old in '63 I'd listened to Ella's and Pete's records in the kitchen. Folkways was probably the first brand name I learned, so I'd been Moe Asch's customer since long before I wrote that check in San Francisco. (After Moe died in '87, the Smithsonian Institution took over Folkways. They still run the company.)

We didn't open till September 7. By then Ella had returned from Europe to tour in California. Her manager Bernadelle and I settled on the day after Thanksgiving for her concert.

Our store was doing fabulously. At our opening party I'd told Jo Podagrosi, sister of Victor, my Child's Play Touring Theatre boss, that we'd booked a series of Saturday shows with professional performers. They'd be free. We hoped customers would spend enough to offset the performance fees. Jo had just started as a publicist. She asked what media I'd alerted. I hadn't considered this; I was planning to buy ads. "You can get publicity. You shouldn't pay."

"How?"

"You need the Chicago Press Club's membership book. I'll drop mine off Monday. Grab names of journalists at every radio and TV station, newspaper and magazine that might be remotely interested. Features people for sure, but news too. For TV make sure you get names in news planning: they decide who's covered. Send one-pagers to everyone, every show. Follow up with calls. Don't forget community relations directors. They're in charge of PSAs: public service announcements. Some even have shows."

This sounded like work, and I thought she was unrealistic about us landing on TV or in papers. But when she remembered to stop by with several contact books, I figured I'd better take her seriously. I typed two hundred media names into a rudimentary mailing list software program. Seeing there *were* hundreds of neighborhood news-papers and radio and TV stations made me think Jo was right. They had to report about *something*; what we were doing was new.

Even though independent bookstores like Stuart Brent's had hosted author-reading programs for decades, only one store Chris and I knew of frequently hosted children's per-forming artists: our namesake, Judy and Hy Sarick's place, The Children's Book Store in Toronto. So we did have some-thing to promote. Following Jo's instructions we attracted media attention; the publicity lent us cachet; the customers came.

We featured performers who were friends. Ed Wilkerson brought a band from the Association for the Advancement of Creative Musicians. A hundred and fifty kids and parents sang with Rita Warford to Ed's bouncing roar. Multi-instru-mentalist Howard Levy presented Music Around the World. Jamie O'Reilly brought her Irish singing troupe, The Rogues. Packed store; strong sales.

My parents, sisters, and brothers-in-law came for Thanksgiving. Our mood was up: my sister Nancy had been promoted from copy editor to managing editor at Harper & Row Junior Books, the house responsible for Margaret Wise Brown's *Goodnight Moon*, E. B. White's *Charlotte's Web*, and Maurice Sendak's *Where The Wild Things Are*. We'd become quite the children's book family.

The store was closed Thanksgiving Day. Ella Jenkins was due for our biggest concert yet, the day after Thanksgiving. We arrived early to move fixtures.

Something was wrong. Stuff had already been moved.

We'd been burglarized Thanksgiving Day. The stereo and a toy robot were missing. Teens. Who else would steal a toy?

Worse, with the excitement of family in town we'd left cash in a drawer. Gone.

Two hours later Ella arrived with two hundred parents and kids. We'd built bookcases on wheels to clear floor space for audience seating. We were lucky no city inspector ever stopped by for a thrilling show like that one.

Our store was on an entertainment block, so we were open nightly till ten, after Thanksgiving till midnight Fridays and Saturdays. Lots of grown-ups bought books for themselves. At closing time we'd have twenty people balancing stacks of books, waiting to check out.

Chris and I worked constantly. I'd read our books as they came in. People were amazed I knew what was in them and that I had elaborate opinions. My literature courses, reading in other fields, and travel around the world somehow made it easy for me to peg customers and guess tastes. My five years in children's theater had familiarized me with the types of texts children liked. I'd always loved talking books; children's literature unexpectedly emerged in my life as a genre I knew by heart.

We assembled a staff that loved children's books: librarians, avidly literate parents, children's performers. It was Mary Swanson of the Children's Reading Round Table who alerted us when local legend Kathy Larkin fell out with Kroch's & Brentano's over their buying. After fifteen years cultivating an enormous clientele, Kathy was now selling clothes at Burberry.

Chris and I'd seen Kathy in action one afternoon in '85. We'd been scoping out the Kroch's children's department, and Chris had picked up a new biography of Georgia O'Keefe. A conservatively dressed woman bustling past with an armful of books had remarked with a hint of an English accent, "It's all very well, but there's still no children's biography of Michelangelo."

I'd asked, "Really?"

She'd halted, looked me in the face, and launched into an expert assessment of the current condition of art history publishing for children. At the time I'd felt it odd she'd make negative comments to customers who were admiring a book. But I'd certainly taken her seriously.

Now that we'd been in business for a year and were overwhelmed with work, having Kathy on our team sounded terrific. We called Burberry. Kathy was delighted to reenter her children's bookselling niche. On her first day a man who'd been shopping with her for years arrived at Kroch's from Florida. Kathy's friends told him where he could find her. I was startled to notice at mid-afternoon Kathy ringing up a big stack of picture books and fantasy novels.

Even more shocking was the number of such clients Kathy imported. Every month a dozen devotees left loaded with several hundred dollars apiece of Kathy's recommendations. She knew her customers so well she accumulated labeled piles for them in the downstairs office. When one arrived she'd dart down, scoop, zoom up, and talk.

Boy could she talk: author anecdotes, histories of oddities, and classics. Especially: cat books. Kathy pegged everyone as cat person or not. If you loved cats, Kathy would sell you all books with a whiff of one. She was so persuasive customers didn't dare refuse titles she pitched.

People complained they spent too much, then came back for more. Many had theories about her: they'd ask if she was a retired librarian from England. She did love things English, but no, she grew up in Indiana. People thought she was the owner. We did make her our frontlist (new title) buyer.

This seemed essential as she was also buying for her clients: many books she brought in were pre-sold. But I don't think ownership would have suited her. She loved putting books directly in peoples' hands. Kathy worked with us ten years. I never heard her say an unkind word about a customer or bookseller. She had clarity of purpose, professional presence, openness to all who asked her assistance. And if you wanted to see her face light up, you just said "cats."

All sorts of people came to us for advice: preschool directors, schoolteachers, therapists. Education professors like Bill Ayers arranged field trips for grad students so we could promote the use of books in the classroom. Our reputation spread nationally: *CNN*, *Los Angeles Times*, *New York Times*, *USA Today* called or visited for quotes on issues relating to children's books. Part of this was a by-product of Jo Podagrosi's suggestions. I'd included on our press-list local correspondents for national news organizations. Our mailings and follow-up calls to these contacts made them think of us when they needed content for articles. Plus, when journalists stopped in unannounced, they had a surprising experience. Our elegant fixturing, with plum-and-cream color scheme, pleased people used to seeing children's books displayed like toys in bright-colored bookcases with annoying loud music overhead. Our thrust was quality: we stood for arts, humanities, sciences. We projected respect for our customers: all ages.

When I was growing up in Rochester, New York, there were two great stores selling children's books. One was a large photography supply place called Light Impressions, one corner of which was set up incongruously as a children's bookselling area run by a guy who had a radio storytelling show called *The Spider's Web:* Jim LaVilla-Havelin. Jim was friendly to teenage me browsing folktales. I remember one book he recommended when I was searching for a present to give a girl: William Steig's illustrated romance *Abel's Island,* about a mouse, swept from his lover in a storm, who endures Robinson Crusoe–like toughening on an island before fighting his way home, where his lover-mouse *had* waited for him, though everyone else thought him dead. I think this was the first time anyone had hand-sold me a children's book. I later used Jim's style as a reference when developing my own hand-selling technique.

Another Rochester store with a great children's section was the Ox Cart Bookshop, an Eastern religions specialty place on Monroe Avenue run by Rafe Martin. We had a few conversations; mostly I browsed his fantasy collection. In '85, sitting at the American Booksellers Association convention Children's Book & Author Breakfast, I read the Lucile Micheels Pannell Award brochure. Who should have won the first Pannell but Rafe! In '83 he'd run the storytelling series Women's National Book Association had judged did the most to bring children and books together. I loved the idea of going after the same award. Perhaps even more because Rafe had moved from bookselling to full-time storytelling and then writing children's books. It seemed to me the Pannell Award might be useful in our future transitions as well.

Of the 150 special events we ran in '86, the most elaborate was a project with Child's Play Touring Theatre that was straightforward for Victor Podagrosi and me, since we'd done it together hundreds of times while I worked for him. We publicized the store was taking submissions for a show featuring children's writing. I ran writing workshops using a scenario-building technique we'd developed at Child's Play. I read submissions; Child's Play performed the best at the store.

Our friend Craig Alton had a children's show on public radio with Steve Hart. A week after the Child's Play performance, Craig and Steve hosted an in-store broadcast. We performed children's contest submissions, and six-year-old author Anna Madden read her own "My Lucky Day," about an outing with a dinosaur. I'd sent the story to my sister Nancy at Harper & Row, and she joined the show by phone, discussing why Harper wouldn't be able to publish Anna's story but what any author could do to try get their book published.

The All-City Writing Contest was the sort of programming the Pannell Award committee liked: interesting outreach; replicable. Combined with the other events we presented that year, and topped off by our candidates' story hours featuring Mayor Harold Washington during the February '87 election, we didn't have a hard time winning, according to Marilyn Abel, the Women's National Book Association's Pannell coordinator, when she called with the news.

□   □   □

Despite our outward success, however, Chris and I were increasingly isolated as individuals. Surrounded by customers and employees we'd lost our privacy. We'd had small circles of longtime friends and now we had no time to see them. We spent our days keeping up a front. Our first newspaper interview was with the *Chicago Reader*. We were completely honest about how we'd stumbled into children's bookselling, and when they printed what we'd said it looked awful. We shaped up fast, telling a story that went, "Take one cup Chris's bookstore background and one cup Andy's children's theater life and *Voila!* The Children's Bookstore!" Everyone loved this fairy tale. It matched the apparent existence of the store as an entity.

I never saw the store as an entity. When I looked around I confronted a million independent decisions, many erroneous, all arbitrary. But customers constantly asked, "Is this a chain? Where are the other stores?" If I answered, "My wife and I own this store," they were perplexed, unable to grasp they were admiring a new community institution created from scratch. "You *own* it? Did you buy it?" When I explained, "We opened it," I'd get, "You *opened* it?! Is it a franchise?" Every few weeks someone would ask us how to open their own children's bookstore. Again, we had to learn how to answer this since it made so much less sense than questioners could possibly understand. Typically such a query came from someone who'd never even worked in a bookstore. When we said, "First get a job in a bookstore to see if you like working there," they'd say, "Oh I don't want to work in a bookstore. I want to *own* a bookstore." If we asked why they were thinking about owning a children's bookstore, they'd say, "I just love children's books and I'd like to have my own store so I can read the books all day."

There was no time to read. The number of tasks was astonishing. People were slobs. Make a swell display; it's a wreck in ten minutes. Alphabetize a section; in a day the titles are subtly rearranged. And the paperwork! I spent the first fall on the sales floor nonstop, while Chris and an assistant manager from our B. Dalton days worked downstairs managing business operations. On New Year's Day we had

$50K in the bank. Exciting! Somehow we thought it was profit. In January I opened a drawer filled with invoices. Neatly filed. All unpaid. I added them up. $39K. Then we discovered *whoops* we hadn't filed any sales tax forms. We calculated: $12K. We brought in a professional inventory team. They discovered *whoops* a lot of books weren't there. When we did our own book-by-book inventory we realized there'd been *theft.* A lot of those wonderful customers had been helping themselves while I was recommending books to their friends. Science toys, baby books, stuffed animals had walked out the door hidden in coats. We'd been worried about theft, but there's only so much you can do when you're overwhelmed with customers. You've got to sell, sell, sell, right? Who'd have thought so much would be stolen?! It was disgusting.

Our plan had been for Chris and me to launch the store, and then for me to gradually pull back out into children's theater, or return to college. I'd work part-time. This wouldn't happen. No time to reflect. The phone ringing. Customers demanding, demanding. "Look up the publication date of this book for my daughter's report. Goodbye." "How can I get an author to appear in my school? Thanks, goodbye." We'd become a fantastic resource but were losing money. How were we supposed to make it work? The American Booksellers Association financial materials had told about stable bookstores during normal circumstances, but this was a runaway train. Zena Sutherland had been right: there were lots of people who wanted the full service we were offering. But no one wanted to pay, they took everything they could for free. Though we were selling books, the cost of operating left little room for error, and we were making errors. In '85 from September through December we did $150K and when we finally got our bookkeeping done our wholesale cost of goods, including inbound freight and theft, had somehow come to $121K. That left $29K for everything else. Employees, shopping bags, printed bookmarks, newsletters plus postage, rent, yellow pages, heat, and of course Chris and me living our lives. Terrible. We booked a big loss.

Start-up expenses are standard, right? Everyone has them, right? Wrong, not us. We weren't business majors. We hadn't made this life decision just to get wrapped up in cash flow management and budgetary fine-tuning. That's why people loved our store! *Who we were* was written all over it. Not business types: arts and culture people with a social agenda. And now we were becoming secret misanthropes. I got mad at Chris. Chris got mad at me. We traded places. Chris started supervising management, operations, staff, merchandising, and the sales floor. I moved downstairs and became business manager. I'd gone through calculus in high school. I hadn't taken a math course in eight years but I knew I'd have an easier time swimming in the numbers than Chris had. After all I'd studied the ABA materials and constructed our financial plans two years before.

The other plus for me of moving downstairs was I'd developed a loathing for our customers. They didn't know this of course. They thought I loved them. I was courteous, upbeat, knowledgeable, friendly, witty, on my toes. My customers were always right, I gave the lady what she wanted. But I couldn't stand it. Why? Consider, here I am, a twenty-six-year-old guy who loved working with children, and I'm stuck working with their parents! These people were of absolutely no interest to me. Where were their kids? They came to The Children's Bookstore and left their kids at home! Then they'd ask, "What can you recommend for a three-year-old?" There were thousands of terrific books for three-year-olds in that store. Why couldn't people make their own decisions?

Perhaps you think I was alone in this irritation with the people in a store. Not at all. Every retailer, every restaurateur, every salesperson struggles with hatred of the customer. That's why there are signs posted in backrooms saying: "Remember, without our customers, we're out of business, and you're out of a job." It's brutally tough to be nice to customers. Now, mind you, after work, closing at ten, exhausted after a roaring day of business, Chris and I would head down the street to the fabulous restaurant Fricano's, and eat, and drink wine, and have dessert, and I didn't care what the waiter or cook or hostess or busboy or guy who cleaned toilets or Mr. Fricano himself thought of me. All I wanted was great food, great atmosphere, great service. To paraphrase Walt Kelly's character Pogo: "We have met the customer and he is us." But what I hadn't known was how it would feel to have a private self of the kind that emerged inside, and how far divorced that version of me would be from the public self I'd be enacting for the customers. I was lucky in one way, though: I was a theater person. I knew the difference between the character you play for an audience, and the actor, underneath. But being the owner of The Children's Bookstore was a matter of playing my part twelve hours a day.

People used to say, "You must love working in such a wonderful place." I wasn't working. I was doing it because it had happened. It was my path. All I had it in my power to do was make art out of whatever self-sacrifice I was capable of enacting, and it happened that I had, collaboratively with Chris, created *this* particular pyre of art, which we were moment by moment keeping lit feeding flammable books to flaming children. The subject of this art act, and its object too, could only be direct action for social transformation and personal liberation. I'd discovered that this profession, bookseller—unsanctioned, uncertified, unavailable only to those who did not freely claim it—most lent itself to the collectivist ethos I appreciated, since among all the mulching markets of goods, services, theories, and futures, bookstores alone existed solely to disperse the turmoil of free, personal authorial arts escaping uncontrollably from bodies of books to minds and lives of readers who helplessly passed these untamed ideas forward to root and regenerate, enriching forever the social soil for other emergent selves.

But I also knew that children, those most uninhibited members of society, were the chokepoints for social transformation, generation to generation. I knew there was no position of greater influence than that of children's culture worker. I'd discovered this as a college student immersed in wildly imaginative free-form creative dramatics workshops inside low-income housing projects. Once in the middle of a game with a group of kids, in '78, an eight-year-old had pulled a knife from his pocket. Another boy had countered with his own; the two circled rapidly. I'd leapt between them and, continuing the game, nudged their characters toward a resolution they improvised, a plotline that credibly permitted them to put knives away and shake hands. Then I'd shifted the group smoothly to another game (I did insist they hand me their knives before continuing, which they both did voluntarily). As a self-proclaimed professional children's bookseller, I knew every time I sold *Goodnight Moon*, written by Margaret Wise Brown whose mother was a Theosophical follower of mystical Hermeticism, I was handing that book's one-year-old reader a manual of magical spells empowering this baby Hermes to take command of the cosmos.

Crying: *Goodnight Moon!* Establishing intimacy with the world's night light, the face of the sky. *Goodnight Room!* Relaxing back the walls of that earthy green room to reveal the profoundly roomy universe. *Goodnight Comb and Goodnight Brush!* Discarding concern for public nicety, ending presentation of self to world. *Goodnight to the Old Lady Whispering Hush!* Deflecting the spell of hushing to strengthen the outward rushing of hyperbolically expansive baby mind. *Goodnight Stars!* Eyes tight shut spark stars in dark: "The brain is wider than the sky." (Emily Dickinson) *Goodnight Air!* Rhythmically inhaling and exhaling night, transmuting the texture of spacetime to a substance engulfed and extruded by creator baby's body. *Goodnight Noises Everywhere!* Extending authority over all event, all sensation, all action, all consequence.

> The Brain is just the weight of God—
> For—Heft them—Pound for Pound—
> And they will differ—if they do—
> As Syllable from Sound.

You see, I took pleasure acting the agent of that secret society, the authors and illustrators of our era's incendiary children's literature, propagandizing subversion of social control by shipping those unwitting grown-ups back to their children's nurseries nursing the fuel I knew would burn bright to incite the macrocosmic minds of those recklessly romantic babies to rip-roaring realization. Which fuel was: *Alice Through The Looking Glass*, *Madeline*, *Peter Rabbit*, *Yertle The Turtle*, *The Phantom Tollbooth*, *Curious George*,

Charlotte's Web, The Very Hungry Caterpillar, Where The Wild Things Are.

DAMNED BENCHMARKS

Are you scared of owing money?

Look, since opening The Children's Bookstore we've been carrying so much personal and company debt it would make me nauseous if I hadn't developed this strange philosophy about money.

It's just this: I don't believe in money.

Money is a convention. It's a language of power. It's an informational feedback system emerging from and reflecting social life. It has no absolute meaning. No absolute value. It's endlessly mutable.

When you go through the bizarre experience of writing a $100 cash-on-delivery check for a batch of cheap toys, selling them in two days for $500, and depositing the money in the bank just in time for the COD check to cash against that deposit—well, that's what I'm talking about.

Or, when you miss paying your federal taxes and can't catch up for years, and in the meantime you start two or three completely new businesses, sell half a million children's books, raise half a million dollars for schools and charities, and finally make a bunch of profit and pay off the back taxes—what can I say?

So, everything I'm about to tell you about structuring your store's finances is nonsense. But you have to start with some standard model to begin to understand how to approach breaking the rules. These benchmarks I lay out below hew pretty close to the American Booksellers Association guidelines. My follow-up attacks on the benchmarks certainly do not represent the opinions of my much more financially responsible colleagues in the ABA.

Since so many independent bookstores have gone out of business, there is cause to attack the standard operating procedures of sound management. In my opinion rational judgment killed us. And, too many innovative individuals who are hankering to open a bookstore are paralyzed right now because prudent analysis proves they'd fail.

It's you, not me, creating this book in your hands, by reading and criticizing. If you don't disagree with me sometimes (or always!), you're not holding up your end of the bargain.

Okay. What's the most important question you need to answer to determine what size bookstore you're going to tackle? This one: How much personal income do you need to earn annually?

Do you want to earn $100K per year? You'll need a bookstore that does $1 million in annual gross sales. That is, plan to take 10 percent of your store's gross sales in personal income, *max.*

(Of course you may figure out ways to buck this. We did it at Children's Museum Store by selling toys, which are more profitable than books when they're sold in a bookstore as sideline products. Plus, as I mentioned earlier, when sidelines flip your identity into a *museum store,* they may even spark more gross sales and profit purely through this image shift.)

Now, operating a $1-million-per-year bookstore is a

huge amount of work, and lots of initial investment may be required. There's significant risk: you could fail to attain your sales targets. Losing money is awfully easy. The reason you might design a store that would yield a lower personal income would be to reduce risk.

You will *not* be able to reduce the workload. No matter what, you'll be working flat out. Unless it's a hobby, which is okay, and in which case the question of personal income can be set aside to an extent.

However, consider. If you do remove the personal salary from your calculation, you're almost guaranteeing you'll be running your bookstore less productively than possible. That's a bad indicator for long-term marketplace success.

It's great to not need an income. But plan to draw an income, strive to draw an income. If you fail, book that missing income as a loss. What you mustn't do is tell anyone you're not getting an income from your store. That's humiliating. If the word gets around, this information will damage sales by hurting your image as a professional. But you do have to know, for yourself, that you're not drawing a salary and that this matters since it indicates untapped potential in your project.

Chris and I didn't get paid for three years in the mid-nineties, during a period when we had a rapidly mutating company: closing The Children's Bookstore and opening Children's Museum Store. (Our families helped tide us over.) When things settled back down we were making three times as much personal income annually as we'd been earning before the drought. We'd built up a huge debt during the transformation that took a while to pay off. It was scary. But the whole time, we knew what was happening. We didn't tell people, *of course,* because they would have felt we were incompetent during the time we weren't making money.

Why is deciding what you need by way of personal income the very first financial question you have to answer? Because you have to have *some* first question, right? The fabric of your future business is woven of threads, so you have to establish some thread first, to start weaving with the other threads.

Okay. Let's say you want $100K in annual personal income for the full-time, hard, scary, risky, exhilarating, fulfilling, exhausting, restorative work of running your bookstore. So, this means you want to generate $1 million in sales at the cash register. Now, the second question: How much hard cash will it take up front to get this business going?

This varies with personal circumstance. We managed to borrow $40K on credit cards several times: in '92 when starting Children's Bookfair Company, and in '95 with Children's Museum Store.

But it's great to have cash. When you have a lump sum of cash you've saved, inherited or assembled, and you spend that cash starting your bookstore, you feel safer. At least it's not borrowed. You don't have to pay it back.

But that's a lie. All money is borrowed. If you hadn't spent that cash on bookcases and computers and light fixtures, it would be sitting in an account earning interest. So you're losing the opportunity for that cash to be growing itself in the bank or stock market. No money is free.

Am I evading the question? No, just couching the answer. Most professionals will tell you that starting a bookstore that aims to gross $1 million per year requires at least $250K up front. This could be composed of some borrowed money. Maybe it would be safe to have a third on credit. For the rest, you need real investment capital: cash. Either your own or from family and friends. Angel investors. You won't find serious venture capitalists in this small-business marketplace.

And don't try to guarantee yourself or your backers they'll get their money out when you sell the business or expand. This isn't fair to any of you. So many of these projects turn out as painful but unavoidable learning experiences, ending in simple store closure with loss of capital.

Even people who've gotten as far as building regional chains, with this (super-speed growth) being their mechanism for repaying early investors, have often seen their get rich plans collapse under the weight of concerted attacks by larger national corporations.

Can't raise $170K in cash and $80K in debt? Better scale back your personal income goals. For a $50K annual income, you'll need to run (at minimum) a $500K per year store. That'll cost $125K to launch (at minimum). You'll need $85K in cash and $40K in debt. (More cash and less debt are always safer.)

Is this unrealistic for you? We've reached the urban/rural chokepoint. If you're going to be living in or around a metropolis, running a bookstore full time, to accept much less that $50K per year means you're not paying yourself what your effort is worth. If you start a smaller store in this kind of marketplace, you'll find you still have to work flat out, but you won't have a chance to be properly compensated. But if you live in a smaller city, or a rural town, getting paid less per year matches cost of living locally. So you might decide, okay, let's see about a

$25K per year owner's salary, a $250K target annual sales level, and a $65K start-up cost. Your start-up capital would be composed of $45K cash and $20K debt.

I'm not saying moving to a small town is a surefire solution to the problem of not having enough cash to safely start up a bookstore. After all, now your market is smaller. Who's going to buy $250K worth of books and sideline products from you in a small town?

Well, some of the most successful indies, for instance our shop at The Eric Carle Museum of Picture Book Art, are located in small towns. It costs the museum little to house the store, and our visitors from around the world like supporting the museum's mission by shopping. Meanwhile, over the Internet, our self-published exhibition catalogs, posters, and postcards, plus museum-branded items, author-autographed books, imported sidelines, and discounted publishers overstock would sell no matter where the physical storefront was located. Gift shop opportunities like this are available in museums, libraries, and community centers nationwide.

If it seems impossible to do $250K per year in a small town, it should seem just as impossible to do $1 million in a city filled with superstores.

They're all impossible. All the options. Impossible. Just in different ways. Requiring the invention of different alternate realities that you inject into the existing world, transforming this world into a new one. And in that altered world, which already *includes* your astonishing, remarkable breakthrough concept in bringing readers and books together, it's no longer impossible for your bookstore to exist and thrive. Instead, it's inevitable: a *fait accompli* no one questions.

CHAPTER FOUR

HOLDING ONTO SHORTS

It's important to sell books to children because we must become a nation of readers.

—Alice Gueno, owner, Adventures in Reading Bookstore, in *The Art of Selling Children's Books,* a film created for The American Booksellers Association by Andy Laties and Loretta Caravette in 1992

The ABA? Them again? You know, there are two ways to run a race. One way is, you try to run faster. The other way is, you try to hold on to someone else's shorts.

—Leonard Riggio, Chair, Barnes & Noble; in *New York* magazine, July 19, 1999

Literary reading is in dramatic decline with fewer than half of American adults now reading literature. The rate of decline . . . has nearly tripled in the last decade.

—National Endowment for the Arts, July 8, 2004

☐   ☐   ☐

At the '87 ABA convention, Chris and I received the Lucile Micheels Pannell Award at the Children's Book & Author Breakfast. Up on the dais, I sat next to American Booksellers Association Executive Director Bernie Rath. He whispered, "So how did you get started in bookselling?"

"Chris hired me into the B. Dalton on North Michigan she was managing."

Bernie thought this was funny. "You'd be surprised how many independent booksellers started off with the chains. No one gives the chains credit for training this generation of independents—but every independent owner who started with the chains will say the same thing: the chains teach terrific operations technique."

What's amazing about the great battle of the bookstores is this whole story of exactly how independent bookselling made its huge comeback in the eighties.

By the late seventies, chain stores were slaughtering independents everywhere. B. Dalton Bookseller was the effort of Bruce Dayton's Dayton-Hudson Corporation to computerize a national bookstore chain for the first time. Carter-Hawley-Hale's Waldenbooks chain was much larger than Dalton in the early seventies, but by the end of that decade those two megachains were neck and neck. Crown Books was famously the outgrowth of a guest seminar at Harvard Business School where young Robert Haft questioned American Booksellers Association stalwart Eliot Leonard—also a key player in the growth of B. Dalton—on the use of discount pricing as a bookstore marketing strategy. Leonard had said you couldn't run bookstores on reduced margins. Haft took this as a challenge, and, coming from the Dart Drug family, tapped his old man for the funds to prove Leonard wrong.

The tussle among Dalton, Walden, and Crown between '79 and '83 was disastrous for hundreds of independents caught in the crossfire. It would have been easy to write off independent bookselling as a by-gone era's approach to book distribution.

So why was it that by the end of the eighties, ABA's membership had doubled, with new independents opening all over the country? Why had the chains entered a period of disastrous retreat?

Why had Dayton-Hudson abandoned their B. Dalton experiment by selling the chain for $275 million worth of Michael Milken's famous *"greed is good"* Drexel-Burnham-Lambert high-interest junk bonds to the New York store Barnes & Noble, owned by independent bookseller Leonard Riggio, who was also running a college bookstore company and an intellectually oriented discount-books catalog?

Why did Waldenbooks stall at 1,100 stores, then become a creature of a *much* smaller company that grew out of a single store in Ann Arbor, Michigan, created by brothers Tom and Louis Borders?

Why was Crown Books being ripped apart by family strife in the early nineties, with the elder Haft—Herbert—declaring to *Publishers Weekly* that Bob Haft had let the other chains eat his lunch?

Chain stores' own employees took them down. My path and Chris's—from Dalton to independent—was followed by many booksellers: we all became friends later through ABA. If you worked for a chain, you learned its weaknesses. You got irritated with the bossy general office. When you headed out on your own, you competed intelligently since you had inside knowledge and friends staying on to spy, feeding you secrets.

But we couldn't have been as effective if we hadn't been welcomed into a club eager to jump-start us. In the eighties, under Bernie Rath's leadership, the American Booksellers Association changed its face dramatically. From being an old boy's network, it became aggressively inclusive. Its Prospective Booksellers Schools promoted bookstore ownership, and these six, three-day seminars held annually for people considering opening a bookstore were consistently sold out: 500 people each year paying $800 apiece to get intensive pre-opening training from respected, established independent booksellers.

On top of that, there were Professional Booksellers Schools and Advanced Booksellers Schools: more three-day seminars that trained hundreds of working bookstore owners in better techniques—again, providing as faculty the owners of other bookstores. Seasoned bookstore financial managers coached uneasy new owners on obsessive inventory control and sophisticated cash allocation, all of us trading war stories at the bar into the wee hours.

ABA programs had terrific impact, and you didn't have to attend a booksellers' school to benefit. You could get financial info, handbooks, and educational reprints from *American Bookseller*—all created by professional booksellers freely sharing hard-won knowledge.

In August of '87 I was working in the basement of The Children's Bookstore when Chris came quickly down the stairs. "Andy, Ed Morrow and Bernie Rath are looking around." I darted up: Ed was incoming ABA president. He'd been our financial management instructor at the '84 Boston booksellers' school. Ed said, "This is what a children's bookstore should be." I knew his Northshire Bookstore in Vermont had that warm, library-like feel we'd striven for. We'd even copied his store's newsletter, having picked one up at the Boston school. I showed him ours: he found this amusing.

Several months later, after publication of my "Showcasing Your Store" articles in *American Bookseller*, Ed called and asked me to chair a committee he was establishing. The Children's Bookseller Task Force would address children's booksellers' complaints.

I worked with the Task Force for a year: in the introduction to our detailed final report I wrote, "The years ahead hold opportunity and risk for every children's bookseller. In both general and specialty stores, we must raise our standards of management and marketing to such a level that we keep many children reading right into adulthood. If we work together through ABA, we will succeed in creating an enthusiastic new generation of book readers who become book buyers." Then from '89 through '92 I served on the Education Committee, steering Task Force proposals like the *Art of Selling Children's Books* video to completion.

In the midst of this flurry of association work—meeting a dozen times around the country with ABA's other committee members—Ed Morrow additionally named me one of six children's booksellers to serve with six children's book editors on the American Booksellers Association/Children's Book Council Joint Committee. Our task was to design a day of children's book programming for ABA's upcoming 1990 convention.

At our group's first meeting, in New York, I suggested our day of events should launch with a readers' theater radio play to humorously depict issues that bedevil the bookseller-publisher relationship. Another bookseller said, "Andy, you're the actor. Write a script and we'll look at it during our January meeting in Chicago. Aim for a fifteen-minute piece." The other committee members seemed enthusiastic: I accepted the commission.

I didn't get around to the play until New Year's. Two weeks before our meeting at the American Library Association convention, I found myself floundering with boring characters and a mushy plot. I was puzzled by the ambivalence of the book industry—but this was what I needed to capture. Only if a problem is defined can it be attacked.

I hit on the idea of taking the film *Casablanca* as template. The story about good people wrestling with moral questions in an amoral landscape seemed a perfect analogy to booksellers' and publishers' business quandaries. Here we were striving to make and distribute literature—yet *having* to do this in a hostile world of down-and-dirty cutthroat money-grubbing.

I wrote rapidly and came up with what I thought was a hilarious script:

> **Ingrid:** *Rick, Victor has taken all the proofs, mock-ups, and original art from the Higgledy House offices in New York. He'll be coming into Miami International today. Rick, we've got to get to Colombia, where the pop-ups come from, to publish the book ourselves. Rick, we need your help.*

But something was missing. I needed lots of the pungent one-liners that pepper those Humphrey Bogart/Sydney Greenstreet/Claude Rains movies. I thought of my friend Art Plotnik—publisher at the American Library Association—who'd written the bestselling *Elements of Editing.* Art was a funny guy; he agreed to spend an evening tightening up my script. For four hours we brainstormed Bogartesque quips:

> **Sydney:** *You've become quite the do-gooder, Richard. Don't I remember something about you and Laszlo's wife Ingrid, something as romantic, well, as a Sweet Valley High? Why would you want to help Laszlo now?*

> **Rick:** *Sydney, I'll level with you. Ingrid's here selling remainders. I haven't seen her since New York. She's better than ever. Why she could sell Judy Blume to the Moral Majority!*

By the day of the meeting I was sure I had a satire that pushed everyone's buttons:

Rick: *Sam, the best thing about being a bookseller is . . . customers kind of feel like you wrote all the books.*

Sam: *But you only have to stock the good ones. If you're in publishing, you have to answer for all your dogs. And I don't mean Clifford and Spot.*

I was right. I'd pushed all the buttons:

Victor: *Why should my message to the ages be compromised by the short-term financial needs of a shipping conglomerate? I will publish 5,000 copies myself. I will distribute in any way possible. The edition will become a rarity, grow rapidly in value, and eventually, as an unfindable classic, be profitable for some insightful, humane publisher to revive, 20, 50 or 100 years from now.*

Rick: *And you're gonna live on library hand-outs and draw greeting cards until that happens.*

But I hadn't realized how ignorant these senior publishing people were of the issues their companies' standard business practices presented for us booksellers.

Rick: *The problems of three little word merchants don't amount to a stack of returns in this oversold world. Someday you'll understand that. Not now. Here's buying from you, kid.*

In the Chicago conference room where our ABA/CBC group gathered, the other booksellers sat silent as the editors ripped into the piece.

"This is not what we asked for."

"How can I defend this to my boss?"

"This isn't even funny."

One irritated editor snapped, "It's too long. Even if we cut it—and there's no time to cut it—no way will this ever fly." A more diplomatic editor suggested, "Maybe this would be appropriate for ABA to present in a session of your own."

Later in the morning, downstairs in the ballroom among publisher displays, I ran into Art. "Andy! How did they like it? What did they say?"

"Art, I'm the first author in history to be rejected by six publishers at once."

By the early 1990s, The American Booksellers Association was coming under intense pressure from its membership to save them from the onslaught of the new chain superstores: Barnes & Noble, Borders, and Supercrown. The association was at a turning point. The question we had to answer as leaders was to what degree a trade organization could assist particular members during their competitive efforts to survive in the marketplace.

Clearly, each store was an independent economic entity. Did ABA *have* a role in saving its members? If so, how could this be legally enacted? What about stores that were being run poorly, so the new competition had nothing to do with their imminent failures? Stores that were undercapitalized? In poor locations? Stores that had made fatal mistakes? ABA needed a hands-off approach to dealing with its members' anxiety. Along what avenue could the industry transformation be directed?

To gain insight into these questions, ABA ran strategic planning sessions using a consulting firm. I participated in several during '91 and '92. Survey data revealed one overarching demand from the membership we could arguably tackle: leveling the playing field. There was a perception— and significant anecdotal evidence—publishers were cutting deals with chains that weren't proportionately available to us independents, as antitrust law required, via the Robinson-Patman Act.

In February of '92, with our own store headed into battle, Chris and I decided I couldn't spend so much time volunteering for ABA. What I know about the ABA leadership's activity between '92 and '94 is hearsay. I read in *Publishers Weekly* about ABA members' complaints; I heard about the '93 annual meeting where booksellers shouted in anger at the board. We arrived at the '94 Los Angeles show with the same information as the rest of the membership. We'd been through hell the previous year: five superstores had opened within two miles; some were discounting all books 20 percent. Our sales were off sharply.

ABA Show Daily contained a bombshell announcement. ABA had sold a 51 percent interest in our convention to Reed Exposition for $18 million and had then turned around and—planning to use this money—filed suit against five leading publishers, claiming violation of the Robinson-Patman Act. These publishers were being enjoined by a judge not to touch any records until a discovery process could be carried out.

ABA had taken money we'd earned serving the publishers to sue these same publishers and caught them *in flagrante:* as the discovery proceeded, it became clear there'd been lots of favoritism. The superstore chains' rapid growth had indeed been sped by outrageous advertising deals, long repayment terms, and cheaper prices paid for books.

The publishers knew their defense wouldn't wash. ABA hadn't requested money damages; only that these practices cease. Over the next few years, all five publishers signed consent decrees: not admitting wrongdoing, but promising they wouldn't offer any deal to any retail company that wasn't provided proportionately across the industry.

On first announcement, though, the outcome wasn't obvious. Publishers were officially furious. Independent booksellers were elated. Chris and I spent the '94 convention walking on air. It was great our side had struck a blow for what was right.

Sunday afternoon our friend David Schwartz stood up from among the membership at the ABA annual meeting saying, "All weekend I've been going booth to booth, and people at all levels of management from all publishing houses—in particular, the houses targeted in the lawsuit— have been thanking us. They're saying things like, 'We had no choice. We were over a barrel. Maybe this will help us say no to the chains.'"

Because the chains were so powerful—capable of providing or withholding shelf space nationwide—these publishing people were protesting they hadn't been able to refuse chain-store demands for extra marketing dollars or preferential discounts. Their jobs depended on placing their houses' books into the superstores.

Shockingly, the big publishing houses were actually hurt by the actions of these employees. American publishers became weaker during the nineties: many lost independence and were gobbled up by foreign conglomerates. The result of these publishing houses' blindness was that thousands of their books never achieved adequate representation in the marketplace, since the superstores alone couldn't possibly have made room nationwide on their centrally programmed bookshelves for the full diversity of titles published each year.

Only a vibrant independent bookstore sector, with thousands of opinionated owners choosing a crazyquilt assortment of titles for display in their quirky stores, could ever have provided opportunities for the majority of non-blockbuster titles to find readers.

Publishers needed chains *and* indies, but, individual by individual, the bookstore lovers working in publishing houses felt they couldn't help destroying us independent booksellers. Their heartfelt professions to David Schwartz that they'd now depend on ABA's lawsuits to help them be good were appalling, especially because these publishing people *did* hope some sea-change might take place.

And the change came, for a time. As the national sales manager for a major publisher explained to me in '95, shortly after he'd closed a deal to place his house's books into Walmart—the biggest sales coup of his career—ABA lawsuits made it possible for him to say to Walmart's buyers not what they wanted to hear—"You're getting a better discount than anyone else"—but *rather* a phrase much more profitable to his house: "Nobody's getting a better discount than you." When those Walmart buyers had protested that their mammoth buy rated the best discount in the industry, ABA's antitrust lawsuits enabled my friend to respond, "Here's the phone number for the company lawyer—he'll explain why I can't offer you a better discount than the best discount we give our other top customers."

That huge publishing house saved millions over several years because of protection the aggressive ABA legal strategy provided; across the industry, ABA lawsuits certainly saved publishers billions.

How did big publishers repay ABA? With spite. Most dramatically, Penguin USA shot themselves in the foot by pulling out of the next few annual conventions. Then they were found in violation of their consent decree when a group of their collections agents freelanced millions of dollars in extra discounts to Barnes & Noble. A judge assessed the largest punitive antitrust settlement in US history: $25 million in damages, payable to the ABA membership. The Children's Bookstore received $1,000 from Penguin as part of this settlement.

If the big publishers had been managed as cleverly and aggressively as the chains—instead of embracing roles as sycophantic lackeys licking the boots of those chains—there'd be more independent bookstores still in business and more books sold over the last two decades. When superstores pushed, publishers could have pushed back. We independent booksellers were trying to work with those publishers. We opened over 3,000 new bookstores in the eighties, many more than the chains did. We invested hundreds of millions of dollars: our own private equity. That wasn't good enough for the corporate publishers. They still couldn't pull themselves together to work with us energetically, though they were selling unique, copyrighted products and needn't have behaved as if these marvelous books were commodities whose only selling points were low, low prices.

The big publishers should have held out for decent prices from their chain-store buyers without waiting for ABA to hold out our helping hand the only way we could: by socking those publishers in the gut.

Did ABA lawsuits force readers to pay more for each book? Exactly the opposite. My contention is that it was chains' manipulative approach to working with publishers that drove readers' payments for each new book purchased through the roof in the 1990s and into the 2000s—decades when prices for competing information-technology products were falling and cheap e-books were on the horizon. These price hikes reduced the number of books each reader judged he could afford.

The chains' strategy of filling hundreds of superstores by ordering and returning many more books than readers would buy increased publishers' administrative, warehouse, and shipping costs. (Admittedly, the closure of 3,000 indie bookstores in the nineties partially compensated for these increases by reducing publishers' cost of marketing and field sales.) Chain overordering additionally forced publishers to buy excessive print runs: though a house might project sales of 50,000 copies, it would print 75,000 to fill chains' supersized orders, knowing 25,000 would be used to plump up displays before being shipped back to the publisher's warehouse, then to be destroyed or dumped at a loss into the international discount market. The inflated print runs in turn helped send paper prices higher by ratcheting up demand for specialty papers when mills were running full tilt.

Publishers, struggling to cover higher operating costs while providing chain stores with illegitimately preferential wholesale discounts off of preprinted suggested retail prices between '87 and '95 found themselves informally changing their longtime rule-of-thumb system for selecting the suggested retail prices on which are based (insanely!) all payments in the book industry (reader to bookstore; bookstore to publisher).

For decades, these preprinted suggested retail prices of trade books (books sold in bookstores) had routinely been set at an average of five times the cost of buying the paper and printing and binding the book (this expense is called PPB). If a trade book's physical production cost was $2, the suggested retail price printed by the publisher onto that trade book would generally be $9.95. But during the late eighties and early nineties, under pressure from rapaciously expanding chain stores demanding higher retail profit margins and more dollars to spend advertising so as to capture customers from other bookstores, trade book publishers found themselves forced to raise their suggested retail prices much faster than the general inflation rate.

While the size of the trade book market was barely growing, against their best instincts, publishing people, department by department, unsystematically implemented an undefined emergency agenda to jostle their books' suggested retail prices upward toward a new 10 times PPB paradigm: $2 in physical production costs now translated to $15.95 or $19.95 in suggested retail prices. Only in this way could the publishers—forced to offer new deep wholesale discounts and extra ad dollars to the chains—continue to produce enough cash income to provide any hope of covering their operating expenses.

I was there. The excessive returns were on every publisher's lips. In just a few years the suggested retail price of a typical hardcover children's picture book jumped from $9.95 to $15.95 or more, and my customers started buying fewer books—although they were parting with the same amount of money! I argued with editors, publishers, marketing directors, sales representatives, other booksellers, and readers as this phase transition set in across the book industry.

Readers' payments to *bookstores* were now determined by stores' thrilling new systems of everyday discount percentages: 10 percent, 20 percent, 30 percent off suggested retail prices!

Hooray! Too bad that since suggested retail prices were by the mid-nineties inflated as compared to similar or identical titles' suggested retail prices only a few years before, readers were really seeing their dollar payments jump. What good is a 20 percent bookstore discount off a suggested retail price that's been kicked up by the publisher 60 percent or 100 percent *before* that 20 percent in-store customer discount is applied?

In practice it turned out there were titles customers wouldn't purchase within the new pricing regime. Readers quickly demonstrated that many books saleable for $9.95 wouldn't move at $15.95-minus-20-percent.

(Publishers often selected especially high prices for books they hoped would become *New York Times* bestsellers, since official bestsellerdom would guarantee books a 40 percent in-store discount, bringing readers' true cash outlays back to earth. This bet-the-moon marketing strategy—often driven by the desperate need to recoup an inflated author advance—frequently backfired, leaving the unlucky bestseller wannabe to fail solely because it was saddled with an outrageously high preprinted suggested retail price.)

At newly inflated suggested retail prices, guaranteed author access to print media, radio, TV, or the lecture circuit became essential to sales success, since publicity alone ensured customers would actively seek out and pay for specific titles at bookstores.

Editors had been accustomed to evaluating which prospective books probably wouldn't attain profitability. Now they shifted strategies, cutting back on titles, authors, and categories newly deemed least likely to succeed, while ambivalently acceding to Barnes & Noble's internal bookbuyers' provocative *suggestions* for ways titles still in development might best be designed and edited to offer a greater chance of ultimately landing that essential B&N buy.

Thus, Barnes & Noble was informally encouraged by publishers to shape the form and content of books subsequently distributed through *every* channel (including of course libraries, classrooms, and foreign markets!).

But how, except by acting on B&N book buyers' suggestions, could publishers have hoped to remain competitive with Barnes & Noble's *own* proprietary publishing program?

Though this newly expanded B&N product line was composed largely of resuscitated decade-old nonfiction, insipidly translated literary classics, and garish Australian and British production-house doorstops, B&N-published mediocrities were nevertheless receiving prime instore placement, and shouting unbeatable prices.

In the proprietary publishing model, few author royalties and no concerns about returns were permitting old-time five times PPB retail pricing. As junk-bond king Michael Milken told *New York* magazine reporter David Kirkpatrick in 1999, "I went into Barnes & Noble one day, and a big, beautiful multicolored dictionary was on sale for about $19.95—about 30 percent of what ones like it were being sold for in other bookstores. Riggio told me that it only cost him about $3 to print it under his own Barnes & Noble imprint, and I concluded he knew more about marketing books than anyone I ever met."

Dr. Frankenstein brand-name publishers were competing with the generic output of the monster bookstore they'd so optimistically nurtured, and on which they depended. ("You are my creator, but I am your master; obey!") This force-feeding of readers got worse as the 2000s progressed. Financial analysis website *TheStreet.com* reported in February 2002, "Barnes & Noble currently publishes about 3,000 books, which account for around 3% of its $3.62 billion annual bookstore sales. The [new] publishing initiative, announced . . . with the appointment of [Len's brother] Stephen Riggio to chief executive, is expected to expand that percentage to 10% in the next five to six years." Just four years later in 2006, *Barrons Magazine* reported that B&N had attained this 10 percent objective. While small and mid-sized independent houses, university presses, and Internet self-publishing tried to join the big publishers in holding up the free-press flag, the shelves of fancy superstores gorging on customer eyeballs were challenging of access for almost every publishing company, unable as most were to mobilize adequate risk capital for payola-style shelf-placement payments now required to ensure in-chain display.

Raising suggested retail prices, focusing on big books that would appear to be worth more to cost-conscious consumers: what else could publishers have done short of reaching out to their natural allies the indies? Expensive special deals demanded by chain stores had to be paid for. Readers were maneuvered by publishers into subsidizing chain attacks on readers' own favorite indies.

Ah, irony: Len "Captain Ahab" Riggio, forcing risk-averse publishers to focus on sure-thing titles, suppressing the very title diversity readers said they shopped at 150,000-title superstores to enjoy.

You *can* fool all of the people all of the time—for a time.

(To be marginally more empathetic, the view from Barnes & Noble included only the bankruptcy option: as Chris and I knew well in the early eighties, B. Dalton Bookseller was in trouble during the several years it was informally on the block. Not only were former Dalton employees running indies wrecking profitability; but plenty of current employees were allegedly stealing. Insiders—the extended Dalton family—knew B&N had swallowed a fishhook in assuming $275 million in junk-bond obligations with Dalton's stores as poisoned bait. Many thought Barnes & Noble was doomed after that crazy acquisition. Dayton-Hudson had been lucky to finally shake Dalton loose; how could much smaller B&N revive the dying leviathan? The turnaround Riggio pulled off was astonishing. He had no option but to use the one indisputably valuable piece of the B. Dalton package: their half-billion dollars in annual sales. This huge percentage of the US trade bookstore marketplace had to be somehow reallocated inside B&N's corporate structure. Hence the rapidly rolled out 500-superstore chain with simultaneous closure of 300 B. Dalton storefronts (the threat of a gigantic B&N bankruptcy hanging, early on, over the heads of publishers). Hence, indirectly, the sharp publisher price hikes to readers all went to ensure B&N could pay its junk interest and turn Dalton's unprofitable book sales to sustainable account. Dammit, Len, why did you hold onto other indies' shorts? You were only able to buy Dalton for a song because we upstart indies had destroyed its profitability! From '82 to '86—before your takeover—Dalton had closed hundreds of stores. Why didn't you hang back, let indies finish drowning Dalton, then join with newcomers in sharing the remaining half billion in old Dalton business? The culture would have been better served. Well, gentle readers, it's never too late: B&N and Borders Books—a company whose own rapid growth was largely a defensive response to, and oligopolistic function of, B&N's expansion—have turned into dying leviathans themselves. True descendents of boring Walden and Dalton, Borders and

B&N have already closed a thousand storefronts. Their losing battle against warehouse clubs and Internet booksellers is opening myriad markets to energetic indies.)

Indies have joint power now, and we had it back in the nineties. ABA lawsuits halted the expansion of anticonsumer practices foisted by overpowerful chains on the culture. If we hadn't leveraged the asset value of our popular industry convention (whose worth we'd systematically stoked for a decade, against just such a rainy day), then used those funds (which our adversaries hadn't anticipated we could muster) to gain access to the courts, impeding behind the scenes hanky-panky, each reader would have paid a far higher price.

Meanwhile, we indies of the nineties were surviving not by hiking end prices to consumers, but by increasing our productivity: keeping operating costs constant while pushing up the number of books we sold, aggressively attracting more readers to more books.

The Children's Bookstore's solution to this desperate need to sell more books anticipated the industry's next transformation, as implemented a few years later by newcomer Amazon.com. In '94, we'd decided to wring some extra promotional dollars of our own out of the publishers. We'd launched a catalog called *Children's Book Reports*, for which the blurbs were written by students in local schools and their parents. This idea of having readers write the text for a retail catalog was adapted from Child's Play Touring Theatre's central concept of inviting our student audiences to send stories they'd written so we could arrive at their schools prepped to perform the best of each school's stories for the entire student body.

At the time when The Children's Bookstore developed *Children's Book Reports*, no other bookstore was relying on a sales catalog composed of reviews written by that bookstore's prospective customers.

We worked the '94 ABA convention: that very show where the big lawsuits against the publishers had just been launched. We sold advertising in our catalog: enough to cover 60 percent of its production cost. Publishers bought our ads because our idea was unheard of: we'd arranged ahead of time to distribute 40,000 copies of this thirty-two-page catalog, written by students and parents, back into the very schools the student book reviewers attended. Any orders placed by families in those schools would generate a 20 percent premium, in book credit, for the schools' libraries.

This was several years before Amazon.com and its fundraising Amazon Associates Program existed (i.e., "click this link on our website to visit Amazon.com to buy this book; a percentage of the purchase price will be donated back to our organization").

It was all part of our Children's Bookstore Partnership. By '93 we were presenting 350 free special programs in our store each year, and we'd arranged for 100 schools and preschools to distribute our quarterly literary events fliers to all children; in exchange, every parent purchase in our store was generating a 10-percent book credit for that parent's school, *plus* a 10-percent cash discount to the parent.

We'd reached the point where we were distributing 160,000 fliers each year into those schools that would be passing out our *Children's Book Reports* catalog.

We'd invented this elaborate feedback system under pressure, as an effort to compete against the many new chain superstores. This tough business environment was forcing us to do our most creative work!

Did Amazon.com learn about—and draw inspiration from—our novel mechanism of using incentive payments to entice organizations to deliver us their members to write book reviews pitching these members' favorite books to other members (John Hagel III and Arthur G. Armstrong: "Amazon.com has . . . [also] established 'Amazon.com Community,' where members are . . . encouraged to post their own reviews . . . such devices . . . encourage a feeling of greater involvement."—*Net Gain*), while simultaneously providing payments to these same members ($2 in book credit for each review submitted), to convince them to invite additional organizations of which they were *also* members to sign up all *their* members for bookstore programs, and so on, and so on, in a widening circle of customer-recommended reading?

Our assemblage of interlocking business concepts was diffusing through the industry. I'd told Roger Williams of Wit & Wisdom bookstore in Princeton, New Jersey, about our marketing campaign during a 1993 ABA school instructors' meeting and then sent him a packet of our painstakingly developed consumer publications and institutional policy sheets. He'd implemented our entire community partnership program with great success. Here's a typically incorrect—but generally accepted—analysis by Evan I. Schwartz, author of *Digital Darwinism*: "There is no perfectly apt analogy for affiliate networks among traditional business models. It's like a pyramid scheme without the pyramid. Or maybe it's more like multilevel marketing without the multilevels. Or perhaps it's akin to franchising without actually offering exclusive franchises. Essentially, affiliate networks are the Web's unique way of roping others into doing your marketing for you."

This matters because the web-based version of the incentive- and book-review-driven sales referral mechanism has become integral enough to Amazon's business to permit the states of Arkansas, Colorado, Connecticut, Illinois, North Carolina, and Rhode Island to use it as the basis for e-fairness legislation mandating sales tax collection, based on the presence in-state of thousands of Amazon Community affiliates earning income from referred Amazon sales. The American Booksellers Association is encouraging more states to join in recovering sales tax revenue to pay teachers, firefighters, and doctors, while leveling booksellers' playing field. Amazon has shown its true anticommunity colors by fighting these sales tax collection mandates in court, meanwhile casually discarding established relationships with thousands of loyal affiliates who had referred millions of customers, all to maintain the critical *no-sales-tax-added* Amazon advantage over storefront booksellers.

Perhaps Amazon.com did invent the affiliate network marketing system independently of indie booksellers. But either way, founder Jeff Bezos hadn't been a bookseller himself; he'd studied our industry as he'd found it, adapting the best of our community bookselling techniques to the needs of netizens. Amy Jo Kim points out some of the adapted techniques in *Community Building on the Web*: "Whenever I log onto Amazon.com . . . I'm greeted by name and invited to check out some recommended books. . . . This is . . . somewhat similar to a bookstore clerk's getting to know you and what you might like." And Patricia B. Seybold points out in *Customers.com*: "The *experience* of shopping in a good book and music store is hard to beat. You can browse to your heart's content, picking up and sampling books as you roam through the shelves. . . . Knowledgeable employees will recommend books to you. . . . How could a virtual bookstore ever hope to compete with the experience of going to a really good physical bookstore? The best way was to make the experience of shopping at Amazon.com as rich and fulfilling as those described above. . . ."

Bezos's resulting special order mail-out, direct-sales company was subsequently marketed to Silicon Valley venture capitalists and Wall Street speculators as an opportunity to profit by investing customer charge card payments, a potentially huge aggregate cash pool tantalizingly useable interest free for the 45 days or more between the dates of initial product shipments to customers and the dates of final payments by Amazon to publishers and subcontracted drop-ship distributors like Ingram Book Company. Bezos's specialties had been financial management, investor psychology, and software design, not community bookselling. We ABA indie bookstore activists were creating tools for anyone to use. From '83 to '98 we went to the trouble of reinventing the industry, in the process slowing several generations of chain-store marauders while providing inspiration and ideas for the new wave of online booksellers. We're not finished: as long as there are free-spirited book lovers, innovative brick-and-mortar storefronts will be launched to keep up the good work of selling all forms of books. Indies, chains, and online operators are today training thousands of tomorrow's rebel booksellers.

MAKE IT UP

Suppose you can't raise $65K. Suppose you can't raise a dime. Does this mean you can't open a bookstore? Not at all. You can always open a bookstore, even without cash. As I mentioned, we started our most lucrative bookstore—Children's Museum Store—with no cash. We didn't tell anyone we had to do this, or that we were doing this. We told them all sorts of evasive things. People get confused when you talk about where the money's coming from and where it's going. But we did know we had no cash for the start-up. For that matter, the time before, when we'd started our school bookfair company, we hadn't had any cash either.

How is this done? It only works insofar as you have personal relationships that do the work the cash would have. I mentioned credit cards. You can't go to a credit card company and say, "Please give me a new card so I can run it up to the limit to buy bookcases for my new store." You have to get the credit card ahead of time.

But, if your child is in a daycare center, you can ask the director if she'd like you to run a holiday book sale. You'd offer to provide 30 percent of the gross sales to the center, in the form of free books. If the director said yes, then you'd open an account with a book wholesaler. You'd develop a book list you hoped would result in good sales, perhaps by asking the daycare workers, or some teachers, or by browsing in a bookstore or on the Internet. You'd project sales levels based on whatever benchmarks you reasonably chose ($30 per family?); you'd order books from the wholesaler; you'd pay them using whatever short-term cash float you could come up with—maybe a credit card. You'd run the sale, inviting the daycare director to choose free books afterward worth 30 percent of the gross sales. You'd return any remaining unsold books to the wholesaler for a credit against your credit card and use some of the cash from the sale to pay off the rest of the credit card bill. You should be left with some profit.

You're a bookseller. You can go to other daycare centers and offer the same service.

Now, as someone who's run hundreds of bookfairs, I can assure you there are only a few booksellers focused and disciplined enough to be able to consistently pull a decent salary from this kind of company. It's hard to make it work well. But this is one frequently used way new booksellers break into markets, establish clientele and reputation, and, critically, create an excuse for systematically opening a set of wholesale accounts with publishers.

Once you've opened a lot of publisher accounts, you'll have a new way to borrow money to launch your storefront. In fact, you'll be joining a select group of borrowers. The superstore chains and all independent bookstores are financed in large part by publishers.

Publishers give long payment terms, and books are fully returnable for credit. Some bookstores, when they get into trouble, pay for portions of old invoices by returning newly received books to publishers for credit against those old invoices!

Strange businesses: publishing and bookselling. Inspired by an earlier Simon & Schuster mass market initiative, bookseller Harry Schwartz convinced publisher Alfred Knopf, in the thirties, during the Great Depression, that the only way trade-book publishers could be sure trade booksellers would take chances on the huge number of new titles published each year was to guarantee books could be sent back if they didn't sell. So, since bookselling is essentially a consignment business, you can take advantage of this to help finance your store.

Of course, you should normally pay for the books a few months after they arrive. Unless they've sold, or unless you return them, at this point, you'll still need that fresh start-up capital you're finding it hard to lay hands on. So, publishers might argue that the fact they extend credit to booksellers doesn't mean it's cheaper to open a bookstore than any other genre of store.

Yes. True. It's possible to utilize credit provided by vendors in every kind of retail operation. From grocery stores to hardware stores to gas stations, all retailers rely on credit provided by their suppliers for capitalization of their inventories. Many stores of varying kinds own almost none of the inventory on their shelves: it's on credit from their vendors. But when the product is fully returnable, no questions asked, as books are, a retailer can borrow a lot more from his suppliers by intentionally ordering larger and larger quantities in excess of what he can possibly sell, systematically returning this excess merchandise, and receiving returns credit to use as a sort of scrip to pay very old bills.

(Marketing directors frantic to get books onto store shelves will always overrule credit managers frantic to collect ancient debt: ask former indie Barnes & Noble about this brazen "owe a billion, the bank owns you; owe a trillion, you own the bank" financial strategy. In the months leading up to B&N's '92 initial public offering—in anticipation of which Standard & Poor's had issued an "avoid" warning—publishers already owed millions by B&N were privately joking they might have to buy stock to keep the chain going. This according to Bernie Rath, as quoted in a *Wall Street Journal* article on September 11, 1992, "Risky Plot: Barnes & Noble's Boss Has Big Growth Plans That Booksellers Fear," the tone of which attracted a demand from B&N for an apology.)

Self-published authors are another source of financial credit. City Lights Books in San Francisco, St. Mark's Bookshop in New York, and Quimby's Bookstore in Chicago all run lively consignment sections featuring self-published books and zines: authors are paid after their books sell. Amazon.com handles millions of self-published and small press books on just such a zero-risk, consignment basis.

As you explore your new field, you'll find that on the one hand you're living in the world of art, literature, education, child rearing; on the other hand, it's competition, sleight-of-hand, inside deals. In particular, if you don't learn to play a little rough, you'll be handicapped when conditions change and you're caught off guard.

Cash. It's easy to say there's never enough. I disagree. You can always substitute personal relationships for cash. You can always substitute inside knowledge for cash. When you transform a mechanical interaction into a personal encounter, in business, this equals cash. When you act in a way only specialists understand, this equals cash.

When you provide appreciated, altruistic service to the community, this equals cash.

In fact there are risks associated with having too much cash when you're launching your store. Having cash makes you blithe. So you spend too much. Then it haunts you, because down the line you realize you spent it wrong.

When we opened The Children's Bookstore, we spent a lot on musicians and theater troupes. Only when we realized this was unsustainable did we figure out we could create special events for free: Making the store available for public recitals by kids taking music lessons at private instructors' homes. Inviting troupes to perform scenes from plays, as teasers to promote ticket sales.

We spent cash until this was impossible, then under duress figured out how to provide free community service while attracting media attention without using cash.

Rules must be broken. The standard, tried-and-true rule that you need $250K in cash and debt up front to start a bookstore that will generate $1 million in annual sales is a rule you have to break.

But break it because you've found a way to do better. Simply use The First Rough Rule of Rebel Bookselling:

ADA
(Adapt, Don't Adopt)

As before, the best place to look for novel financial models is other industries, other professions, other periods in history, other social structures. Once you move beyond the lockstep mentality of publishing and bookselling, you'll recognize amazing approaches no one has implemented and powerful social networks no one has tapped.

These discoveries are *yours.* However obvious they seem, if you share them with book industry insiders, that old guard will knock you down. This is a good sign: when insiders are blind to unusual opportunity, there's room for newcomers to join the game.

If you can implement your great ideas in practice.

Just remember, if those ideas do work, everyone else will steal them (and deny they did). So you'll need more breakthrough plans by then.

CHAPTER FIVE

SYMBIOTIC SOLUTION

Even in the face of big publishers' nearly criminal lassitude, independent booksellers did have opportunities for success. Unfortunately, many indies failed to understand uniqueness was their strong point. Why were so many apparently *only* complaining when it was *sauve qui peut*—every store for itself?

For years I'd been lecturing at the convention and in the ABA schools about aggressive community outreach and media-oriented marketing. Why weren't other stores featured on their local TV newscasts? Why weren't they being regularly written up in the papers?

After a presentation I gave at the '92 Los Angeles convention, a bookseller approached. "That was a wonderful talk. You're doing so many interesting things. But I could never do those things. I don't have time."

I answered, "You have to make time. I don't have time either. You don't have time not to do these things."

Luckily Chris and I did understand our image in the community was our greatest asset. The question was how to cash that asset in.

We finally realized we needed look no further than our chain-store adversaries for inspiration: they'd creatively pioneered several innovative moneymaking techniques we could fruitfully adapt.

We established a separate corporation: Children's Bookfair Company. We'd learned that publishers sold books for 10 percent less to businesses calling themselves *wholesalers* than to businesses calling themselves *retailers*. The Borders Books & Music superstore chain was owned by such a wholesaler: Book Inventory Systems (BIS). This corporate structure was originally developed so as to sell inventory management services to independent bookstores such as Schuler Books in Grand Rapids and John Rollins Bookstore in Kalamazoo.

Now, however, BIS was selling directly into its very own proprietary chain of Borders superstores. When we learned the Borders expansion was a case of a wholesale company selling to the public via a captive retail chain, we were intrigued publishers would knowingly permit such flagrant abuse of their own discount schedules. Then, when Borders superstores appeared in Chicago and started competing with us, we were outraged. (The Borders brothers sold out high to Kmart Corporation for $126 million in '92 while their outfit was structured this way.)

In '92 we lost patience and copied BIS, forming our own wholesale company, using our bookfair operation as the foil, and got many books 10 percent cheaper than before. We were stunned to find all publishers' sales representatives assisting us in this process of cheating to survive: helping us buy low, as wholesalers, and sell high, as retailers.

The traveling sales reps helped us cheat because they liked our store, and because they foresaw they'd lose their jobs if too many independent bookstores closed.

We knew Barnes & Noble ran stores for colleges. When I was growing up, my dad chaired the University of Rochester Bookstore faculty committee, so I knew how Barnes & Noble went about convincing colleges to outsource. In '92 we approached Chicago Children's Museum and offered to do for their new gift shop on Navy Pier—the city's rehabbed waterfront promenade—what B&N did for colleges. After three years of talk, in '95 we got a long-term contract—because we'd already established an excellent reputation as fundraisers. Children's Museum Store turned out to be our lifeboat and privateer: we handed the museum $800K over the next seven years out of an operation that had yielded essentially no profit to them previously, while pocketing over $1 million in salary for ourselves.

Well, it wasn't that straightforward; our reincarnation required every iota of good karma we'd accumulated over the previous decade.

In October of '84, getting hammered with Victor Podagrosi in a Korean restaurant after a day in the schools with Child's Play Touring Theatre, I learned of his great ambition: to found Chicago Children's Performing Arts Center, a brand-new, stand-alone building that would provide a showplace for all Chicago's outstanding children's performers (at the time there were 150 groups on the Illinois Arts Council roster).

Victor was a man of action. Two years later he founded Chicago Alliance of Professional Performing Artists for Children: CAPPAC. He brought the membership near the 150 mark within a year. He applied for grants to the Build Illinois program, through which the State was helping non-profits create cultural arts buildings. He received $80K in State funds and hired Brad Morrison of Minneapolis, a leader in theater development, to conduct, first, a needs assessment survey, then a design survey. Two thick books of data and plans emerged by '92.

Victor had invited me onto the planning committee for

Chicago Children's Performing Arts Center (CCPAC). I'd missed most of the meetings. In July of '92 I did make one: on Navy Pier. CAPPAC was assessing the possibility of establishing CCPAC on the newly redeveloping Pier, right across from the future location of Chicago Children's Museum.

There was a scale model of what Navy Pier would look like after the redevelopment. Astonishing, the transformation they were planning. From a sea of abandoned parking lots, the place would turn into a major waterfront tourist attraction.

While the meeting was in progress, as it became clear Metropolitan Pier and Exposition Authority (MPEA) was serious about having Chicago Children's Performing Arts Center be part of the project, I saw The Children's Bookstore should also move to Navy Pier. It was clear that located next to Chicago Children's Museum and CCPAC we'd be enormously successful. The free literary programming we could bring would be a draw for the Pier as well.

But I realized the museum would have a gift shop. How to ensure our store wouldn't run up against the museum's need for revenue?

I remembered the restaurateur's trick. If you have a successful restaurant, you open another across the street with a different cuisine. Competing with yourself, you capture all the traffic and protect your company from an outside competitor. I decided we could open both our children's bookstore and an educational toy store that would be the museum's gift shop. I knew the Barnes & Noble model for concession agreements with colleges and figured we could adapt this to the museum.

A few days later, after kicking the issues around with Chris, who agreed it looked like a good opportunity, I called the museum's founding president. We'd never met her though she'd been running Chicago Children's Museum since '83. Brought in by the Junior League, she'd taken the museum over when it was a couple of exhibits in the hallway of Chicago Cultural Center and grown it, via two major moves, in conjunction with first a $1 million capital campaign, then a $5 million campaign, to the twenty-seven-thousand-square-foot institution it was in '92, at North Pier, a redeveloped lakeside wharf. She was in the middle of her third capital campaign, aiming to raise $14 million for the museum's move to Navy Pier.

The museum's president was the kind of person we felt had probably shopped at The Children's Bookstore but not introduced herself. Chris and I had a lot of undeveloped relationships like this. We knew her the same way, since we'd visited her museum regularly with our children Sam and Sarah, age five and three.

The president was intrigued by our offer to run her gift shop. I didn't mention we were thinking of opening a bookstore across the hallway as well. I realized midconversation this would not be to her liking.

She asked us to send a proposal.

This put us in a quandary. If we sent one we'd have to reveal we intended to compete with the store we were proposing! Would we rather just put The Children's Bookstore on the Pier?

We decided to pursue MPEA itself for a storefront slot first and hold off negotiating with the museum. Only after eighteen months of courtship with MPEA, culminating in a decision on their part to lease instead to a local general bookstore—Barbara's Bookstore—did we send the president her proposal.

In the meantime something happened that helped guarantee the museum's acceptance of our offer. But we didn't know it was happening.

Six months after CAPPAC's meeting on the Pier, in January of '93, Clara Coen, one of our buyers, came through our back basement door, returning from the bookfair company barn with an armful of books.

"Andy, I just got a call from my friend. A group of parents from Francis Parker School are bringing in the *Anne Frank in the World* exhibit six weeks from now for a one-month show at Chicago Cultural Center. They need a bookseller to handle sales of the *Diary* during the program. They're about to ask Bookvine to take the job, but we can bid for it if we'd like."

"How much do you think Bookvine will offer?"

"Bookvine usually gives clients 20 percent of the gross."

"Tell them we'll give twenty-five. Wait." I realized I was getting ahead of myself. "Did your friend give an estimated attendance figure for the event, over the course of the month? And how much space would we have? Could we sell any books other than the *Diary*? Won't everyone who shows up at an exhibit about Anne Frank already own the *Diary*?"

Clara was still holding her armload of books. The phone was ringing. She said, "I'll call her back and find out," then squeezed past through our tiny office out to the downstairs sales floor.

A few minutes later Clara was back. "In Portland, Oregon, the show's attendance was 75,000, and the bookseller there did $41,000 selling ten Anne Frank–related titles. All schoolchildren bought the *Diary*."

I was flabbergasted. "Seventy-five thousand people came

to an exhibit about Anne Frank in Portland? That's impossible! The book's been out for forty years! No matter how good the exhibit is, how could that many people show up? Are you sure?"

I knew Clara was overloaded with work that day. "Andy, she said 75,000."

"OK, wait a minute. Only ten titles? There must be hundreds of titles that would match a Holocaust exhibit. What would that be, a room-sized show?"

We'd hired Laura McVey back from Doubleday Bookstore the previous fall to be Children's Bookfair Company's manager. Six years before, Laura had put together our Mayoral Story Hours; now we'd asked her to develop a full adult trade-book inventory to grow the sales at our largest bookfair accounts. She'd done a terrific job. Working with Margaret Wroclawski as children's book buyer, Laura had produced a $200K fall season, including $50K in adult trade-book sales. But the spring bookfair contracts were clustered in March, and we were trying to decide whether to lay off most of the outstanding booksellers she'd picked off from Doubleday and Kroch's & Brentano's. A month-long February bookfair at the Cultural Center looked like perfect timing to keep the crew paid until the spring season kicked in.

I knew Laura would love putting together a sale that focused on a topic like this: teaching people about all the horrible things that had happened around the globe and throughout history because of racism and discrimination. There could be fiction, history, atlases, of course lots of children's holocaust literature like *I Never Saw Another Butterfly* by the children of Terezin, and *Rose Blanche* by Roberto Innocenti. "Clara, will 25 percent be enough to pick this up?"

The Anne Frank committee—actually it was the local chapter of the organization Facing History & Ourselves—accepted our 25 percent offer. We'd have five six-foot tables, for a month right inside the room with the exhibit. Laura was bursting with ideas, and our entire team—thirty remarkable people—started brainstorming titles we could sell.

Chris and I had planned a trip to Mexico; January was the month we could get away since it was slow season. While Chris, Sam, Sarah, and I were hanging out on Isla Las Mujeres and climbing pyramids at Uxmal and Coba, Laura and Margaret prepared for our month at the Cultural Center.

When we finally got back, Laura asked me to sit down. "Andy, I don't know if I've got enough of the *Diary* in paperback. It was out of stock at Bantam Doubleday Dell. I had to call wholesalers all over the country." She paused. "We own every copy of *The Diary of Anne Frank* that was sitting in any warehouse. BDD says no one else will be able to get any till May."

This sounded disastrous. We'd calculated if 75,000 people had attended the show in a small city like Portland, which surely didn't have a large Jewish population, Chicago should be able to pull 150,000. To run out of the *Diary* itself would be inexcusable from the perspective of the Facing History sponsors, and of course we'd be missing a ton of business ourselves. "How many copies could you come up with?"

"I've got 2,000 in Barney Nibble's." (In honor of the new Barnes & Noble that had opened a mile away, nibbling our sales down 20 percent, and because we had mice in the bookfair company's barn, Laura had nicknamed it Barney Nibble's.)

Two thousand copies of the *Diary:* this seemed like a

lot—and also not enough. I said, "This just puts more pressure on us to round up a diverse title base."

Laura took me out back and gave me a tour of the books she'd brought in. An amazing, terrifying inventory: five hundred titles, in multiples of from ten to thirty copies, conveying the horrors of history while staying within the boundaries of excellence. Novels, art history, poetry, reference, biography, photography—yet every title was one you'd normally have qualms about stocking. I picked up this book, or that, and each, in a special way, practically *burned* me. Looking at so many personal statements from humanity's darkest days— Native American, African American, Latin American, Chinese Cultural Revolution—was overwhelming.

There were the works of Elie Wiesel, who'd be presenting at the Cultural Center during our month. Those were among my sister Nancy's favorites. Here were my own sixties childhood influences: *The Autobiography of Malcolm X* and Richard Wright's *Black Boy*, in new editions. Books about the Japanese-American World War II concentration camps in California. Books about the Khmer Rouge.

A week later, we were loading our boxes into the Cultural Center through its back alley. The same alley behind the big B. Dalton on Wabash where I'd unloaded boxes thirteen years before, when I'd helped combine our North Michigan Avenue Dalton book returns with the downtown B. Dalton return shipment. Now B. Dalton was a Barnes & Noble– owned company, and we were selling books behind its back. Laura enjoyed this too: her Doubleday Bookstore at North Pier had been acquired by B&N the previous year. She'd leapt to our bookfair company a few months later, bringing most of her staff.

The Anne Frank exhibit was powerful: it documented the

Holocaust in a personal way, using Anne Frank's life as an organizing principle. I tried to imagine 150,000 Chicagoans choosing this as an educational experience.

It didn't sound like the Chicago I knew.

How could Portland have drawn 75,000? How could this dark subject have become the focus of such attention? This exhibit didn't contain revelations. Were so many Americans in '93 eager to expose themselves to awful truths?

Traveling in Holland in '77, my friend Susy Elder had insisted we visit The Anne Frank House. I hadn't read the *Diary* at the time: during childhood I'd thought of it as a girl's book.

Susy and I'd gotten lost. After a frustrating hour when I kept suggesting we forget it, she noticed I was holding the map upside down.

When we finally arrived, it seemed the famous Secret Annex was just an upstairs room.

Looking back from my '93 bookselling perspective, surrounded by the evocative *Anne Frank in the World* exhibit, I saw Anne Frank House's curators had been forced to choose between turning the annex into an exhibit and leaving it the spare space it had been in Anne Frank's experience.

They'd made the right choice. Somewhere between Hannah Arendt's banality of evil and Alberto Moravia's idea of the terrible fruitfulness of boredom lies the value of seriously contemplating an empty room where something tragic happened. The unprepared tourist walks away yawning; sixteen years later he begins to understand.

Our completed book display was shocking. Poring over those titles made me feel we were doing something worthwhile. If many people could be induced to contemplate this, our world, through the eyes of the remarkable individuals whose experiences informed these narratives—well could they? Would anyone dare to browse these terrible book tables?

I was worried. The exhibit's hours were nine to five, seven days a week. The staffing budget had startled me. Most bookfairs rely on volunteers; here we were bearing all this expense. For Saturdays and Sundays, we'd scheduled two booksellers. Other days we were hoping one person could manage the crowds.

The crowds. This was the key. With enough traffic, the costs would become insignificant. Even if we ended up returning a lot of books to the wholesalers. Even if we needed to bring in more booksellers to sell all those copies of the *Diary* to thronging schoolchildren. With enough traffic, the thing would pan out.

The exhibit opened.

One day—one *hour*—told us there wouldn't be enough traffic.

Plenty of people came opening weekend. But weekdays were slow. Worse, most schoolchildren already owned the *Diary.* Author events were held in the evening, in another room, and generated few sales since authors didn't come by our tables to sign books: I didn't meet Elie Wiesel or Cesar Chavez, although they were there.

Why in hell had Portland seen 75,000? The exhibit wasn't poorly attended; on the contrary, thousands of people were coming each week. But our expectations had been out-landish, and we'd bought books to match them. The last 2,000 *Diary of Anne Frank* paperbacks in the country were in our barn, and we were selling what, twenty a day?

Facing History had created a second exhibit: children's art depicting racism. The young artists came one afternoon to be honored. I was working our display, and business was slow, so I wandered to the atrium. Thirty students aged eight to eighteen sat in five rows of chairs. An organizer, to my surprise, introduced Oprah Winfrey.

I wondered how she'd handle them. These kids were being honored for artwork showing they'd encountered horrific bullying. They were scarred. Scars don't just go away. They take a long time to heal.

Oprah was upbeat. "Everyone on your feet. Come on, stand up." The kids were not awed by Oprah's star power. They rose, giggling. Even stragglers—sixteen-year-old boys—finally stood up.

"Now, raise one arm." She did this herself, and I did too, at the back of the group.

"Reach that arm high. Imagine you're Michael Jordan at the basket. You might need to get on tiptoe." We strained with our fingertips.

"Now, take your other hand, swing it up fast and *give yourself a high five*!" Swinging our free hands up to clap forced us to jump. Everyone laughed.

"When things aren't going well—you're having a bad day—give yourself a high five. Come on, raise—up—that—arm—streeettttchhh—*give yourself a high five*!"

The exhibit concluded. Attendance had been 15,000. Excellent, great. Very strong. Terrific. The fact this many people had chosen to consider Anne Frank's life, in February '93, in Chicago, was a good sign.

We'd done $38K in business. We had 1,000 copies of the *Diary* in the warehouse, and an average of 20 copies each of 500 other titles: we'd be doing a massive $100K return to our suppliers. After paying the 25 percent premium—

$9,500—to Facing History, and taking into account staff expense plus freight on the returns, I figured we'd book a painful $7K loss on the event.

Throughout the month, one coordinator had been an ongoing presence. I'd been introduced to her briefly as a force behind Facing History. She didn't talk much; at least she didn't talk to me. But she smiled. I knew she thought we were doing a good job. All the Facing History people had been warm and complimentary.

On the last day, I pulled the van in to the loading dock of the Cultural Center and came upstairs. Laura was boxing up the display. She said, "Andy, can I see you for a second?"

"Sure, what's up?"

Laura pulled me out of the exhibit hall into a corner of the atrium. "I was talking with the coordinator about attendance. You know why they had 75,000 in Portland?"

I was shivering. "Yeah? Why, what?"

"The Ku Klux Klan picketed. It was all over the news. People came to support Facing History and oppose the Klan."

I was angry. "But why didn't Clara's friend or the coordinator tell us to begin with? If we'd known, we wouldn't have overbought!"

"They didn't tell *anyone.* They were worried if word got around, the Klan might picket *here.*"

I recalled the Klan's march in Skokie, in the seventies. Even in Chicago you have to worry about the Ku Klux Klan.

"They could have told Clara!"

"They didn't feel they could tell *anybody.*"

We didn't complain. We paid the $9,500 premium. No one heard our side of this story.

We'd passed the test. There was something else we didn't know.

Facing History's coordinator was also board chair of Chicago Children's Museum. Two years later her name was on the contract giving Chris and me the right to run the museum's store on Navy Pier.

High five.

HE WHO CANNOT, TEACHES

love brainstorming with working booksellers, but please, preserve me from reliance on professional industry consultants. If we hire experts to give us all the answers, we're dead. Why? Because now we've evaded our responsibility to innovate. We're chickening out, we're cooked, and guess who'll eat us for lunch?

Of course the pro consultants may say I'm a hypocrite since I'm writing this sentence. Well, I taught bookselling for ten years for the American Booksellers Association and never got paid a dime. Which makes me not a consultant. By not taking money for my thoughts, I've always been free to speak my mind. And the whole time I was teaching, I was also running my own bookstore. I'm still running my own bookstore. Five days a week I'm at the register.

If I were an industry consultant I couldn't spout absurd ideas like *rules are useless.* Paid sages need dependable ways to stimulate short-term improvements. They can't risk being too original because they have to worry about clients failing to benefit from disruptive suggestions. Instead, consultants derive theory and technique from industry data and lore, then convince clients (you and me) we'll succeed if we apply these so-called methods in our markets. If their fossil formulae don't breathe life, they can safely complain that we demonstrably received wise counsel, propounded from studied practice and bench-mark, so it's clear that we're just not implementing correctly.

Hired guns must defend themselves. Many clients fail despite everyone's best efforts; a key task is to ensure clients accept blame for dying. (Fair enough.)

People who pass out answers aren't educating. Good educators don't lead, but encourage creativity, learning from students while pushing them forward and away. As Viola Spolin says in *Improvisation for the Theater*, "We learn through experience . . . no one teaches anyone any-thing. . . . Through spontaneity we are reformed into ourselves. It creates an explosion that for the moment frees us from handed-down frames of reference, memory choked with old facts and information and undigested the-ories and techniques. . . . Spontaneity is the moment of personal freedom when we are faced with a reality and see it, explore it and act accordingly."

Now, some of my own best friends are professional consultants. I've learned to take their advice in one way: I avoid doing as they suggest.

That way my bookstores stand out in the marketplace.

CHAPTER SIX

TRADING PLACES

In January of '95, American Booksellers Association education director Willard Dickerson called me up and asked me to sit down. "Andy, how would you like to be dean of this fall's booksellers school in Latvia?"

The Children's Bookstore was headed into a demanding year. Since October of '94 we'd been running a small full-time outlet at Chicago Children's Museum's location on North Pier. Now we were immersed in planning the museum's much larger shop at Navy Pier, to be opened in September of '95. We also had seventy-five bookfairs on the docket. The count of superstores in the Chicago area had risen to eighteen, six of them close to us.

But how could I say no? I'd taught at several ABA schools, and I loved them.

ABA's Eastern European program had been going for several years—it was a function of the Soros Foundation's Open Society Institute. OSI had identified bookstores as some of the threatened institutions to try to assist in their transition from the centralized economic system of the Communist era to the free-for-all capitalist marketplace now emerging, since bookstores perform a vital informational and educational function in every free society. I'd been on the American Booksellers Association education committee when this overseas schools program had launched, and I'd alerted Willard I'd like to get involved.

I took a preliminary research trip to Latvia and submitted findings to John Mutter at *Publishers Weekly* that I felt would be of interest to US booksellers. Unfortunately my article kept getting bumped back week after week. *Publishers Weekly* eventually decided not to publish it.

Maybe they decided it was a bit biased against American chain superstores.

FACE TO FACE

One week last May I traveled a thousand country miles visiting two dozen small-town booksellers in preparation for a special American Booksellers Association seminar. Until 1992 their bookstores had been linked to a central warehouse, which took care of all inventory management. The booksellers' tasks were to unbox, shelve, and handle cash. They could place orders, but these would often be ignored. Still, their stores were well stocked, their clientele devoted.

Then, with the regional economy in a severe slump, these booksellers were forced to abandon their longtime practices and begin to manage their stores independently.

Some of them couldn't handle the slew of new responsibilities. Their towns lost bookstores. Others rose to the occasion, their creative energies unchained, and achieved startling success.

I was touring Latvia, courtesy of The Soros Foundation. The American Booksellers Association school there would be our seventh in Eastern Europe and the former Soviet Union.

To get an idea of bookstore privatization in Latvia, picture a huge bankrupt retail chain whose branches have been sold off to its employees. Most embraced their newfound autonomy, discovering within themselves the strengths, skills, and instincts required to operate a community bookstore.

Some booksellers have become entrepreneurs, buying multiple outlets. Some are importing books from Germany and Britain. One launched a lottery to underwrite town reconstruction. Another conducts a weekly literary-trivia contest in a local newspaper.

Several put in copy shops or cafés, or subleased space to currency exchanges. Many launched in-store reading groups, or off-site book clubs. One store put together a festival featuring a parade with costumed book characters and a sausage-and-vodka giveaway.

And there were newcomers as well, like the popular schoolteacher who convinced a publisher to underwrite a children's bookstore for her.

Several booksellers were participants in the revolt that brought Latvian independence, and one was particularly influential. Rebelling against the Soviet bookselling establishment, Inara Belinkaya took it upon herself to assert the historical identity of the Riga bookstore she managed.

Shortly after the rise of Gorbachev, in 1986, Belinkaya initiated a letter-writing campaign to restore her bookshop's pre-World-War-II name: Janis Roze Gramatnica. Janis Roze was the principal independence-era publisher and bookseller. Beginning in 1917, he produced 850 Latvian-language titles. A living symbol of the nation's cultural revival, Roze was sent to Siberia when the Soviets invaded in 1940. There he was starved to death.

His location was re-opened as a Soviet bookstore in 1949. Belinkaya started there in 1965. Her efforts to rename the store bore fruit in 1988, when petition drives, street rallies, and media coverage forced Moscow's hand. In the midst of the huge public renaming celebration, Belinkaya found herself face to face with Janis Roze's grandson.

Ainars Roze is a former beekeeper and boxing champion turned chair of the department of commerce at Latvian University. With the arrival of post-independence privatization, Roze was awarded ownership of his grandfather's storefront. He and Belinkaya became partners in Janis Roze Gramatnica.

Roze's activist approach to business strategy perfectly complements Belinkaya's gift for management and marketing. When I visited in 1995 there were three Roze bookshops in Riga, including a gorgeous new English-language store.

Inara Belinkaya, who in 1993 founded the Latvian Booksellers Association, recounted the history of Janis Roze Gramatnica as we dined in a fashionable jazz café in central Riga. Listening, I thought of the Soviet bookselling apparatchiks who hired her in 1965. They could never have expected that a young student of dance and English would catalyze an independence movement. Knowing the fate of Janis Roze should have kept any bookseller in line.

But it is a function of large institutions to train rebels. The martyrdom of Janis Roze had not frightened Belinkaya. It had inspired her.

"They could have killed you," I said. Smiling, she answered, "Of course."

The ongoing efforts of booksellers like Inara Belinkaya have blessed the former Soviet captive states with a diverse community of independent bookstores, acting as agents in the essential, never-ending process of individual and social transformation.

American booksellers, engaged in a difficult struggle to revive and strengthen community-based bookselling, can draw inspiration from Janis Roze, Inara Belinkaya, and all our independent-minded colleagues throughout the world.

□   □   □

After the first day of their September booksellers school, the forty Latvian booksellers were visibly uneasy. We'd been told one of the difficulties was tension dating from the period when they'd been locked together into the Soviet bookselling bureaucracy. Some of the booksellers had done cruel things to others. Now they were trying to run their shops like independent competitive capitalist enterprises. It wasn't easy for them to relax and act collegial.

At dinner I announced there'd be a special lecture and everyone should assemble back at the hall at 8:00 PM. No one was happy about this but they did all come. My colleagues—Stan Bolotin of Harvard Bookstore, Tracy Danz of Zondervan Publishing, and Valerie Lewis of Hicklebee's Bookstore—presented impromptu storytelling performances and songs before my lecture, so the Latvian booksellers were alert something unusual might be coming.

I stepped to the podium, cleared my throat, and launched into Kurt Schwitters's classic forty-five minute dada poem, *Ursonate.*

After a few seconds, when Berutha wasn't translating, the Latvians began to get irritated. She interrupted me excitedly. "Is it German poetry? From the early twentieth century? Is it Christian Morgenstern?" I was delighted: Morgenstern was a predecessor of Schwitters by a decade. I told her what I was doing, and she gave the booksellers a rapid explanation. She had a degree in poetry!

I continued with *Ursonate* and realized something was

happening I'd never experienced in my decade presenting the piece in Chicago venues with Art Institute instructor Lynn Book. Our audiences had always been composed of English speakers, so the nonsense was non-English. But here, the nonsense was equally non-English and non-Latvian. And, although the day had been spent communicating via translator, here were words requiring no translation. The text dropped down into the space between our languages. Valerie, Tracy, and Stan coached the group to join in chanting: they transformed to a jolly ensemble.

When we'd finished, the Latvians asked us to sit down, because now *they* were going to perform for *us*. They launched into an hour of rousingly rapid Latvian tunes with complicated rhythms and choruses. Lots of laughter. I'd read Latvian folk songs are a full-scale literary tradition. A nineteenth-century scholar compiled a comprehensive edition in multiple volumes.

They're bawdy.

Suddenly we were on our feet learning circle dances. One, called "Adam had Seven Daughters," required someone to go to the center and snatch someone to join him. There, the two would entangle into an impossible position. Each person in the circle then had to turn to his neighbor and wrap with her into the knot invented by the dancers in the center. This *could* involve the removal of clothing, but that night we didn't get farther than trading jackets and shoes.

The next morning I opened Valerie's and my talks about marketing and customer service by singing the Malvina Reynolds song "Magic Penny" as a means of explaining our theories of bookstores as community centers (love, given away, returns multiplied). On our final day, Tracy introduced his discussion of the publishing process by getting out his guitar and singing David Mallett's "Garden Song" (asking blessings for seeds sown).

After the lectures we had a final question-and-answer session. A seasoned bookseller who'd spent decades running a technical and intellectual bookstore in Riga asked a question that really gave pause: "What if you go bankrupt?"

I heard my voice answering, "You still have yourself," and explaining that even though out of the 130 bookstores in Latvia before the Soviet break-up, sixty had gone under, this was only because the economy had lost its linkages. Once the reforming economy developed new links, this well-educated country of book lovers would be able to support its bookstores again.

I pointed out that we American independent booksellers were facing the same risk of failure for opposite reasons. My store had been surrounded by six super-sized bookstores in a two-mile radius, and we might soon have to close. Our response had been to form a symbiotic alliance with another institution—Chicago Children's Museum—and our new store should be able to survive even if the old one couldn't. I advised a similar approach: the Latvian booksellers should look for unconventional allies. New networks didn't appear spontaneously; they had to be created.

In following years some of those booksellers' stores did go out of business, but others' thrived and expanded.

PUKE APOTHEOSIS

There's one set of consultants we must listen to: the people we suspect need our help, the people we live to serve, our customers. (Who also serve us, since they permit us to serve them.)

Thus, one day three field trip groups from three different schools—over a hundred children—swarmed into Children's Museum Store. Soon children were screaming chaotically, and long lines formed at both cash registers. I was staffing the store alone, and found myself rapidly shuttling between the registers, ringing up both lines of small customers simultaneously. A heroic adult male voice rose above the fray. "Does anybody here have a MOP???"

At first, I did not hear this voice. Insane rushes at that store did happen, especially at field trip bus-departure time. I'd learned to ride the waves of panic teachers send through frantic children. I'd entered my zone: fingers top speed, breath slow, rapid sentences voiced for the nth time, no mind. The man had to call out again before I realized I was the only person with whom this voice could possibly be trying to communicate. "Does anybody here have a MOP???"

I surfaced and stopped. The clamorous lines of seven-, eight- and nine-year-olds whose school buses, lined up outside the museum, were leaving in five minutes, quieted, as now no one was ringing on the cash registers.

"Does anybody here have a MOP???" The teacher stood at the center of a huge cluster of children. They were staring at the floor, holding their noses.

I came to an understanding. I darted out from behind the counter, into the back room, returning with mop and bucket. I pushed through the crowd. There, at the center, was a puddle of vomit.

Baloney sandwich, not digested.

A child's vomit has a special purity. The room still held a hundred people but was now intensely quiet.

I realized my mop was useless. I pushed through the crowd, rushed behind the counter, found a roll of paper towel, dove back through, down on the floor, and carefully sopped up the puke.

All eyes were on me. No one moved.

My brief task complete, I ran back behind the counter, put the towels in the trash, and began ringing the young customers again. They were now stunningly polite. None pushed or jostled. Each quietly presented his purchase, accepted his change, and waited nicely with his teacher. Soon I'd finished ringing all the children and they'd gone to the buses. The store was empty.

Those children, those teachers, are the only business consultants I'll ever pay attention to. Because I am those children; I am those teachers. So are you. We're all we've got.

Rabindranath Tagore explains, "[The] moral sense of man . . . enables him to see that he is not true when he is only restricted to his own self. He is more in truth than he is in fact. He truly belongs to individuals who are not included in his own individuality, and whom he is never even likely to know. As he has a feeling for his future self which is outside his present consciousness, so he has a feeling for his greater self which is outside the limits of his personality. There is no man who has . . . never sacrificed his selfish desire for the sake of some other person, who has never felt a pleasure in undergoing some loss or trouble because it pleased somebody else. It is a truth that man is not a detached being, that he has a universal aspect."

This is why you can trust yourself more than you can trust a consultant. Because it really matters to you, on a personal level, what you do, as a bookseller. If you understand your customers' vomit, you will never need a professional consultant, and you can understand your customers' vomit. Without their vomit (that is, without their pressing urgent needs), you can't and don't and won't exist as a bookseller, serving the public in whatever way these people deign to demand of you, which it is your privilege and honor to do.

Right? Why did the store fall silent as I cleaned up the kid's puke? Because everyone in the place realized that this moment epitomized something inexpressible in all our lives. The moment before, in that store, for those hundred people, shopping furiously, spending irrationally, noisily, thoughtlessly, everyone dizzy, exhausted, emotionally out of control, children screaming, teachers frantic, me a subhuman robot, that moment was *nauseating!*

The transformation of the scene into an enactment of abasement and humiliation—a theater of vomit cleansing—revealed us all as human. We found ourselves together, locked in the disgusting moment, with pure focus.

We became one. The moment required all of us to become aware of all of us. That was our vomit.

There's no such thing as *independent* bookselling. Who are we fooling? We have every one of us been dependent from the day we were born. Interdependent. That's what being a person means. None of us exists without all of us.

When you open a bookstore, you're acknowledging and celebrating your dependence on all the people you hope to serve. You're inviting them to bear you up on their shoulders. They alone can create your new identity as *their* bookseller. You're humbly requesting they do you this honor. You hope to be elevated to this status. You're also planning to abase yourself once you've been so elevated. Your customers will rarely be conscious of their roles as electors in your election. Rarely will you be cast as the star of a scene like my puke apotheosis.

In return for our customers' creation of our roles in their lives, we booksellers are also, importantly for them, pledging to assist them in depending on each other. We may provide our most important service in this area, and perhaps this is where you will find your breakthrough success mechanism. You're a nexus, a knower, a locus in your community. You're bringing in, as new members, all the artists of word and image who've contributed, individually and as an informal collective, to the future of humanity: you're representing these authors and illustrators in your neighborhood. You hope your customers will appreciate your services and establish new relationships in your beneficent presence. They'll become more themselves as they helpfully recommend the artworks called books to one another.

CHAPTER SEVEN

THE CONQUEST OF CHICAGO

When Children's Museum Store opened in September of '95, there weren't many other shops on Navy Pier yet, so our place didn't have much competition selling to the hundreds of thousands of visitors.

Omigod. Just like when we opened The Children's Bookstore, we were riding a crazy wave of success, so much business it was practically unmanageable. We built the staff up to twenty people by November, an outrageous number for a fifteen-hundred-square-foot place. Since we had only a tiny back room, the store had to be run out of Barney Nibble's: all receiving was happening three miles from the Pier, and we delivered the books and toys after ten every night, often working until two in the morning.

The entire value of merchandise on display was selling through every month, a rate more than three times the industry average.

At the same time, sales at The Children's Bookstore back on Lincoln Avenue were down again, despite another season of special events and publicity. And the fall bookfairs were off, which we felt resulted from the proliferation in book-buying opportunities parents had in all the new superstores.

With bookstore and bookfair company barely breaking even, and neither yielding a salary for Chris or me, the success of the museum store was forcing a choice on us. If we kept running the older businesses, they'd be living off the museum store. If we closed them, the museum store could pay down the bookstore's accumulated debt over two or three years.

Victor Podagrosi had died suddenly, at age forty-one.

As a long-time Child's Play board member, I resolved to assume Victor's grant-writing obligations for the coming year.

This made our choice even clearer. In December, we decided to close The Children's Bookstore on February 15. Child's Play's building on Armitage Avenue had a vacant downstairs office. From there we'd operate the museum store, and I could run upstairs and work on grant writing and development for a few hours each day.

In the midst of this we received a call from Linda Bubon, co-owner with Ann Christopherson of Women & Children First Bookstore. Linda had decided to convene a buy-local organization that could make the point to the public that indie bookstores were worth saving. The Independent Booksellers of the Chicago Area (IBCA) would also help us share skills. In other regions of the country such organizations had been in place for years—in fact indie booksellers were helping catalyze a national buy-local movement—but Chicago's extremely competitive retail climate had interfered with indie store owners getting to know one another.

IBCA's first meeting, at the beautiful new location of Howard Mandel and Gayle Seminara's store—Transitions Bookplace—was remarkable. There we were, twenty-five Chicago bookstore owners chatting amiably as if we'd always been friends. As we realized we should have been. We came up with all sorts of ideas, but best was the feeling none of us was alone in this time of trouble.

Surely the most surprising presence at that meeting, though, was that of William Rickman.

Bill had devoted his life to Kroch's & Brentano's, rising through the ranks to CEO. At its largest, in '89, Kroch's had operated twenty stores with a total $40 million annual market share. Since Chicago was at the time, according to the Book Industry Study Group, approximately a $400 million annual trade bookstore marketplace—the second largest in the country, after New York City—Kroch's was still as late as '89 very much the big brother.

Papa Kroch—that is, Adolph Kroch—founded what grew to be "the big store" on Michigan Avenue in 1909. Scholar Barbara Brannon says of the era, "The climate for bookselling in general had ranged from apathetic to dismal since the turn of the century; price-cutting by the large chain department stores made it difficult for independent bookstores to stay afloat, and this mass-market approach did not foster quality among the books most people bought. . . . Trade watchers complained that bookstores often did little in the way of actively seeking to create readers, or to pursue proven buyers with thoughtful suggestions. The time was ripe for change in a moribund industry."

By the thirties, Papa Kroch had gone into a loose partnership with Brentano's bookstore of New York and Paris: Papa Kroch had the rights on the Brentano's name in Illinois, but the store was the Kroch family business.

Adolph's son Carl took over management, and in the fifties pioneered the concept of the suburban chain bookstore when he opened branches of Kroch's in several new shopping centers. His formula was to open Kroch's & Brentano's outlets exclusively in malls anchored by Marshall Field department stores: his assurance of quality.

When Walden, Dalton, and Crown entered the Chicago market, Carl Kroch was confident the Chicago consumer would stay loyal to the hometown bookstore chain. He dismissed the idea that the computerization of Dalton meant he too must computerize, and he declined to match Crown's bestseller discounts.

In '86, Carl Kroch essentially walked away. At a moment many booksellers recognized as a time of major change requiring significant new investment—this was the year Dayton-Hudson sold B. Dalton, exiting the bookstore business, while Len Riggio bought those B. Dalton stores, committing his own company Barnes & Noble to a gigantic expansion—Chicago bookselling thane Carl Kroch telegraphed his intentions cross-country by bluntly informing *New York Times* reporter Andrew Malcolm, "The independent bookstore—you know we're almost dinosaurs in this country; I'm fearful for the future."

Kroch had no reason to fear for his own retirement: in '85 he'd cashed in with a cynical business move that had sealed the fate of his small chain and devastated the futures of his longtime employees. This maneuver had been touted as an innovative action designed to fend off an unnamed suitor who'd tendered what Kroch had described as "a tempting buyout offer." (Guess which ambitious New York discount bookstore chain had recently received an $18 million infusion from Anton Dreesmann of Dutch retail giant Vendex, promising this foreign investor rapid national expansion?)

Kroch's response to the not-tempting-enough offer was to instead launch an ESOP: an Employee Stock Ownership Plan. That is, he sold a large ownership stake in Kroch's & Brentano's to the employees themselves.

ESOPs are supposed to be a way to guarantee employee input into management. But in K&B's case the purchase of the store from Carl Kroch was made by the employee pension plan. Money that had been invested relatively safely was paid to Carl Kroch, in exchange for pension plan ownership of part of the company. Kroch had the pension's cash; the plan was left holding half of Kroch's & Brentano's, the remainder to be bought out over five years.

Although he had plenty of personal wealth—he owned part of the Cincinnati Reds baseball team, and he helped fund a library at Cornell University that cost millions—Carl Kroch did not make further adequate investment in turning his stores around. In particular, even in the late eighties after Barnes & Noble had bulled its way into Chicago via the B. Dalton acquisition, K&B didn't computerize chain wide. Several more stores were opened, some were refixtured, but when a Borders superstore arrived outside Chicago in Oakbrook Court Mall, in '89, just before a pilot Barnes & Noble superstore in Edina, outside Minneapolis, with rumors of a national superstore rollout on the horizon, refusing to computerize Kroch's & Brentano's twenty-store operation was tantamount to corporate suicide.

Only in '92—a year when several outside superstores opened in the Chicago market—did K&B seriously begin to computerize its inventory. And of course it encountered enormous difficulties making its new system work since it had a huge corps of longtime employees used to established paper-based systems.

Computerization couldn't save Kroch's. Nothing could, because the entire book industry was abuzz with insider gossip about K&B's precarious situation. Its failure became a self-fulfilling prophecy: $40 million in market share in '89; bankrupt in '96. The national chains were just moving in to make sure they picked up K&B's share when the regional chain went down.

An average superstore needs to gross between $3 million and $8 million per year. The inevitable closure of Kroch's meant eight or more superstores could live on the leavings. But since Barnes & Noble was closing down B. Dalton storefronts as rapidly as it opened B&N superstores, trading market share with itself, and since Borders (recently purchased by Kmart, which also owned Waldenbooks) was closing Waldenbooks locations when it opened nearby Borders superstores, also trading share with itself, and since Crown Books was closing regular Crown locations when it opened new Supercrowns, much more than the $40 million Kroch's share was in play. What with the ongoing collapse of a variety of independent booksellers, the entire $400 million Chicago market was up for grabs.

Borders was based in Ann Arbor, Michigan. Barnes & Noble was based in New York. During their early years of expansion—'88 to '91—the superstore chains informally staked out regional territory. Borders was expanding in the Midwest; B&N was putting outlets on the East Coast and in Texas, where it had purchased Bookstop, a regional chain. But because B&N owned B. Dalton, based near Minneapolis, B&N also launched a Midwest expansion strategy that overlapped Borders's. Chicago became a battleground where each chain was determined to establish dominance. Since Crown's strategy was also strongly regional—in Washington DC, Chicago, Texas, Los Angeles, and Seattle—Chicago looked set by '91 to play host to a three-way.

Unaccountably, the British chain Waterstone's, recently purchased by heavyweight W. H. Smith, had decided to launch its own superstores in the US. In '89 and '90 it opened one store each in Philadelphia and Boston. In '91 it came to Michigan Avenue in Chicago.

Waterstones stuck to one local outlet, but Barnes & Noble, Borders, and Supercrown did not limit their ambitions. Each peppered the Chicago region with stores, building close to one another. On the corner of Clark and Diversey, a mile from The Children's Bookstore, there were suddenly a ten-thousand-square-foot Supercrown, a twelve-thousand-square-foot B&N, and a twenty-thousand-square-foot Borders. Two miles south of us a forty-thousand-square-foot Borders opened next to a twenty-thousand-square-foot Waterstones. Two miles west of us a ten-thousand-square-foot Supercrown opened that was joined in '96 by a twenty-five-thousand-square-foot Barnes & Noble.

By '95 the superstore shakeout had begun. Waterstones went first, just four years after opening. In 2000 most Supercrowns closed when the chain went bankrupt. But B&N and Borders, in ensuing years, still pumped one new store each into the Near North and downtown markets. Superstore employee gossip said they did this to act as spoilers to one another.

During this period dozens of established Chicago bookstores closed: Adventures in Reading, Aspidistra, Barbara's Bookstore on Broadway, Barbara's Bookstore on Clybourn, Booksellers Row, The Bookworm, Child's Garden, Children's Reading Corner, Dan Behnke Books, Doubleday Bookstore, Le Grand Tour, Guild Books, all twenty Kroch's & Brentano's, Oak Street Books, Paul Rowe and Son, People Like Us, Platypus Bookstore, Rizzoli, Season to Taste, Toad Hall, Wilmette Book Gallery. Ironically for Chris and me, our erstwhile competitor from B. Dalton days, Stuart Brent, announced his legendary store's closing the same week we announced ours.

We decided The Children's Bookstore would go out with a bang. We condemned our superstore competitors with a fifteen-thousand-piece mailing to our customer list, plus press releases to 250 journalists.

We never received so much attention. Strange how with good news we had to work hard to get press but with bad news the media were at our service. Major articles appeared in the *Tribune* and *Sun-Times*. We were on radio and TV. Most reporters, some of whom had become personal friends over the previous ten years, kindly permitted us to make our socioeconomic argument. Other journalists, perhaps aiming to inject humor into the story, presented our politicized essay as an understandable emotional outburst: "Chris and Andy the sweet bookstore couple yell, 'Screw the chains!'"

A few writers, maybe wishing to ensure balanced coverage of a business story, attacked our ideas in a breezy way.

They were right in one respect: "Superstores are bad" wouldn't have made sense. But we hadn't said anything so simplistic. Our essay discussed the superstores' practice of buying way too many books then returning huge quantities unsold and how this caused financial problems for the publishers, who covered their costs by hiking suggested retail prices so sharply that consumers were now paying more for each book they bought.

We also explained that when a few chain-store buyers in New York can keep books off the shelves of bookstores nationwide, publishers lose confidence in putting out unusual or controversial books, endangering the free flow of information in society.

Although they gave us our say, no one in the media continued to explore this debate. It was one-shot coverage. Case closed. Most Chicago editors thought *human interest*, not *politics & society*.

Of course we knew reporters needed to subtly offer their

public that other more pungent story: "It's so sad when the little mom-and-pop store gets beaten up by the big corporation, but hey, they had it coming because that's the way the world works." The subtext is how nobody should stick his neck out and act fancier than the rest of us. Survival of the fittest. Eat or be eaten. Pride comes before a fall. Get regular jobs!

CNN put together a sob-spot on our closing and Stuart Brent's. ABA school instructor Steve Cogil phoned to say he'd been stuck in the Miami airport and the piece had been running every thirty minutes on airport TV. Not long afterward Tom Ehrenfeld of *Inc. Magazine* called with the news he'd selected The Children's Bookstore for his obituary column, which profiled significant business failures. This I felt was a bit much since our company hadn't failed and we were headed for a great year at the museum store. Still, I did love the idea of getting an obituary while we were alive: like Tom Sawyer attending his own funeral, or Robert Graves finding he'd been listed as dead, during World War I. I asked Tom to make sure to mention we were running a profitable spin-off company, and I thought this made his obit read oddly: "They're dead. Boo hoo. (Wait—they're alive?)"

So Bill Rickman of Kroch's did join our first Independent Booksellers of the Chicago Area meeting, and he generously hosted the next, on the second floor of the big store, down in the Loop. This surreal experience—meeting with other indie booksellers in the Kroch's inner sanctum; being befriended by a chain from which a few years before we'd been grabbing customers, and which had thought of our stores as flies at a picnic—was made especially odd by Bill's acting as though Kroch's was just another indie like the rest of us, instead of the huge company against whose backdrop all our professional careers had played out.

I don't know whether anyone shed a tear when Kroch's & Brentano's closed. The employees were already bitter: they'd lost everything, since their pension plan's investment in the K&B ESOP was essentially worthless to most of them. The customers preferred the new superstores with their superior locations and long hours. The only people to be simply sad were independent booksellers.

This surprised no one so much as us. We realized a strong Kroch's & Brentano's—one that was not overly ambitious—had made our existences possible. By appearing intimidating, K&B had kept the outside chain presence in Chicago limited. Fancy-schmancy on the outside but stolid and workmanlike internally, K&B had left niche and neighborhood markets unserved. For decades Carl Kroch had been declining opportunities to put a big store into Lincoln Park on the North Side—where many independents like Guild Books and The Children's Bookstore opened in the seventies and eighties— merely because there was no Marshall Field department store in the neighborhood for him to open next to, as was his wont. And yet when the new superstores appeared, they all located in this gaping (from their standpoint) hole, and wiped most of us indies out. (Altogether, we North Side independents who closed represented perhaps $10 million in market share: a tidy sum to tack onto the Kroch's bounty.)

Linda Bubon also invited us to participate in a smaller collaboration, aside from the IBCA launch. She'd cooked up a plan to grab the upcoming Hillary Clinton autograph event away from the forty-thousand-square-foot North Michigan Avenue Borders.

Clinton was promoting *It Takes a Village and Other Lessons Children Teach Us* with a national tour. Since a big-name autographing can sell thousands of books, a title like *Village* retailing for $20 can generate $40K. Linda felt several independent bookstores could collaboratively produce the event at a major downtown site. We'd propose to rent Chicago Theatre, a grand old landmark seating two thousand. Barbara's Bookstore, The Bookstall at Chestnut Court, The Children's Bookstore, 57th Street Books, and Women & Children First would among us undertake to sell presigned books, and the purchase of a book at any of our locations would provide a voucher good for admission to our downtown event. We'd split the total proceeds evenly: five ways among our five companies. To spin the proposed evening out, June Podagrosi and I promised excerpts from Child's Play's '96 show, *Kids for President,* plus a performance by The Happiness Club, choreographer Gigi Faraci's socially activist troupe of child dancers. Maggie Daley, the mayor's wife, joined our team, agreeing to be Hillary's introducer should we land the deal.

Our proposal looked better than Borders's to the White House and Simon & Schuster. We won the right to produce our program.

We all promoted Clinton in our newsletters: Chris and I built this pitch into the mailing announcing The Children's Bookstore's closure. Chicago Theatre was jammed, but everything went off smoothly. After our children's theater program, Hillary gave a talk describing model community development programs. Then row-by-row the entire audience came to the stage to shake her hand.

As the event wound down I asked Hillary how the tour was going. She expressed amazement at the intensity of interest: "In Detroit, people waited in a line that stretched outside Borders for four hours. In the rain!"

This was diplomatic. I could tell she felt we'd done better than the Detroit Borders. We'd delivered an exceptional experience to our customers. Linda Bubon's collaborative strategy had been right on the money.

WHAT'S SELLING

The most important business consultants you'll have are your customers. However, you'll be ignoring the words coming out of their mouths, in taking their advice, because they don't know what they need you to do. Instead, you must watch what *they* do. It's often the reverse of what they say.

To make these observations, you must set up situations where you can 1) see them in action, and 2) retain the flexibility to react to your research. So I *will* advise this, specifically, in terms of your set-up plans: Flexibility in all things.

Initial fixtures: Flexible. Initial systems: Flexible. Initial staff configurations and staffing levels: Flexible. Initial hours of opening: Flexible. Initial products and services defined, offered and priced: Flexible.

As soon as you've placed an order for twenty bookcases from that major fixture supplier, you've ruined your flexibility in display. As soon as you've hired your friends the qualified retail manager and the qualified bookkeeper, you've risked ruining your flexibility in systems and staff levels.

Luckily, the most important element of any bookstore is inherently flexible. I mean the inventory. You can test any book, and if your customers love it you can order more. If your customers appear to not even see some title you're testing, you can mark it down to move it out, or send it back where it came from and use your return credit to order something you think your customers will notice.

Now, the big stores have 150,000 titles. So they say. And, if you look back at the Book Industry Study Group's many years of of book-buyer surveys, you'll see that the majority of readers have said the number one thing they want in a bookstore is breadth of inventory.

However, this has been a case of customers saying one thing and doing the opposite. In fact, bookstores have consistently observed exponential power laws in play among customers, in patterns related to Vilfredo Pareto's century-old observation that distributions of assets and earnings in market economies fall along curves. Such empirically observed power-law patterns are usually referred to as "80/20 rules."

The bookstore industry's most commonly cited 80/20 rule of thumb says 80 percent of revenues come from 20 percent of titles: most people buy mostly the same books as their neighbors.

At The Children's Bookstore, we kept an average of thirty thousand different titles in stock. We consistently observed that the 80/20 rule was true. We also observed a 50/5 rule. That is, fifty percent of sales came from five percent of titles. During a $500K sales year, $250K came from fifteen hundred titles. The next $150K came from forty-five hundred additional titles. The last $100K came from the last twenty-four thousand titles.

What an astonishing figure! Out of a thirty-thousand-title bookstore, twenty-four thousand of those titles accounted for only a fifth of the sales! How horrible! Why carry all those sluggish books?

Well, consider the superstores' 150,000 titles. In a typical superstore, doing, say $5 million per year—120,000 of the titles are responsible for $1 million, and 30,000 titles or fewer are responsible for the other $4 million! *New York* magazine reported on July 19, 1999: "According to Barnes & Noble merchandising executives, just 100 of the more than 45,000 new titles in its superstores make up 20 percent of new-title sales revenue; just 500 titles make up the same portion of revenue from more than 500,000 backlist books [that are sold chainwide]. The book industry, says the retail consultant Paco Underhill, increasingly tends to sell books the way Baskin-Robbins sells ice cream—stocking 31 flavors to sell just 4."

And so we see when customers inform survey takers they need breadth of inventory to be convinced to shop at a particular bookstore, they're really saying they need that breadth as décor!

ABA Executive Director Bernie Rath once told me publishing executives referred to all those rows of bookcases at superstores as wallpaper.

A discount-book wholesaler told me the Borders discount-book buyer had boasted much of that chain's nineties-era profit came from sales of publishers' overstock discount books in the small area near the cash registers!

And, consider this: one of the fastest growing sectors of storefront bookselling is nonbookstore locations. That's right: whether in warehouse clubs or The Eric Carle Museum Gift Shop, every year, people are increasing their storefront book buying at nonbookstores more than at bookstores.

At Children's Museum Store we carried fifteen hundred

titles. Our book sales there were only half what they'd been at The Children's Bookstore, where, once again, we used to carry thirty thousand titles. Boy, did we have a better return on investment selling books at Children's Museum Store than we'd had at The Children's Bookstore! Customers turned out to love a tiny title base. They'd simply never have admitted this to themselves.

I'm not suggesting you open a bookstore with fifteen hundred titles. Our fifteen hundred titles sold so well because our customers' expectations were not geared toward *bookstore,* so they didn't feel critical of the small selection. They were thinking *museum store* and they regularly praised us for our *large* selection!

Now, perhaps you thought I was going to advise you which books to buy for your new store? Is this because buying is the aspect of ownership you thought would be most enjoyable? Oh dear. Everyone wants to be the buyer. Every owner, every employee, every expert customer: "Always keep X book on the shelves!" Or, "Those stores have no taste; ours will have an exquisite selection." Again, bookstores need wallpaper, and our favorite books make great decoration.

Unfortunately, we will never be the buyers in our stores. Our customers are the only buyers. We shape their purchases, but much less than we may wish. Rather, we learn what books they need, and provide these for them.

Keep in mind booksellers buy from publishers on a returnable, consignment basis. So, bookstores don't really *buy* from publishers. While it's true that our customers may return books they buy, their purchases are generally final. So, in all that collaborative, incestuous family of authors, agents, editors, illustrators, book designers, printers, sales representatives, and booksellers, there are no buyers. The true buyers are readers themselves and the professionals who serve them (teachers and librarians).

I don't mean to suggest there's no such thing as prescriptive bookselling. Naturally we should leave ourselves in a position to enlighten the unenlightened as to the very best books. But remember the reason 5 percent of the titles account for 50 percent of the sales is that those 5 percent are flying off the shelves by themselves. For some reason there are certain titles in any market that customers snatch up. We can't stop them. These may be titles we don't like. Or, we may be delighted these are the books that sell.

It's not up to us. What *is* up to us is to make sure titles that demonstrate they act in this way are always in stock, in stacks, in our stores (not easy: we're monitoring thousands of books and we're very busy).

As Leonard B. Meyer explains in *Music, The Arts, and Ideas*, "Democracy does not entail that everyone should like the same art, but that each person should have the opportunity to enjoy the art he likes. . . . Respect and esteem for the dignity of other human beings—which I take to be central to the democratic ethos—does not, fortunately, depend upon aesthetic taste and sensitivity."

So when you discover some title unleashes guaranteed buying in your customers, don't ignore this knowledge. This is the key to your survival. Your customers show you by their actions what titles work in your store. But if you've bought two copies of a title, and if they sell in two days, and if you don't immediately bring in two more copies, then two more, then five—and if you don't discover at what pace and in what quantity this title must always be reordered so it's never absent from your shelves: well, you're dead.

This is The Second Rough Rule of Rebel Bookselling (with thanks to leading bookseller Eliot Leonard):

SMOWS
(Sell More Of What's Selling)

You can see you don't need me to give you a booklist. What you need to assemble is any assortment of titles you think people who'll claim your store as theirs will love. You need to keep close track of what sells each day, even to a trickle of customers. *(Read: computerized inventory system from day one.)* You need to re-order every title that sells. You need to continue this process, while watching for trends. You need to research additional titles complementary to those that are selling and seriously consider phasing out poor performers. Your reward will be a unique inventory of books that's perfect for your community.

CHAPTER EIGHT

DEBTORS' PRISON

I paid no attention to our bookstore's liquidation: Chris was left to run this awful process by herself, with the assistance of our staff. We rented a huge dumpster. Over the course of weeks the thing filled up with paperwork, spinner racks, scrap wood, damaged books. It was hauled away, and we needed another.

We were sitting on more than $250K in vendor debt. In retrospect we should have closed the store two years before: after Supercrown had joined Barnes & Noble at the corner of Clark and Diversey and our customers had started confessing to us at the register that they *had no choice* but to shop at the superstores because all books were 20 percent off. But we'd decided that if we closed on Lincoln Avenue our negotiating position for a new location would be destroyed. Instead we'd ramped up our promotional campaign. Our school-partnership fundraising program, the creation and operation of Children's Bookmobile, all our activity had functioned as a smokescreen to ensure we could continue negotiating from strength.

The strategy had worked. But its cost had been this debt. By the time we'd started buying inventory for the museum store it was incredible to me anyone would extend us credit. We were lucky to be relying on different vendors.

Children's Museum Store had to be an educational toy store with a limited book inventory since Barbara's Bookstore, two doors down, was watching to ensure we didn't exceed the 20 percent of floor space our contract permitted for books. Operating a toy store meant we were selling products that traditionally received a much higher markup than books. We needed that money.

But there was an unexpected additional benefit to being a nonbookstore.

Doubling a product's cost to arrive at its final retail price is called *keystoning*. Specialty toy stores assume most products will be keystoned at the very least, whereas in the bookstore business, with its products oddly sporting preprinted suggested retail prices and fully returnable for vendor credit, retailers rarely can sell to customers at keystoned prices. Children's Museum Store, however, fell under the gift-store banner: our old friends the bookstore sales representatives weren't allowed to call on us. Instead, gift-store sales reps turned up to sell us the very same titles the bookstore reps had been selling us before.

We were invited to choose nonreturnable terms and receive standard 50 to 55 percent discounts off publishers' suggested retail prices, yielding keystoned profits on books.

We'd been uneasy buying as wholesalers, into our book-fair company, and illegitimately reselling into our retail store. Now we were being offered the chance, as a gift store, to receive that same wholesaler discount level, as long as we agreed to the gift-store standard no-returns clause. This was a no-brainer since books we placed into Children's Museum Store were chosen because they'd sell fast. If they sat around instead, we could mark them at 60 percent off to move them out as sale books.

Who needed return privileges? Returns for credit had

been wasting not only our vendors' money, but ours as well. (Since '96 we've bought nonreturnable whenever possible.)

I didn't have the stomach to deal with the day-after-day screaming phone calls from collections agents and lawyers. This task was left to our bookkeeper. When I darted down from Child's Play to the museum store office in the middle of the day I'd hear her telling outrageous lies on the phone. I'd never told her to lie to the collections agents, but I didn't tell her not to. I knew what those guys were like. Scary.

I heard her say, "The man who signs checks comes by every two weeks and he was through a few days ago."

I wanted to run back upstairs.

Sometimes a sales rep would be in our office selling to our toy buyer. These meetings would go on for hours with the rep pulling out more and more catalogs, and our buyer placing orders from many. She knew each order she placed with a new vendor might yield a shipment we wouldn't pay for until months later. The toy reps loved us! Everything they could get us on account we'd consider.

Watching this drove me up a tree. How long could the charade continue?

Chris couldn't stand it either. We handed a lot of autonomy to our staff—and since their responsibilities hinged on one another, we began to see conflict.

Back at The Children's Bookstore, Chris and I had been around to troubleshoot, but now both of us were wrestling with a desire to ignore the crisis at the heart of our so-successful store.

In July, several staff members had a nasty turf war over salespeople's right to unilaterally modify product displays created by buyers. The lead buyer quit; Chris and I fired the store manager and several employees. The crew that stayed started its own feud shortly afterward. By October more people were out. In December, after we'd announced everyone's hours would be cut because sales had settled in at lower levels, most of the remaining staff quit.

The reasons for our staff infighting were threefold. Yes, there'd been turf battles. Yes, Chris and I hadn't been fully present during '96 because closing The Children's Bookstore had eaten us alive emotionally. But worst was the simple experience of working at Navy Pier.

Back when The Children's Bookstore had opened, we'd found it challenging to maintain our sanity among the customers. But we'd become accustomed to them and even come to consider many as friends.

Most significant was the effect our children had on Chris's and my lives as Chicagoans. The kids had gone to daycare and school. We'd hung around at playgrounds and thrown birthday parties. Among other parents, our identities as owners of The Children's Bookstore were comfortable masks.

By the time we closed, we'd been offering six free story hours each week for years. I'd been presenting two of these myself, while talented staff members had each performed weekly as well. Our story hours had been well attended: ten to thirty families each time, plus daycare groups and field trip classes. Our styles had been diverse: each storyteller had developed a faithful following.

So in eleven years Chris and I had passed through an entire cycle. We'd become part of the lives of many families, and they'd become part of ours.

Surely an unacknowledged reason we hadn't closed back in '93 was that it would have been embarrassing. We lived in Chicago, our children went to school, what would we *say* to friends?

Perhaps the scheme of landing the store on the Pier had been a cover for this wish not to confront the truth that we couldn't stay "Chris and Andy from Children's Bookstore."

By '96, everywhere I went, I knew people and they knew me. I'd become a personality bookseller—like Stuart Brent—and it was fun. Being Andy-from-Children's-Bookstore had all sorts of nuances. I helped schools raise money, told stories to kids, had the perfect present for any child's birthday. When a tragedy filled the news, therapists rushed to me, and I found books for their practices.

I felt useful.

But Children's Museum Store was in a tourist mall, so there was no neighborhood clientele. The thousands of customers we knew from The Children's Bookstore each came to the Pier once a year. They greeted me warmly as an old friend, told me how their family mourned the loss of The Children's Bookstore, and commented on how awful Navy Pier was.

Staring in amazement at the tourists, they'd say, "Why would anybody come here? It's crowded!" Tell me about it. Those crowds were our new customers.

I used to joke, "We've died and gone to retail heaven." The only problem was we never wanted to be retailers: bookselling is different because it has a social agenda. It has meaning. Where's the meaning in selling a Superball, T-shirt, or plastic monkey mask?

The world was at Navy Pier, each person a first- and last-time visitor. On Saturday nights I'd hear five or six languages spoken by the hundreds of customers swirling in, around, and out of the store. Women in saris, evening gowns, burkhas, ripped T-shirts. The lines could build so I was ringing nonstop for four hours: $2,500 in $10 increments.

Each customer would have *nothing* in common with the one before.

Here's a guy from India buying presents for his children. Then a family of five from West Virginia: the boys bouncing balls wildly. Hovering behind are three ladies from the North Shore in elegant dresses and heels buying *cuuuuute* baby books. Next, a biker couple. His thick arms ripple with tattoos; she's a Goth incarnation with spiky hair and purple lips; they're buying a frog puppet. And while they wait they're grabbing handfuls more: a plastic cockroach, a harmonica necklace, a lollipop with a cricket in it.

The words that came out of their mouths!

Many of these people were straightforwardly unpleasant—to each other, to their kids, to us. Men, lewd about women; teens, nasty about mentally handicapped adults; whites insulting blacks, blacks insulting whites. Bald-faced stuff.

Day after day, we were drawn into repulsive interactions. In '95 and '96 our staff became walking anthologies of horror stories. All you had to do was ring on a busy afternoon, and you'd be guaranteed several unpleasant adrenaline rushes.

One of our part-timers used Children's Museum Store tales in her nightclub stand-up routine. Another taped customer comments and used the recording for a University of Chicago linguistics paper.

Our big problem was shoplifting. We settled in at an astronomical 10 percent theft rate. Staffing heavily didn't help. We could have eight staffers staged throughout our small store, but when 100 customers were swirling through there was nothing we could do to keep people from stuffing things in pockets and disappearing into the crowded mall.

But since tourists at the Pier *bought* toys when they were

marked way up, we could pay for shoplifting by identifying junk that sold when overpriced. Bring in a sparkly ring for five cents, sell it for 50 cents, and if you sell four and a fifth is stolen, it's just cost 25 cents to earn $2.

Making this shift to selling marked-up garbage was our only option.

And then, Chris and I made money. No matter how many awful experiences we had in that store, at least we could pay down the old Children's Bookstore debt.

Our staff would never be able to make this accommodation, though. When I'd arrive from Child's Play at 6:00 PM to begin my evening stint on the Pier, our salespeople would be seated on stools behind the register regaling each other with tales of incredible customers. I knew the stories were true. All humanity was at Navy Pier. The first year's official count was nine million. Thus the destruction of the staff. Chris and I were left, in January of '97, with a breathing space. Midwinter was slow. We knew a busy spring break was around the corner. But must we hire more staff? If we did, would we then watch these unfortunate workers be destroyed in their turns?

And here, incongruously, reappeared a familiar friendly presence. Willard Dickerson, still ABA's education director, had invited me to teach marketing and customer service at the Specialty Store booksellers' school in Nashville.

The school got off to a strange start. One of the instructors—Sally Jordan of Jeremy's Books in Houston—had to cancel at the last minute. So Willard asked me to teach advertising and publicity, which I'd done before, but for which I hadn't brought any supporting materials.

No problem. Our team—Clara Villarosa of Hue-Man

Experience Bookstore in Denver, Jay Weygandt of Logos Bookstore in Springfield, Ohio, and Willard himself—had worked ABA schools in various combinations.

But—another problem. The box filled with handouts and overhead transparencies Willard had shipped from New York had gone astray. UPS tracked the errant box to a sorting facility, then couldn't find it. We had to run the school without these materials.

No problem. We're booksellers, dammit. We're tough!

(Was I still a bookseller, though?) I didn't voice this internal query and, as in Latvia, acted hearty about our deal with Chicago Children's Museum and confident that anyone can make new networks, and throw ten things against a wall to see which sticks.

Besides, I knew I was still a children's bookseller. It was obvious, teaching those owners with their struggles, that I with my million-dollar location and eager customers buying their marked-up junk qualified as the luckiest damned businessman on the planet.

In '96 we'd sold $250K in children's books on gross museum store sales of $908K.

That's a lot of children's books. You can take the children's bookseller out of The Children's Bookstore but you can't take The Children's Bookstore out of the children's bookseller. So *there.*

On the other hand, working with those sixty booksellers, I felt keenly that we weren't running a bookstore, but rather a touristy toy store with books as a sideline.

I began to feel lost. I didn't know how to think about the coming year. I knew we couldn't hire; I was determined not to bring in staff just so they could flip out. But how could we run such an insane store without hiring?

One evening in the hotel bar I told Willard what was going on. He'd been in business since the mid-sixties, founding three companies. The last had grown to become the eighty-member Logos Bookstore Association. He'd *retired* to run ABA's education department. I'd first taught alongside him ten years before, in '87.

Willard leaned back in his chair. "What are your two biggest fixed expenses?"

"Well, I don't have any fixed expenses."

Willard scrutinized me. "Rent?"

"It's a percentage-of-the-gross deal. Rent varies with sales."

He sat up, puzzled. "There must be a minimum."

"They expected me to do a lot less business. I told them I'd probably be doing $900K per year, but they thought I couldn't do more than $500K and they set the minimum on that basis, at a low level, as it turned out."

His face brightened. "So if your gross sales *dropped* then your rent to the museum would drop? No problem of bumping up against a minimum alternative payment?"

"Right," I said. "Strange, huh?"

He raised his eyebrows. Then he said, "Okay, occupancy cost isn't fixed. What about staff? What percentage of the gross are you spending?"

I groaned. "At this point I have practically no staff, and I don't think I can bear to hire anyone. The setting is stressful: it destroys people. The customers can be incredibly rude, there's so much theft—"

He interrupted me, "So, your staff costs *right now* are low?"

"Yeah."

"You have control over your two largest expenses: rent and labor. How low do you think you can keep your labor costs?"

"I don't know. I'm expecting to work a ton of hours

myself. It's dead in the evenings at least through spring, so I can put orders together and receive merchandise at the register. I can run the two registers at the same time when there are crowds. I still have a bookkeeper working half time. Chris can relieve me for a few hours in the middle of each day; I'll have part-timers working Sundays. I think my labor costs are going to stay low, yeah."

"Andy, you don't have problems. You're in an ideal situation. If you can run that store with the level of staff you're talking about, it will be extremely profitable. You might even consider—" He paused.

"What?"

"You might even consider *raising* your sideline prices until the number of items you sell *drops.* Your margin will increase, and you'll see more dollars of bottom-line net profit. You may cause your top-line gross sales figure to *decline* by doing this! Still, the trade-off is you'll be handling fewer products, so that's less receiving, fewer items crossing the counter. It will be less work for you to run the store. Now, if your gross sales do decrease because you've increased your prices, of course your rent payment to the museum will drop, but that's not an important number to you. You only care about your dollars of net profit. And I'll bet you can get an increase in net profit if you carefully increase those prices, while also reducing your workload and reducing the likelihood you'll have to do much hiring."

Willard was advising me to do with sidelines what the mega-publishers had been doing with books: raise prices and reduce the number of items sold!

When I returned to Chicago and explained to Chris this way we could avoid hiring employees, she felt I hadn't understood Willard, and in any case not hiring as we headed into spring break would destroy our family life. But I was desperate for a break from employee management. I insisted on working the eighty-plus hours each week. I felt I was doing the only possible thing.

Most of the year our store hours—mandated by Navy Pier—were 10:00 AM to 10:00 PM; during the summer, Friday and Saturday till midnight. I worked all the hours except Sundays. The Sunday crew had stayed sane and survived. So even though my days were extremely long, it was only six days a week. Except—during the summer I worked Sundays from 6:00 PM to 10:00 PM on my own as well.

Our new buying strategy was the opposite of the one we'd used in '96. We reduced inventory diversity, paid cash up front, and kept fast sellers in stock. We pushed prices up until people complained to one another (no one notices dumb cashiers listening), then reduced prices hour by hour until we discovered what most customers would pay.

In this way, between February and April we identified fifteen hundred books that sold rapidly and a thousand toys that could sustain a high markup.

How was it different working alone at Navy Pier? The strange little con games, the phony travelers' checks, the spilled soft drinks, the abusive parents, the random insults: all were the same as in '96. But I had no one to tell the stories to. Without someone to turn to with an exasperated smirk, or with livid outrage, I was forced to accept these people.

And I did. I became more outward-facing. I could tell myself, "Calm down. Relax. Relax. It doesn't matter. Shhhhh."

One of the first things I changed was the way I'd respond

to queries about the store itself. In '96 I'd always called us *Children's Museum Store*, not *Chicago Children's Museum Store*. When people had asked who I was, I'd called myself the owner.

Now though, all alone at the cash register, sixty school-children marauding through the place, an angry teacher demanding a special educator's discount insists on speaking to the manager. When I say, "I'm the owner," I am greeted with simple disbelief. The self-righteous teacher thinks I'm lying.

"You're *what?* I'd like to speak to your supervisor right now."

"I. Am. The. Owner."

Oh no, this was not a functional exchange.

Instead I learned to act the lowly cashier. This worked well. It matched everyone's expectations. Here's this slob, a man no less, wearing an apron, what's he earning, $7 an hour?

I'd calculated I was personally earning $50 an hour, 80 hours a week, 52 weeks a year: a $210K annual salary.

Knowing this did help me somewhat.

Consider: we'd cut sixteen people and were pocketing all their paychecks.

So I acted the poor cashier. And it worked! People were constantly sympathizing with me.

"Are you alone here?! Why don't they give you any help, dear?"

"Oh, I like to work alone."

"Well, they should give you some help, you should make them, they *have* to! Look at all these kids, how can you *stand* these kids?"

"Oh, I'm used to them."

I became incredibly fast on the registers. Because we'd narrowed our product base to twenty-five hundred items and puzzled over every product and its price, I could glance at someone's pile of stuff in her arms and ring the whole thing up. When she deposited her goodies on the counter expecting the transaction to *begin*, I'd tell her the total and begin bagging the merchandise. As she recovered from her shock and began to fumble for money, I'd zip to the other register and ring someone up over there. I'd be back at register one in time to take the money or credit card that slowpoke had finally come up with, and then—after swiping the card, but before the approval authorization came through—zip back over to register two to take *that* person's money. I'd complete the cash transaction on register two and reach over just in time to grab the credit card slip printing over by register one, flipping it onto the counter for the original customer to sign.

In this way, I kept my lines of customers moving even when I had one of those overwhelming days when I was ringing nonstop for hours at a stretch.

One March morning I was deluged by field trip groups: dozens of seven-year-olds zooming around the store, while their teachers and parent chaperones chatted by the door. After ten minutes, adults shouted that buses were leaving. Kids crowded around the counter.

The phone rang. I jammed it between cheek and shoulder. "Children's Museum Store, this is Andy."

"I have David Schlessinger on the line. Will you hold, please?"

"Yes." David was founder and CEO of the Zany Brainy toy store chain. This call could mean any of five things, some good, some terrible, and I thought of them all immediately.

I continued to ring on the register.

He came on the line. "Is this Andy?"

"Yes. David. Nice to get a chance to say hello."

"Right. Do you have a minute? I was wondering if we could talk."

"Well, I'm alone with sixty schoolchildren frantically throwing money at me. Could we schedule a call for tomorrow? Or this afternoon?"

He said, "That's nice: to get back to the customer sometimes. No, I'll be coming to Chicago next month; I'll transfer you to my assistant so you can set up a time to sit down. Goodbye."

I begged his assistant to call me tomorrow. She agreed. As I continued ringing the kids I reviewed each of David's words. Why would he want to sit down with me?

He'd hired away our bookfair company manager Margaret Wroclawski during the fall '94 season. I'd learned from her that David was using ABA's *Art of Selling Children's Books* film as a staff-training tool in all his stores. Margaret had starred in the film, which was how David had known to headhunt her.

Fine. Business is business. I hadn't begrudged her the chance to become Zany's national book buyer: I'd been proud.

I'd finished ringing up the children; the store was empty.

I thought about David's words, "That's nice: to get back to the customer sometimes." He'd been fumbling for something friendly to say, to relieve embarrassment I might feel about having to work at my store's register.

I knew he'd started his first used bookstore when he was nineteen, grown it into a chain called Encore, sold this chain to Rite Aid Drugs for $13 million, and launched Zany Brainy a few years later with Microsoft cofounder Paul Allen as his key investor.

"That's nice: to get back to the customer sometimes." Here I was, pinned to the customer, unable to escape the customer. Our entire operation was there in that store, and he was building an empire. He had three dozen ten-thou-sand-square-foot educational toy superstores already. Margaret had told me he'd reach a hundred and fifty loca-tions within two years.

What had happened to us? We hadn't wanted to create an empire—Chris and I hated the idea—but why hadn't we been able to control the entity we *had* created? And what was *his* motivation? His stores were disastrous for small operators like us. What was I doing, thinking about him in this pleasant way? He was our enemy.

(Well, yes, in my prior year's identity as Child's Play Touring Theatre's Director of Development I had bitten the bullet and approached Zany Brainy as a supplicant. David had responded to my Fed-Ex'd proposal with an e-mail: the fundraising packet had been forwarded to his marketing people. After which there'd been no response to my repeated phone messages.)

But today David had called me at Children's Museum Store. This couldn't be about Child's Play.

Anyway, who cares if everyone says he's a nice guy? Every superstore I'd ever met had tried to kill me. Why was he calling? Why didn't he *say* why he called? Was he trying to drive me crazy to soften me up? Planning to threaten and extort something?

I'd arranged for a breakfast meeting since I couldn't leave the store once we opened at ten. David came by at eight, and we walked from the Pier toward a diner on Grand. He said, "Margaret's been wonderful to work with. You know she put together a summer reading program featuring the *Magic Treehouse* books: we sold 17,000."

"Wow. That's amazing."

He said he didn't know what I knew about him, but that he'd come out of the bookstore business. He'd gotten the idea for the Zany Brainy company browsing in the children's department of a B. Dalton in Atlanta. The books had been jammed onto the shelf spine out: he'd realized if those covers were face-out they'd sell better. He'd decided to open a store that sold children's books with all the covers face out. He'd already wanted to get into selling children's CD-ROMs: no one was doing a good job, and he'd been certain there'd be a huge market soon. But he'd felt he'd have to sell books at ten percent off to be competitive, and that CD-ROMs couldn't have a high markup either, so he'd looked for a category with higher margins: he'd settled on educational toys.

I was glad to learn David still thought of himself as a bookseller: it made me a little more comfortable. I said, "We're in the same business; we're not alone as booksellers who've learned to make money selling more sidelines than books. Did you know the typical Christian bookstore sells mostly sidelines? I read that in *Publishers Weekly*. I guess we shouldn't call them sidelines, or we shouldn't call ourselves booksellers."

He laughed and said, "It's an oxymoron. We're oxymorons."

I suddenly knew who he was. We could have been two members of a high school chess team.

He continued. "I'm on the board of the Please Touch Museum in Philadelphia. They're expanding, and I've agreed to run their store. I've also been approached by seven other children's museums. I'm trying to decide whether to do any of their stores. I wanted to hear your thoughts about running stores for children's museums."

This directness did surprise me. I'd spent a month waking in the middle of the night wondering if Chris and I would somehow lose our business at this meeting. How could David not expect I'd be scared to meet with him? Of course we'd considered running stores for other museums ourselves. We'd rejected a number who'd asked us to take their stores over, since these didn't seem to offer opportunities on a par with Chicago's. I said, "Well, those museums are right to try outsourcing. How much space will Please Touch give you?"

"They've set aside a thousand square feet. It's too small for anything resembling a full Zany. We've been thinking it could double as a place where people in the city could place orders we'd fill through our suburban stores."

I asked, "So you'd probably be happy if the place just broke even?"

"The problem is it could be a distraction. That's why I'm wondering if we should be opening stores for a number of other museums as well. Maybe the opportunity is the larger project."

We'd picked up pancakes at the cafeteria counter and carried our plates to a table. I told him, "I've turned down five museums: Grand Rapids, Kohl Museum in Wilmette, Dupage, Pasadena, one in Wisconsin, one in Nebraska— actually I've spoken to directors from dozens of museums. A lot have been through to look at Chicago Children's Museum. There are problems with these museum store projects."

"Then why are you running the store here?"

I was having trouble figuring out how much to tell him.

He was talking casually; he seemed to be unaware he was a threat. I decided to assume that since he was doing the conversation, he wasn't intending to attack. I'd use the opportunity to try again to raise money for Child's Play. I'd tell David what I knew about the children's museum store field. It wasn't encouraging anyway.

"The money we're making is because the museum is located on Navy Pier. Our store is open twice as many hours as the museum: they'll close tonight at five, but all the Pier's stores will stay open till ten. During the summer we're open till midnight on weekends, and there's business that late. The store is doing $900K per year. Half comes from museum traffic, but our profit comes from Pier visitors."

"That's a lot of business for a store your size. Why don't you think the museum is responsible for more of your profit?"

"Because what's selling is an inventory we've developed to match actual demand, whereas products the museum wants us to sell don't move fast. See, the museum has five new exhibits each year and asks us to match those with customized merchandise selections. You know when you bring in a new product assortment, you mark down slow-moving products and reorder successful ones, but when we have to develop brand new assortments every two months there's no chance to benefit from data collection. We end up putting a lot of square footage at the service of the museum's mission instead of store profitability."

I continued, "Also, in terms of dealing with the field nationally, there's another problem. Chicago has one of only a few dozen fully professional children's museums. It's usually community groups that launch children's museums; they rely on touring exhibits drifting around the national market. If I do a deal with these kinds of founders I'm at the mercy of people who aren't necessarily doing quality work."

He asked, "Why not concentrate on the strongest museums?"

"The benchmark inside stores at the best children's museums is two dollars in sales per visitor per year. Boston Children's Museum has a $900K store and they have 400,000 visitors. Chicago has 500,000; I'm stuck at $900K because I've got competitors in the Navy Pier mall. So if you picked off top children's museums you'd be running twenty locations grossing under a million dollars apiece. Your headquarters would eat up a lot of the income. Anyway, your markets contain only five or six of the big twenty children's museums."

He answered, "Well, it's only where Zany has stores that the children's museums have invited us in. But even there if I give my regional manager a store that's smaller than a ten-thousand-square-foot Zany, that cuts into the time he needs to run his region."

"So, it sounds like you've already rejected the idea of picking up these stores?"

"We're still discussing it. If it were one museum that had asked, it would be easy to say no. But it's happening whenever we enter a market."

"Of course they're asking! They don't care about the profit from an improved store: they want you on the hook for cash donations. You're on every nonprofit's list, and there's no getting off. Remember, even I tried to get Zany to sponsor Child's Play Touring Theatre last year: I pitched your people a full-scale marketing campaign. Fundraisers ask our stores for money because they can walk through our doors and buttonhole a human being. I tried to deal with the demand for donations by growing our bookfair company: we raised a lot for schools and daycares that had been asking for cash, but they still stopped by the store every year wanting more."

He said, "Margaret told me about your bookfair operation. I don't know how you could stand those. You lug all those books to the school, then drag half back to the store unsold. I stopped doing bookfairs when I was running Encore; I concentrated on opening additional storefronts."

"That was smart. I didn't feel we had a choice but to grow the bookfairs: it was the only part of our business we could grow at the time. There've been an awful lot of bookstore players in town. And the bookfair company did lead to our deal at the museum: the board members knew us as reliable fundraisers."

He asked, "What was that idea you sent about the theater?"

I was frustrated he didn't remember at all. But at least he was asking now. I laid out my proposal.

It was getting close to ten o'clock: I needed to open the store. As we walked back, I said, "You know, I've been uneasy about this conversation. After all, we're still thinking about opening other children's museum stores if the right opportunities come along."

He seemed surprised. "You just told me all the reasons it's a bad idea! I assumed you were a one-store person. If I'd thought you were likely to do it yourself, I would never have asked you."

I was surprised, in turn. "You know, you're right. I've talked myself out of it over and over, but every time a museum director asks me, I find myself puzzling about it again. The truth is, I know this store is an interim project. I doubt Chicago Children's Museum will renew this deal at the same percentage when the contract's up, and I can't see paying them more. We're not happy here. I'm trying to figure out what's next. My problem is it seems like every idea I have requires much more money than I can come up with myself, but I hate the idea of not owning a 100 percent of my company. How can you stand sharing ownership? Don't your investors drive you nuts, constantly second-guessing you?"

I opened the store's gate, and we went inside.

He said, "Managing your investor relationships isn't easy. If you ever find yourself needing help with that, I'd be glad to give you some tips."

Zany launched no museum store chain.

In May, Chris and I learned that a friend was looking for a job to help pay her way through college. Chris was emphatic we had to hire her. As it turned out, Rebecca Hatch had done a lot of waitressing: this seemed to have given her survival skills. I was glad Chris had insisted.

You never knew who your customer was at Navy Pier. Rebecca and I were working one Saturday morning when a woman with three children hurried into the store. The woman gave a guy some instructions then led her kids upstairs to the museum.

The store was busy, and it took me a while to realize this guy was piling up a lot of books. He began bringing more and more stacks to the register. He said the woman would choose which books she wanted when she came down from the museum.

After an hour the woman and her kids came back. She sent the kids off with the guy, and started going through the books he'd picked out. When she'd set aside half the books he'd chosen, she started shopping herself, piling up more stacks.

She asked me if we had any books to teach children French. I pulled out *First Thousand Words in French* and started hand-selling it, pointing out the illustrated phrase-book in the back. She said, "Great, this is exactly what I need. Ring these up while I'm at the restaurant. I'll be back in half an hour to sign the charge slip." She handed me a credit card.

I protested, "Wait a minute. Can I ask you—it just seems like you must not have a chance to buy children's books very often. The only other people I've met who bought so many books this way were a couple of regular customers at my old children's bookstore, whose husbands had jobs in the oil industry in Saudi Arabia. They got to the US and shopped in our store once a year."

The woman had noticed our greeting card rack, and as I spoke she was rapidly choosing handfuls of *Curious George*, *Madeline*, and *Wild Things* cards. She turned and said, "Well, I just like these greeting cards, my children love these books. See you in half an hour." She darted out of the store.

Rebecca asked, "Andy, didn't you see who that was?"

"What do you mean?"

"That was Demi Moore."

"No it wasn't. She was too short, and she had short hair."

Rebecca stared at me. "Andy, didn't you hear her voice? You didn't recognize her because she was wearing sunglasses. It was definitely Demi Moore."

"No it wasn't."

"Look at the credit card."

I looked, and it did say Demi Moore.

I started ringing up the stacks of books, but I got confused and had to start again. It took me the whole half hour to get a total: my largest book sale ever to one person.

She'd chosen well, and I was impressed she hadn't bought any toys. I felt dumb about my Saudi Arabia comment, but I guessed I was right it wasn't easy for her to walk into a bookstore and browse.

When she returned to sign the receipt, she noticed the basket of insect finger puppets on our counter. "Do these guys make a cockroach finger puppet?"

"No, but I've got their cockroach hand puppet. Should I grab one for you?"

"I've seen those. But they should make cockroach finger puppets." She was testing out the ladybugs, mosquitoes, and bees. Waggling her fingers at us, she said, "Wouldn't cockroaches be great?"

We handed over several shopping bags heavy with books, but as she was leaving I realized I'd forgotten to give back her credit card. Rebecca called out, and ran from behind the cash desk.

Demi Moore held the card up, smiled at us, and said, "Gotta have it."

Children's Museum Store was able to sell $250K worth of books each year with only fifteen hundred different titles because we'd chosen the books *very carefully.* Every Sunday—my only day off—Chris, Sam, Sarah, and I would visit somebody else's bookstore: city or suburb, indie or chain. My time was spent almost entirely in children's sections, assessing titles. Every Monday we'd order the new books I'd scouted Sunday. If these didn't perform *very well* over the next few weeks, we wouldn't reorder them after they *did* sell. Since we already knew the field of children's literature and had observed the buying behavior of millions of readers, we were able to choose perfect titles for our wildly diverse clientele. Many customers complimented the store's book selection verbally as they made their purchases; others showed their approval by hiding books in their baby strollers and riding the in-store elevator up to the museum without visiting the cash register first.

That's why it was hard to interact with our clientele: they all loved the stuff in our store, but we never knew who was ripping us off. I didn't know for sure even after Demi Moore left whether there mightn't have been some con. It could have been a Demi Moore look-alike doing an identity theft with a fraudulently obtained card. (Could you really get your stage name put onto your credit card? This kind of financial fraud happened regularly at the Pier.)

But once I'd relaxed into accepting this person really had been Demi Moore, I felt great she'd paid us the compliment of finding so many books she could enjoy, even if we had so many fewer to choose from than in the old days at the real bookstore.

PUBLISH, PERISH

We have now attained enlightenment on the subject of opening your new place, discovering two Rough Rules of Rebel Bookselling:

ADA
(Adapt, Don't Adopt)

SMOWS
(Sell More of What's Selling)

Unfortunately, ADA and SMOWS are rules from different dimensions.

You see, ADA is a linear rule. It reads the same forward and back, palindromically. As soon as you've adapted something, your adaptation becomes the target for someone else to ADA! You must promptly respond by adapting from their adaptation of your previous adaptation. You're locked in an arms race.

But SMOWS is a circular rule. You can roll the phrase completely upside down, turning it like a wheel, and the letters still read SMOWS.

SMOWS never stops spinning because the customers never stop changing their minds and making new demands.

Since SMOWS encompasses ADA, you'll find you're responding to your competition just as ADA demands you do, but you're doing this by looking through your customers' eyes at your competitors, responding to your customers' responses to your competitors' actions. This is smarter because your customers are your life, while your competitors are your death. You must view death through the eyes of life because you're alive now. Just so, you must view your competitors through the eyes of your customers.

While SMOWS hands control over to your customers, who by their actions force constant transformation on your store, you're the one enabling this to occur by actively responding to these customers' shifting demands, refusing to allow any new stasis to congeal, keeping your store's nature provisional, not fixed. You're using *Sell More of What's Selling* to stay in flux, morphing moment by moment, thriving on the world's mutability.

There is no bookstore, only people, their needs, and your compassionate efforts to assist them in the attainment of whatever nature of enlightenment they're capable of realizing right now.

There is no book. You've ordered it, but that damned publisher didn't print enough copies, and it's out of stock.

□   □   □

See, that book's strong sales surprised its publisher.

The marketing department thought the author's abrasive personality—he writes satiric graphic novels for that hard-to-reach twelve-year-old-boy demographic—would make the phone-in local talk-radio publicity campaign he demanded a wash, at best. Guided by marketing's cautious sales assessment, the publisher didn't order much of a print run. The annoyingly strong orders mean their whole ten-thousand-copy first printing has already shipped. And now, their Asian printer has a ten-week backlog of orders, so any reprint would take ages to arrive. Since it's a large-format, full-color book with die-cuts and a pop-up page, even using the cheapest top-notch printer in the world, the book has to retail for twenty-six dollars: awfully high for a long-shot title, which is why they didn't dare to order more copies in the first place. The availability of an e-book version won't affect demand for the physical book.

To make matters worse, the truck drivers have just gone on strike, and since the author's publicity campaign didn't launch until a few weeks after the book first hit the bookstores, many superstores had decided at the four-week point to use this deadweight title to generate some return credit to help pay off debt sitting on very old invoices. Several thousand copies of the book were shipped back from stores nationwide, via truck, and now, with this sudden strike, all those books are sitting in trucks and warehouses around the country where no one can get at them.

With the surprising success of the irascible author on those talk-radio shows, all the copies that were available in bookstores when the publicity campaign started have suddenly shockingly sold. So, there are 1) no books available at any bookstore or wholesaler in the country; 2) internal proof at the publisher that the first printing did not sell out, as, obviously, a lot of copies were *returned,* with these returned copies now reported internally as on-hand in the publisher's warehouse (because the superstores have already received their return credit, having called in the tracking numbers for their sent returns).

Therefore, the publisher's system reports that no reorder for a new print run is necessary: there are, after all, plenty of books! (And, informally monitoring the situation, the marketing people and editors are moaning about the ten-week backlog at the printer, were a reorder to be placed.)

The sales reps are taking frantic calls from booksellers, and have placed on back order the limited quantity of books soon to reappear at the publisher's warehouse as returns.

The author's two weeks of call-in interviews on dozens of talk-radio shows, amid this chaotic failure of interlocking systems, have roused him to a pitch. On-air and online he now sounds *just like his target market* of twelve-year-old boys. He has such a valid beef that his rant against mega-publishing conglomerates has begun to strike a chord with a wider public and is generating national news coverage as a human-interest slant on the trucker strike negotiations!

In a moment of anarchistic mania, on a nationally syndicated show, the author instructs listeners to place special orders for his book with every superstore, independent bookstore, Internet bookstore, and warehouse club, to *force* the publisher to reprint. He assures people they can always refuse the mail-order shipment when it arrives and cancel their order when the bookstore calls to alert them it's ready to pick up.

The Twitterverse erupts.

Yes, this is the fabled author from hell. Wow, he's getting popular. Hundreds of thousands of back orders appear on the publisher's system, and the marketing people conclude most are fake multiple-copy orders from people who will cancel at the last minute.

But, truth be told, this is an authentically marvelous book and quite a sales moment. Still, prudently, no new print run is ordered, since it's impossible to gauge real demand for this niche market children's book. It is deemed wiser, to 1) wait until the truckers' strike is over, 2) receive the thousands of books that were put in transit by the superstores, and 3) fill the outstanding back orders—chain superstores and Internet bookstores will have first crack at the limited supply, and their orders are so large that no indies will get any books at all.

The strike does finally conclude. The truckers' drama took two weeks to play out: the exact two weeks when the author was working through his prescheduled talk-radio publicity campaign. Within another week, the books that were in the backward pipeline from superstore to publisher have been reshipped by the publisher and reappeared in the superstores.

These few thousand sell out nationwide in five minutes.

The book is now officially out of stock on all computers. The superstores place huge reorders, and the balance of old, possibly fraudulent, back orders remain as well. The very human individuals occupying choke-point positions at the publishing house have credit card debt, elderly parents, children in driver's ed classes, health emergencies, lost keys, forgotten passwords, dirty underwear. They are over-worked and underunderpaid. They are lovers of literature, scholarship, laughter, who've devoted their lives to serving those whose speech must be heard and whose visions must be shared. A group of coworkers was fired ten weeks ago. Their superiors have daily considered firing them and daily, until the present at least, refrained. But this sheltering sky of management could itself at any time be stripped away, leaving our friends then with their former superiors' job responsibilities to parcel among themselves, in hopes of still salvaging their audacious, cutting edge artists' graphic-novel publishing program for teens.

In their quandary, faced with stunning pressure from the entire company to *just solve it,* they must determine if 1) this book, which they all really like, has gained status as an authentic work of literature, with a fairly long run ahead of it (one year of steady sales in hardcover would be an outrageous dream come true for their department) or, 2) the book's burst of celebrity is a flash-in-the-pan phenomenon that has briefly engaged the attention of a distractible public, but is now fading, soon to be replaced by the new, new thing.

If they do order up a big print run, say a hundred thousand copies—not super-bestseller level, but quite large for this author and only half the number needed to cover existing back orders (if they are real back orders)—and if these books, arriving in November, when shipped to stores, then sell to customers over the ensuing weeks, then this book will have turned out to be the book the whole company has been praying for. It will pay for many titles that didn't succeed this year.

Esteemed Princeton University Press director Herbert S. Bailey Jr. reminds us in *The Art and Science of Book Publishing*, "The history of publishing is the history of great houses that published great books; it is also the history of literary taste, which itself is made in part by publishers. The purpose of the activity we have been analyzing is to produce and distribute books, and it is worthwhile only to the extent that the books are worthwhile—and only to the extent that they are read. . . . If a publisher runs his business well, he has greater opportunities to favor quality, to distribute it widely, and thus to contribute something worthwhile to mankind."

The order is placed. Ten weeks later, stacks of the book are in stores and Internet-company warehouses for the holidays.

The moment had passed. The book, when examined by twelve-year-olds, twenty-two-year-olds, uncles, librarians, is bought by some, rejected by many, mailed back to Internet booksellers by most, for an array of arbitrary reasons. No one remembers the talk-show interviews or the strike.

The book is now selling at the rate projected in the original marketing plan. But with such a large bet placed, this is disastrous. With their stacks of the book generating little profit, the superstore returns are swift and massive.

To avoid paying exorbitant tax on their excessive, non-depreciable inventory (thank the Supreme Court for its 1979 Thor Power Tool ruling), the publisher must quickly arrange to have, at best, no more than a moderate quantity of the book on-hand at the conclusion of the fiscal year. Everyone knows what must be done. They do it often: elements of this scenario play out daily. Get rid of the excess inventory. At first, the thought is to keep ten thousand books in the warehouse, and shed sixty thousand. The thirty thousand other copies from that second, hundred-thousand-copy print run have either been sold to readers, are spine out on store shelves, or are languishing in distributors' warehouses. But the publisher doesn't know how many copies of the book have been purchased and taken home by real readers. So there is no way to judge how many of those thirty thousand copies shipped and still in the field are waiting like time bombs to be returned.

The wisest course, without doubt, given operating constraints, actors' self-interests, financial realities, limits of knowledge, past experience, is to remainder all seventy thousand books in the warehouse.

Remainder?

What would you do to make seventy thousand hardback books disappear? You can't give them to charity. (Not this title.) So—destroy them. But, there are two problems with destroying these books. First, it costs money to truck the books to the shredder then pay the shredder to do the deed, and this book has already cost too much. Second, the publisher might truck the books, and pay the shredder, only to hear a month later from the Midwest sales rep that the grapevine informs him there are an awful lot of a certain book that shady middlemen are offering for sale at a low price to all. Bad trucker! Bad shredder! How could you let those seventy thousand books slip through your fingers, poof? Corruption in the book-shredding trade goes back decades. Ask McGraw-Hill about their old friends at Guaranteed Destruction, Inc.—and *their* indirect acquaintances—via an additional middleman—at wholesaler MBS Textbook, controlled by Len Riggio. See "McGraw Hill Charges Huge Sales of Books Aimed for Destruction," in *Publishers Weekly,* June 19, 1995. This particular shenanigan, exposed when McGraw-Hill hired a private security firm, was settled out of court. Nice: that way no one gets convicted. No such accusations have been made in public for a while, so I guess the shredding industry got religion. Anyway, if we purified the pond, wouldn't the lilies just die?

Fortunately we don't need to think about shredding because just in time arrives the solid, respectable, and efficient remainder dealer. The man everyone in the industry—except the unfortunate author—secretly loves the best. (It's true that a book remaindered is one on which no royalties will be paid to the author, but who cares about that hack scribbler's cash flow? It's a big book and has a life of its own.)

Why does everyone love the remainder man? Well, the mission of every toiler in the high-rise publishing conglomerates is to provide *compassion for all readers.* Ditto for booksellers. (Plus, we all want to make a little free cash on the side with no strings. As big a pile of little as possible.) Remaindering is the process that produces publishers' overstock: discount books. So more readers get more books at great low prices, and publishers escape tax liabilities and earn cold cash from remainder dealers to help settle invoices from printing companies.

The publisher announces an auction. Remainder dealers submit bids for some or all of the books. Warehouse clubs and superstores may bid too. Sometimes even authors bid, trying to buy up books they've written so they'll have copies in case this process turns out to be the prelude to being dropped from the catalog, that is, put out of print.

There's time pressure and few bidders: the book goes cheap. One dollar a copy.

The book then finds its way into all sales channels as a nonreturnable commodity. It still bears its preprinted suggested retail price. But now it's nonreturnable: the publisher no longer promises to prop up that oddly artificial price with the legal promise to take back unsold copies. With no publisher providing price supports, and no percentage of income from copies sold predestined for its author, the book's price is suddenly, startlingly at liberty.

Not for long. The market swoops down on the fledgling little price. Several remainder men were lucky suitors for a total of fifty thousand books. They'll offer these to booksellers in the US and around the world for three dollars a copy. The booksellers will ask their customers to pay $6.98: 73 percent off the original $26 suggested retail price!

Meanwhile, during the original auction, superstores and warehouse clubs directly purchased twenty thousand copies, also paying $1 per book and also planning to sell for $6.98. Do you recall I mentioned my contact whose source said his discount-book-buying division at Borders accounted for much of that chain's profits? When your division can buy for $1 and sell for $6.98 the bigwigs *really* like you.

The ordinary bookstore profit margin, established and maintained by publishers through that pre-printed suggested retail price system, is based on a model in which a bookstore pays one dollar and sells to the customer for under two dollars. Oh, occasionally we can buy for under a dollar and sell for the full two dollars, but more often we're trying to retain customer loyalty through price promotions and frequent buyer incentives (Join our club and get a ten percent discount), buying for one dollar and selling for a dollar seventy-five. So, how do you think *you'd* feel if you could get your hands on a special category of current books, that you could buy for one dollar or three dollars and sell for seven dollars: selling for *tons* more than you paid?

In its remaindered form, the book is popular. Customers,

seeing the sticker saying "Sale: was $26, now $6.98," love the bookseller for providing this book at such a low price. While these customers did not enter the store with the intention of buying this book, they now do so despite themselves. Within a year, the actions of our friends at the publishing house have sent those seventy thousand books home with enthusiastic readers. Our author's next book will benefit from this low-priced introduction to many new fans. (If some publisher will take another chance on him.)

There were still some copies of the book, spine out, in the graphic-novels section of the bookstore, on sale for twenty-six dollars. Not for long. Within a short time of the arrival of the cheap incarnation of our book came the departure of every outstanding copy of the old, high-priced incarnation, back to the publisher, with credit for the return being deducted from a very old invoice. Shortly thereafter, these returned books were also auctioned off.

Since so many remaindered copies of the book have flooded the marketplace, no full-priced version will be saleable for a while. Within a year, the publisher has put the marvelous, physical version of the book out of print, essentially forfeiting the funds spent developing it.

Ghostlike, the inferior e-book abides.

CHAPTER NINE

PAYING THE PRICE

One afternoon our former employee Esmé Codell drifted into the store. "Hey, Andy!"

Esmé'd been through a couple of times with her son Russell, but it had always been so busy we couldn't talk.

"What you been up to?" I asked.

"I just finished recording my diary for WBEZ-Radio."

"No way! What? You mean your diary from *that school?*"

Esmé had worked for The Children's Bookstore during '92 and '93, when she'd been getting her education degree. During her last summer with us, when she'd put together the programming for the launch of the Children's Bookstore Partnership school outreach program, she'd also been working for a principal who was in charge of a new inner-city school. He'd been having Esmé buy books for his school's library.

(I'd been especially impressed when she'd told me that after compiling the booklist, which would require a $35K outlay, she'd played two wholesalers off against each other to knock the price down. When one had offered her a ten percent discount, she'd called the other, who'd countered with a twenty percent offer. Esmé had called wholesaler number one back to report this, garnering a revised, twenty-five percent off quote. She'd called wholesaler number two, obtained a thirty percent offer, called number one, received a thirty-five percent bid, been unable to get wholesaler number two to match this, and placed the order with whole-saler number one, at 35 percent off.)

I knew Esmé had started keeping her journal when she was eight years old. She'd created a pen-pal club in ele-mentary school; by high school she was maintaining correspondences with kids around the world.

Esmé had started as a bookseller part-time in Stuart Brent's excellent children's section when she was fourteen, operating his mail-order children's book club. She'd jumped to working for Laura McVey at Doubleday when she was twenty. She'd applied to us for a job when she was eighteen but we hadn't had a slot for her, so Esmé didn't start with us until she was twenty-three, when Laura brought her along to help with Children's Bookfair Company.

No one knew what to make of Esmé but everybody liked her. She had long curly red hair, wore fun makeup, and could nail anyone to the wall with cutting sardonic com-mentary, backhanded compliments, acerbic observations, and witty insights. She was terrific at selling children's books: she could figure out a customer's pressure points quickly and find the exact title he'd want. The summer of '93 she was having a terrible time deciding whether to work at the new school in the fall. She didn't think much of the principal, but he seemed to like her. In pitching her the opportunity to buy an entire elementary school library, he was of course taking advantage of her, but at the same time he was giving her the chance to do something she enjoyed.

I encouraged her to take the job.

"But Andy, just because he likes me doesn't mean I'd be able to work for him."

"Esmé, you've got to break in somewhere. This is your

only full-time offer, right? You don't want to sub. Come on, probably he'll be fine. Everyone has to pay dues."

During her year there, Esmé continued to fill in at The Children's Bookstore occasionally. The updates she delivered about life at her school were hilarious and horrifying. Overall she seemed okay. She brought me in to run a bookfair during an October open house, and showed me her classroom. It was filled with hundreds of her books. I loved the time machine: an old refrigerator box decorated with pictures cut from National Geographic and maps from around the world. You closed the cardboard door behind you then read all the books inside, which transported you to another place and time.

At the bookfair in the cafeteria I was stunned by the family tension. Many parents seemed to be in their teens; they were snapping loudly at their seven-year-olds and each other. The sound system wasn't working anyway: none of us could understand the speech the principal was spouting from his platform.

A few months before—in July of '93—Chris had returned from the American Library Association convention in New Orleans having scored the coup of arranging for the author of Pleasant Company's new American Girl books to visit our store in November. Their Addy character was African American, which was a big deal since the books' accompanying dolls had been targeted to a white market before, and the introduction of Addy meant they'd be creating a black doll. Would this sell in Peoria? Oh yes. Pleasant Company promoted our event to their catalog's entire Northern Illinois mailing list. Connie Porter autographed for five hours.

We'd created an Underground Railroad experience.

Bookseller Jennifer Holmes, in Quaker dress, led families out the back door, down the steps into our basement, and through a darkened passage with leaves on the ground covering crackling bubble wrap. Customers emerged into our downstairs fiction section, where Connie was signing. Costumed booksellers were stationed around the store helping families choose other books until the hour they'd reserved to wait in line. We ended up with $4,400 in Addy sales: pretty good for a few $5.95 titles in paperback.

Esmé had helped plan the Addy event and had asked me to try to arrange a Connie Porter visit to her school as well. Pleasant Company had agreed that a visit to an inner-city school would fit their publicity campaign. Esmé had created a slew of in-school preparatory events so the kids would be psyched for Connie's visit. I heard afterward from Pleasant Company that Esmé's program had gone well, but I'd been too busy to pay attention to what she'd done.

Esmé had phoned the following summer and asked if she could send some books she'd been writing. A week later a packet had arrived, including several picture-book texts and a full-length manuscript entitled *Diary of a First-Year Teacher*. I'd flipped through: her writing was nice, but I'd heard these stories in casual conversation.

So—four whole years later—when she stopped into Children's Museum Store with the news she'd taped the diary for broadcast on public radio, I was surprised.

"Well, your journal was pretty long. Did you record the whole thing? When's it going to play? Will they be trying to syndicate?"

She called me the following month to tell me when the program would be airing, but I forgot to listen.

Another year passed.

Esmé was through the store again, on her way to the museum with Russell. "Andy, I sold my book to Algonquin Press. And that WBEZ tape won an award."

Once again, I was stunned.

"So an editor at Algonquin heard the tape?"

"No, they didn't know about the tape. They accepted the book, and, separately, the radio program won an award."

Was Esmé's book that good?

I mean, I knew she was a good writer—but this was incredible. "Wait a minute. You sold your book? Congratulations! When's the release?"

"Next year. I'll keep you in the loop. Hey, when are you going to write *your* book?"

I rolled my eyes and said, "Didn't you see *You've Got Mail?* People want *that* ending."

She gave me her teacher stare. "No one will know if you don't tell them. When you think you're ready, give me a call. Maybe I can help you."

Another year passed.

I received an advance copy of Esmé's title in the mail from Algonquin. It was a compact book with a yellow cover, like a school writing tablet, called *Educating Esmé.* I buzzed through: I was listed in the acknowledgments, and she described the Connie Porter event from a different perspective than my own.

Strange!

I couldn't believe I was holding a book written by my employee, from the time when she'd been at the bookstore, about her life as a teacher at the school I'd urged her to work in.

I started reading, carefully.

Her stories as related casually in '94 had seemed satiric.

But here were traumatic yet uplifting events. Battling the system had taken a toll, but an unstinting commitment to her students had unleashed awe-inspiring creativity in the classroom.

The book was terrific; I could see this now that it was a *book*, not a typescript. Her spare, sparkling style—veering between verve and whine—was energizing. Juicy. I finished in an hour. I felt great. I wanted to quit my job! Wait, I didn't have a job to quit. Damn.

I started keeping stacks of *Educating Esmé* on the counter: it sold well. It also attracted negative reviews. Clusters of teachers would pass it back and forth.

"I could have written this."

"Any of us could have written this."

"Why does she think she's so great she can go and write this? She only taught for one year. What does she know?"

The book became a national bestseller!

One afternoon, a teacher I knew well stopped in the store. She picked up Esmé's book and said, "I don't know what all the fuss is about this book. I could have written this."

I bit.

"No, you couldn't. Esmé started her journal when she was eight. She's been writing nonstop ever since. That isn't just a chronicle of her first year teaching; it's a brilliant piece of writing."

The teacher was perplexed by my ferocity.

"Well, okay, maybe she *does* know how to write. But I *still* could have written this, and a lot more, I can tell you."

All those evenings at the cash register, I'd tried to start securing our future by creating a socially responsible Internet business called PovertyFighters that raised funds to support microfinance institutions worldwide. As we pumped money into this website, in full view of Chicago Children's Museum's administrators, they got mad. They wanted us to spend that cash refurbishing their store.

We responded with complaints about their weakened marketing campaign.

With a national recession taking hold and sales drifting downward, our payments to the museum declined.

Mutual irritation compounded.

In May 2002, I was informed that the museum's new president required us to invest $150K in fancy fixtures. Since he knew we had only three years left on our contract, this was the same as telling us to leave.

I asked if the museum had a company in mind to replace us, and was told they had been telephoned by Tom Hicks— vice-chair of the right-wing communications conglomerate Clear Channel—with a better deal, one that included a complete refixturing job and much more income.

I did some research and found that Tom Hicks's retail company was the San Diego outfit Event Network; Hicks had recently committed millions to this new museum-store chain. Hicks was the man who had made future president George W. Bush a multimillionaire: in '98 then-Governor Bush had reaped a $15 million windfall when his major campaign donor Hicks had paid the surprisingly high price of $250 million for the Texas Rangers baseball team, of which Bush was part-owner. (Interestingly, back in '96, Governor Bush had handed Tom Hicks's firm the chance to earn huge profits privately supervising the publicly funded University of Texas Investment Management Company.)

Since 2000, Hicks's new company Event Network had been rapidly taking over shops at zoos, science museums, and aquariums across the country, while helping place exhibit/store combinations on subjects like the Titanic into some of these same museums, working hand in glove with Clear Channel Exhibitions, colonizing the nonprofit, tax-exempt museum industry in a manner analogous to Clear Channel's monopolization of radio stations, billboards, and concert venues.

Of course, our client Chicago Children's Museum had no reason to share our jaundiced view of imperial corporations. Just the opposite. The museum's new president was the recently retired CEO of one of the world's largest cosmetics firms: Unilever unit Elizabeth Arden. His mandate from the board's new chair—a scion of the Pritzker family, owners of Hyatt Hotels—was to reinvent the museum, and he'd decided to launch a major capital campaign to expand the place dramatically. Chris and I had known he wanted us to invest in his expansion, but during seven years of working face to face with museum visitors, we'd developed our own perspective.

We had learned it was possible to attract more visitors and revenue through mission-driven innovation after we'd had success with the museum's Oaxacan wood carving exhibit back in '97.

The founding president had involved us extensively in developing this exhibit. At a time when we were suffering under crushing vendor debt we'd succeeded in concealing, at her request we'd invested $15K in brightly painted Oaxacan carvings. She'd arranged for two families of wood carvers from San Martin Tilcajete—Margarito Melchor and son, and the Sanchez brothers—to come to Chicago and demonstrate their artistry. That year's July and August crowds had witnessed these master craftsmen wielding huge machetes to create sophisticated and highly detailed *ale-briges:* creatures of fantasy.

The founding president's instincts had been excellent on the subject of the *alebriges'* sales prospects at Navy Pier: during and after the exhibit we'd brought in over $50K in unanticipated income. When we'd seen how profitable the exhibit was becoming, we'd proposed to pay the museum four times their usual percentage on these sales, then followed through with that cash: *alebrige* sales income (we later learned) had covered two-thirds of the cost to the museum of creating the exhibit. We'd also proactively paid the wood carvers themselves prices averaging triple their usual rates.

In '98 the museum had arranged with American Airlines for Chris and me to make a follow-up trip to Oaxaca to buy more sculptures. When we'd visited the wood carvers, their dramatic earnings from the previous year's program were evidenced in recent housing improvements, new farm equipment, and power sanding tools.

Our interest in playing to the international tourists at Navy Pier with more fair-trade sales programs had influenced our decision to launch an in-store exhibit and Child's Play Touring Theatre outreach campaign featuring the writing and art of children of microentrepreneurs around the world. But this PovertyFighters exhibit had been quashed by the interim leadership committee just days after the founding president's retirement in 2000, although by then we'd pumped $75K into the project. When the interim leadership committee had announced we couldn't use the store's square footage for the exhibit unless we paid a new fee— one committee member had mentioned $10K monthly—I'd been overcome with anger and revulsion at their weak-

mindedness, and I'd let them know it. Our store's relationship with the museum had never recovered.

We hadn't given up. Child's Play's *Writing Our World*
show was picked up by the Goodman Theatre for downtown
presentation, then attracted grants totalling $41K from the
National Endowment for the Arts. Meanwhile, Oxfam
America's student activist training program, CHANGE, had
made use of the PovertyFighters website to run their Colle-
giate Click Drive fundraising campaign.

I'd initially hoped that the new president would view
PovertyFighters in a different light than had the interim
managers.

No.

We'd never been employees; we were *only* concession-
aires, standing outside the museum's front door making the
money to fund the museum's payroll. Now we'd outlasted the
administration that had understood who we were and what
we stood for: only six of the museum's hundred people had
worked there longer than we had.

We didn't want a legal fight. The museum had run a million-dollar deficit the previous year; if the members of the
board were convinced they would double their revenue,
guaranteed, by turning their store over to Clear Channel's
Tom Hicks and his stalking-horse company, we'd get out of
the way.

Anyway, business hadn't picked up much since the disastrous slide following the 9/11 attacks in New York:
because Navy Pier is a tourist destination, even in Chicago
people had stayed away out of fear. I pointed out that we'd
been counting on a busy summer of 2002 to recover losses,
but I couldn't be sure even that revenue would permit us to
abandon our fixtures and inventory without being stuck with

$100K or more in debt. I was promised by the finance director that the case would be made to the president we should be *permitted* to leave at the end of August, then advised, *sotto voce:* "Maybe TCB goes bankrupt." ("TCB" meant "The Children's Bookstore" in contract legalese.)

Well, this was a point. Plenty of our chain-store competitors had done it: Crown Books, Kroch's & Brentano's, Learningsmith, Natural Wonders, and Store of Knowledge. This time, why not us? What was The Children's Bookstore structured as a C corporation *for?*

When I told one collections agent I'd known for years we had to walk away from the $5K we owed, he sighed and said, "There's millions of guys like you, with this 9/11 thing. Back in the seventies, I owned a chain of grocery stores: lost them in *that* recession. They say owning your business is the American dream. It ain't what it's cracked up to be."

On the Internet I discovered a new museum was slated to open in Amherst, Massachusetts, on the campus of Hampshire College: The Eric Carle Museum of Picture Book Art. They were advertising for a gift shop manager.

Of course we knew Eric Carle as the author of *The Very Hungry Caterpillar* and dozens of other children's titles. We'd sold thousands of his books, and Eric had visited The Children's Bookstore in '93 to promote *Animals Animals.* I applied for the job, and three nerve-wracking months later, Eric Carle Museum hired me.

We prepared to pull up roots and move cross-country.

Chris was worried about the way I'd been acting. She felt my obsession with the museum's managerial failings and my refusal to abandon the PovertyFighters website—which was costing $750 per month to maintain when our income was about to drop—proved something she'd suspected for years: I was becoming mentally unbalanced. After arguments about business reality and family history, I finally had a SPECT brain scan done at University of Illinois. To be sure there weren't neurological problems impairing my decision making.

The radiologist was concerned. My brain had dilated ventricles. I had to go back in for an MRI to check for tumors that might be causing a fluid buildup. I spent a week terrified my life would end early like Victor Podagrosi's, but the MRI came back clean. Dr. Pavel concluded my SPECT had revealed a hereditary abnormality I'd had since birth. In his office, he explained the images, pointing out the brown D-shaped spots centered in each blue brain lobe. I asked if there was a name for the psychiatric condition associated with my odd brain structure.

"Hypomania."

"So, that means?"

"A little manic. You should take more time to relax. How about meditation?"

He smiled. I knew he spent his life helping cancer patients and their families. I was the lucky one.

I hadn't needed his diagnosis. I'd known about my dada gene.

SELLING HIGH

What have we learned? We heard if we don't acknowledge the uselessness of rules, we're dead as bookstore owners. We've encountered the bookstore industry benchmarks: I suggested some approaches to sidestepping those. We've skewered the publishers' policy manual, which bears the fifteenth-century-style title *The Amazing Story of How and for Whom a Book Is Born and Kills Itself or Is Murdered but Is Then Miraculously Reborn to General Astonishment*.

Now you and I need to discuss how to think about exploiting our modern-day publishers' policies.

Let's get one thing straight. What was good for Harry Schwartz and Alfred Knopf in the Depression Era is bad for all of us today. If I had my way, there'd be no overstock-return-for-credit system. Books would be like nearly everything that's bought and sold. You buy it, you've bought it. If it's damaged, okay, send it back. Otherwise, you deal with it from now on. This would undercut the weirdly roundabout remainder business. Bookstores caught with stacks of excess books would eat their losses like most other stores.

Chains would no longer have the luxury of ransacking publishers' bank accounts and picking authors' pockets. Industry power would swing back where it belongs: to publishers, authors, and independent booksellers. The national superstores, never able to match community booksellers' hyperresponsiveness to customer needs and now prevented from gaming publisher policies to finance bloated hierarchies, would implode catastrophically like the Cold War–era Soviet bookselling monopoly they so closely resemble.

The big winners would be readers, who'd gain in-person access to a million wildly diverse books, marketed by thousands of new, aggressive indie booksellers, and sold for good old five-times-PPB suggested retail prices: half the current levels and much more competitive with e-book prices. (I'm not the first bookseller to high-mindedly propose the abolition of the overstock-return system from which we've benefited. Top dog Carl Kroch of Kroch's & Brentano's, speaking at the Library of Congress in 1980—a year he was surely looking to strategically stunt the growth of his competitors, return-and-remainder-subsidized B. Dalton, Waldenbooks, and Crown Books—declared, "books [should] be sold on an outright, not a returnable basis. Discounts would have to be adjusted to enable the bookseller to absorb the cost of unsold books. However, disposing of these books would enable the bookseller to have an honest clearance sale which would attract customers to the store.")

Ahem: let's not fool ourselves. From each publisher's perspective return privileges are sadomasochistic bonds securing bookseller fidelity in the battle with other publishers for control of bookstore racks.

Company-by-company positioning trumps industry strategy. It violates antitrust law for competitors to systematically act in concert; publishers will remain powerless to transform the book industry.

So I say congratulations to booksellers who exploit loopholes hapless publishers leave open in their nitwit systems.

If *you* want to induce possession of readers by books and books by readers, then just sell books: where industry behavior is concerned, feel no guilt, know no shame, accept no blame.

Do you deserve a reward for having to wallow in this filth? Yes, and I do too. Now that we're freed of guilt, shame, and blame, we're ready to violate our own unacknowledged taboos. Welcome to The Third Rough Rule of Rebel Bookselling:

BLSH
(Buy Low, Sell High)

"Buy Low, Sell High" transforms nothing to something. When we use inner energy to write, we're buying low and selling high.

When we make dreams come true, we're buying low and selling high. As Ralph Waldo Emerson writes:

> Wealth is in application of mind to nature; and the art of getting rich consists not in industry, much less in saving, but in a better order, in timeliness, in being at the right spot. . . . Wealth begins in a tight roof that keeps the rain and wind out . . . in tools to work with; in books to read . . . giving . . . the greatest possible extension to our powers, as if it added feet, and hands, and eyes, and blood, length to the day, and knowledge, and good-will.

Fighting for simple decency from his unresponsive landlord, in the mid-seventies Ed Sacks formed a tenants union in his building, attracting retaliation and no improvements.

As he waged his battle, he realized he shared common cause with tenants citywide who were paying for apartments with faulty wiring, broken locks, unsafe fire escapes, leaking roofs. Ed had schooled himself in muckraking journalism during his radio newscasting days in St. Louis. He took action, researching and writing *The Chicago Tenant's Handbook,* prefacing this instructional tract with a *Tenant's Bill of Rights* that asserted every renter's right to repair and deduct: unilaterally diverting rent money to essential apartment repair.

Harper & Row published the book in '78 but put it out of print in '79 in response to a landlord-organized media smear campaign. Ed stepped forward to buy the remaindered copies directly from Harper. He offered them for resale to Chris Bluhm at the B. Dalton on North Michigan Avenue. Chris used her discretionary budget to buy hundreds of Ed's book. It sold briskly because if you wanted to read it, you had to buy it: at Chicago Public Library it was, according to librarians, the most stolen book ever. Despite this anecdotal evidence of reader demand, Harper declined to reprint.

Several years later, Ed completed his *Chicago Tenant's Handbook, Second Edition:* hugely enlarged, outrageously detailed, filled with diagrams depicting stove-repair techniques and toilet disassembly do's and don'ts, sections on subjects like How to Win in Small Claims Court, appendices packed with phone numbers of city inspectors and citations of legal precedents.

But Ed found no publisher. Even though his legendary *Tenant's Bill of Rights* had been enshrined in law by Chicago City Council, with no publisher, no tenant would ever crack Ed's exuberantly encyclopedic, dryly sardonic textbook for city survival.

Ed had wired The Children's Bookstore's phones (he'd once worked as a lineman for Western Electric). He'd photographed our special events (he had a photography studio at home). He'd networked our computers (under his Dr. DOS alias he ministered to the numerous computer-illiterati of the late eighties).

He'd written the legal-sounding letters to our neighbors, whose roof spilled floodwaters through our porous brick wall every heavy rainstorm. He'd configured our business software, then for three years been our business manager. Working with Ed while he endured failed courtships with publisher after publisher—all wanted to shear his *Handbook's* copious appendices—Chris and I offered to tap the bookstore's cash flow so Ed could publish himself.

Finally he agreed this might be his last option.

We siphoned $10K off The Children's Bookstore in early '92 by pushing payments to several publishers—Harper in particular—four weeks to arrears. Ed's friends together anted up $8K more. Ed called our venture Pro Se Press. He formatted his book on his home computer and contracted a printing house.

By April, 3,000 copies of *Chicago Tenant's Handbook, Second Edition*—in full-throated 392-page 8 1/2 x 11 inch uncensored glory—filled boxes stacked high in Ed's photo studio.

Because of his influence on city lawmaking, on announcement of publication Ed was introduced by Chicago Public Radio program director Ken Davis as "The Thomas Jefferson of Tenants' Rights."

Acknowledging this fact, and desperate to control their lives, Chicago's tenants bought Ed's *Handbooks* in handfuls from a dozen Chicago bookstores—chain and independent—and Ed spent the year driving around town aggressively replenishing every store's selling-out stacks, not waiting to miss sales before stores thought to reorder. By September the Handbook had repaid its printing costs, Ed had repaid his investors, and The Children's Bookstore had repaid Harper and the book's other unwitting publisher-backers their $10K.

The Chicago Public Library again discovered *Chicago Tenant's Handbook* was its most stolen title. The book's popularity propelled Ed to slots as tenant's rights columnist for *Chicago Sun-Times* and tenant's rights expert on public radio. Extending this path Ed trained as a mediator, becoming a consultant for Chicago Center for Conflict Resolution, working with courts to mediate cases before they reached trial. Ed's next book, *The Savvy Renter's Kit,* found harbor with a new publisher: Dearborn Trade.

In forming Pro Se Press with The Children's Bookstore's backing, and taking control of the trajectory of his *Handbook,* Ed Sacks transformed his life and those of many others. If those big-time gamblers the publishing conglomerates won't support important books—while pocketing due profits—we booksellers *must* step in to publish and promote these books ourselves.

Maybe you'll be the next rebel bookseller to *buy low, sell high*—subversively bankrolling your favorite author's declaration of independence.

Go on.

Improvise your own indie.

Get in the game.

CHAPTER TEN

GIVEBACK TIME

From September 7, 1985, to August 4, 2002, Chris and I had sold a million books and as many toys. We'd kept our stores stocked, staffed, and open to the public almost every day. Now newly arrived in Amherst we were in the unfamiliar position of having no employees, no fears of shoplifters or competitors, and, strangest of all, our evenings and weekends free.

I spent every day poring over publisher catalogs. The temporary office of the Eric Carle Museum was located in the same building as Eric's art studio, and he was actively engaged in the launch. His museum was a startlingly generous project: the outcome of seven years' focused effort and millions in book royalties. Queried (gently!) about his motivations, Eric shrugged and said, "It's giveback time."

It was a busy fall for him. Inspired by the experience of hustling and bustling to create the museum, he'd sat down the previous year and written a just-released book urging exactly the opposite: *Slowly, Slowly, Slowly Said the Sloth*. One week he was on tour, the next week on *The Today Show*. Suddenly he'd been invited to the White House to meet President Bush, who'd pronounced *The Very Hungry Caterpillar* his favorite book (Eric told us that if given the chance he'd request that President Bush not invade Iraq). Then off to a book festival in New York to accept an award. Each time through our offices Eric would whisper into our ears, in his soft German accent, "Faster faster, bigger bigger!"

One afternoon Eric sat at my desk piled in catalogs and asked, "Are you an expert in children's literature?" I considered whether to dodge this question but instead answered, "Yes. I am."

He said, "I don't know much about children's books."

"Oh come on, you don't expect me to believe that."

"Yes! I don't read other peoples' books. I don't have time."

"But Eric, even if you don't read everything, you know so many authors and illustrators. You've been so influential, how could you not know children's literature?"

"I'm telling you, I don't read other authors' books. Maybe you can teach me something."

I didn't know what to make of this conversation though it seemed credible he didn't read many children's books. I'd browsed his shelves when I'd gotten a tour of the Eric Carle Studio: they were packed with art books about Expressionism and *Les Fauves*. When I'd asked him to suggest titles I should stock in his new museum store he'd pulled out a book on Fernand Leger and another on Franz Marc, pointing to images that had informed books he'd created.

On the wall by his desk was a Leonardo da Vinci quote: "The more minutely you describe, the more you will confuse the mind of the reader and the more you will prevent him from a knowledge of the thing described."

Eric remained artistically engaged no matter how busy his social calendar. One morning word came from the studio that no one was to disturb Eric today. Then, at 3:00 PM, we were invited upstairs to see what he'd been doing. On the floor of his studio was an eight-by-sixteen-foot painting he'd created for hanging in the museum's great hall. It looked like something that could have taken a month to paint—

marvelously layered with huge brushstrokes of perfectly complementing shades—but he'd done it in six hours. The next day he completed another huge study in color; the first had been greens, this second, oranges. The following week two more gigantic expressionist paintings appeared, these in yellows and blues.

Eric Carle Studio director Motoko Inoue filled me in on products being developed for sale in the store: *Brown Bear, Brown Bear, What Do You See?* bathroom tiles, *Very Hungry Caterpillar* watches, dozens of postcards and lithographs, *Brown Bear* and *Caterpillar* pins and picture frames. The store was expected to generate significant revenue; I was delighted to learn that Barnes & Noble had expressed unreciprocated interest in operating it.

I was glad to take on the challenge, but worried. I knew too well failure was possible. There was no guarantee parents would bring children to an art museum with none of the *touch everything* assumptions of a children's museum.

Eric Carle and museum director Nick Clark were both quite clear: The Eric Carle Museum of Picture Book Art was an art museum first. It was for all ages. Certainly children had a special invitation, but it was a rather formal invite.

Nick explained we were the next step beyond children's museums, and we didn't want anybody to confuse us with one. His background as art museum curator and education director guaranteed a focus on the finest in children's book art and an informed approach to appreciating it. He wanted to open doors for both children and adults, using original art from children's books as the jumping-off point from which they'd become comfortable launching critical evaluations of visual messages in all areas of their lives. Thus the visual-literacy thrust of the institution. The mantra to be used with visitors—during guided gallery tours—drawn from Abigail Housen and Philip Yenawine's *Visual Thinking Strategies* curriculum—was, "What do you see? What makes you say that? What more do you see?" The idea was to reject insistent focus on artists' intentions and offer authority to viewers.

The Eric Carle Museum crew gave me a birthday party. Eric had made me a sculptural collage; his wife Bobbie handed me a crazy birthday card with an ostrich on it; and I found myself laughing and crying at the same time.

I could put any spin I wanted on the story I told people about that year, but the truth was it was once again terribly hard. Just like the year we'd closed The Children's Bookstore. Yes, escaping Navy Pier had been like awakening from a nightmare, but watching hundreds of thousands of dollars vanish after 9/11, being ejected from Chicago Children's Museum Store, and finally uprooting the family had meant months of denying revolting facts and slogging through emotional quicksand.

And here were these warm, supportive people at the end of the journey.

I told them a story of something that had happened the night before. Chris and I were renting four different storage garages—two in Chicago and two in Amherst—filled with stuff from our house and store. Each garage had a padlock we'd bought from its storage company. On my key chain I had four padlock keys.

Sam and I had rented the garages in Amherst after our first cross-country truck delivery in August. Now, in late September, I'd gone with Chris to dig out some clothes.

We'd arrived after hours. We'd used a password to open

the gate and driven in among the garages behind the office building.

Twenty rows of garages, thirty to the row.

I'd forgotten the numbers of ours.

I called up a mental image. I stopped the car, got out, and looked at my keychain.

There were several possible keys for the padlocks I'd be trying to open, and, looking at the padlock on a garage that I thought was one I'd rented, I realized something was wrong.

I started inserting keys into first this garage's padlock, then the lock of its neighbor.

I thought perhaps I was mistaken and that we were in the wrong row. We drove to the next, but here too I couldn't figure out where our garages might be.

I found myself walking down row after row of garages, inspecting brand names on dozens of padlocks, looking for matches with brand names on my keys.

I deduced that the most common brand must be that sold by *this* storage facility—so I could be sure our units had this most common kind of lock. Beyond that nothing was certain.

I spent nearly an hour testing multiple keys on hundreds of locks. Chris trailed behind me in the car, periodically suggesting we give up and come back tomorrow when the office would be open and the staff could *tell* us where our garages were.

From the outset there'd been one region of the storage facility I'd ruled out: the garages up front, behind the main office. I was certain I had a memory of the look of the area where our garages had been, and it was a few rows to the right, or a few rows to the left of the office. It had definitely not been up front behind the office.

So I hadn't checked those garages. I'd walked up and down every row in the facility, systematically looking at every lock on every garage, and inserting keys in many of those locks. But I hadn't checked the first few garages behind the office.

Finally, having failed everywhere else, I realized I might as well test my keys on those front garages.

And there they were. The fourth and fifth garages back, directly behind the main office. The only place I was absolutely sure they couldn't be.

Sitting at that table in Eric Carle's studio, eating birthday cake, I was awfully glad to be back among children's book people, to be their children's bookseller.

The next morning, Eric and Bobbie stopped by my desk with a package. I unwrapped it to find a large magnifying glass.

Eric explained, "You can use it whenever you lose something."

Bobbie asked, "Andy, have you thought about writing a book?"

By late October I'd finished planning the inventory. I'd come up with a set of elaborate filters to decide whether any given title would earn a place on my shelves. Books about children's book illustration, art history, and arts education comprised a quarter of the collection; beyond that, only titles that featured exceptional illustrations, represented exceptional illustrators, or had a special place in the history of children's book illustration made the cut. I'd brought my plan to show Nick Clark, and Eric had happened to be in the back office too.

I handed Eric my hundred-page, four-thousand-title

computer print-out and said, "This is the kind of book I write," realizing at that moment I *was* an author myself, since I'd created lists like this several times, managing their reinterpretation and revision in collaboration with our many buyers and our millions of child, parent, teacher, and librarian customers at The Children's Bookstore, The Children's Bookfair Company, and Children's Museum Store.

The product of this intensely selective process—one month later—was a store filled exclusively with remarkable books. Chris displayed them elegantly. The crowds Eric Carle and board members Jane Dyer, Barry Moser, Jerry Pinkney, and Maurice Sendak attracted to the museum's opening flooded the store. Our first day was twice as big as any we'd ever run: thirty-minute lines at both registers for six hours.

Bobbie Carle interrupted me ringing up a customer to introduce Norton Juster, whose architectural firm Juster Pope Frazier had designed the museum. I'd mentioned to Bobbie I'd loved Norton's book *The Phantom Tollbooth* as a kid, and I'd toured schools as the Humbug—that whiny but well-intentioned know-it-all who was one of the book's characters—in a college theater production.

Norton leaned close, opened his eyes wide, and shouted, "Were you the best Humbug ever?!"

I was startled, but my pompous Humbug self rose to the challenge.

"Best, sir? Of course! *BEST HUMBUG EVER!*"

CHAPTER ELEVEN

AMAZON ATTACK

JUNE 2010

Expressionist images of protesters crowd the slideshow screen as a voice declares, "Sometimes resistance caused riots. These struggles led to reforms such as public housing and rent control. Roosevelt's New Deal was the result of a militant mass movement. Is such a movement possible today?"

My blues harp is a train whistle. Eric Blitz's cymbals rustle and clang; his snare and tom-tom drive home the question.

Silence. The slide changes; the storyteller continues.

It's Seth Tobocman: social justice advocate, cofounder of the thirty-year-old *World War 3 Illustrated* political comics collective, a man whose iconic, confrontational stencils get spray-painted on walls worldwide wherever squatters battle police. Our act has packed Bluestockings, the Lower East Side bookstore collective that defies the peace and delusion of gentrification to draw forth veterans of the resistance, fellow travelers, youthful recruits. Whenever troublers of sleep like Seth Tobocman need to rally people to a cause, Bluestockings is the vibrant, well-trafficked space in Manhattan that welcomes them, stands for their right to congregate and imagine and act. Five worker-owners and dozens of volunteers pool their efforts to keep lights bright, coffee flowing, bookcases and front tables filled with provocations: voices of oppressed peoples, books advancing alternative interpretations, tracts filled with dangerous propositions. Here, we construct the world of our desires.

Against the odds, since 1999—barely escaping collapse in 2003—the Bluestockings collective has passed a torch, renewing the membership flame from the volcanic resource of its volunteers. The messages emanating nightly from Bluestockings discussions, performances, and readings sometimes dare the city powers to intervene. Other bookstores have played this role through history—bookseller Henry Knox hosted the Sons of Liberty's secret Boston meetings in the 1770s; the British destroyed his bookstore after Knox left town to run the revolutionary army alongside George Washington.

Bookstores are powerful.

"Don't believe what they tell you!" Seth Tobocman roars as he flashes his blistering slides on the screen. I'm boiling on saxophone; Eric Blitz bashes sheet metal. "Their weapons won't save you! You don't have to fuck people over to survive! Or yourself!" His harsh black-and-white images scald the eyes. "The dog imitates the master but only eats the leftovers!" We drown Seth's shouts in rambunctious squeals and explosions. Our audience has come for catharsis.

After this show attacking abusive banks and corrupt officials, praising anticorporate protestors and housing rights activists, Seth Tobocman speaks of a different corporation, one that—like the interest-gouging finance companies portrayed in his book—has infiltrated our lives with messages of community, customer service, and low prices, but which in this case has also asserted control over our voices and thoughts. He says, "Amazon has published a review of my book. They trash it. If you buy the book and read it—I won't tell you what to write—but if you post your review on Amazon, raise your voice, I would appreciate that."

Two days earlier, after our rehearsal in Williamsburg, Brooklyn, we'd discussed it. *Publishers Weekly*, the voice of the book industry, has a deal with Amazon.com to feed reviews onto the Amazon website. Hostile reviews show up alongside favorable ones. Seth Tobocman was not admired by *Publishers Weekly*'s anonymous reviewer: the book we'd be touring to promote—*Understanding the Crash*, published by Soft Skull Press—had been damned in a way likely to harm sales at the moment when readers were deciding whether to buy it.

"You're the expert. What should I do about this?" Seth asked me, as we finished packing Eric's drums into the back of the van and climbed in.

I hadn't seen the book review, but I did have an opinion. "I had the same problem," I answered. "*Publishers Weekly*'s review of *Rebel Bookseller* on the book's Amazon page was nasty. They said, 'Laties is a bitter, bitter man.' But Amazon makes it possible for you to post stuff on your page. So, should you take the bait and respond to negative reviews even though some of what sells may be used copies that don't pay royalties?" We were driving toward the Williamsburg Bridge.

Eric jumped in, "What did you do? What do you think Seth should do?"

I answered, "Took the bait. I wrote in to the customer review section of the page—using my own name, which you don't have to—saying the *Publishers Weekly* review was probably insulting to me because I'd insulted *Publishers Weekly* first, in *Rebel Bookseller*. I also set up an author blog inside the Amazon system and wrote a lot." I pulled onto the bridge and we headed toward the Lower East Side of Manhattan.

Seth asked, "And do you think it helped sales?"

"It probably helped. Other people wrote positive reviews to back me up. The book sold two hundred copies a year on Amazon for a couple of years: I tracked it through my distributor's website. We sold more through indie bookstores, though."

"So you're saying I should do something. Is that what you're saying?" Seth seemed to be irritated with the conversation.

"You could ask friends to write in with reviews. But even if you work at marketing on Amazon, it won't be useful overall. They do 75 percent of sales on their forty thousand bestselling titles, which are less than 1 percent of their long tail of 8 million titles."

Eric asked, "How do you know that?"

"It's hard to get info—Amazon doesn't release lots of numbers. But the founder Jeff Bezos said this on the blog of *Wired* magazine editor Chris Anderson. Think about it. Real world storefront bookstores aim to do 80 percent of sales on 20 percent of titles, but Amazon is doing 75 percent of sales on less than 1 percent of titles. This is what happens in online stores; it's happening in my online store at Eric Carle Museum too. We make most of our money on a really small number of hot items."

Eric said, "Sounds like you'd rather have the indie stores back that Amazon killed, instead of giving Amazon your sales. Anyway, I boycott Amazon; I don't want them knowing what I read."

I dropped Eric at Delancey Street. Seth remarked, "So your book didn't break through on Amazon even though you wrote the blog on the page."

"Not that. I tracked *Rebel Bookseller*'s rank on Rankforest.com. I was usually in Amazon's top couple percent of titles—the top two hundred thousand—but, then, it turned out this translated to under two hundred copies a year sold. I bet it's only their top few thousand titles that account for the bulk of their book sales."

We pulled up to Seth's building. He said, "So you did the work there, you were in the top group, and still you weren't happy with your sales."

"Right. I think it's typical. Nielsen Bookscan has reported that Americans are buying more of fewer titles. Amazon gained control of a quarter of the book market over the past ten years, so I think the shift in reading habits is Amazon's fault. They don't want to help readers or authors; they're a rich-get-richer company."

Seth climbed out and said, "Well, I'm about to go on the road, but I can't ignore Amazon if they're going to attack. I have to do something."

Seth Tobocman's political cartoons have appeared in the *New York Times,* the *Nation,* and the *Village Voice.* He has written six books, but his activism—resulting in over a dozen arrests—has probably impeded his career. He has retained artistic freedom by publishing in the collectively edited magazine he cofounded, *World War 3 Illustrated.* Every 120-page issue is produced by two dozen authors, each of whom contributes an idiosyncratic five- or ten-page comic. Hundreds of graphic artists have participated in *World War 3 Illustrated,* doing satiric and angry work about topics like homelessness, 9/11, the prison-industrial complex, and Hurricane Katrina. Some peers in the shifting collective—which includes among others Mumia Abu-Jamal, Sue Coe, Scott Cunningham, Eric Drooker, Fly, Sandy Jimenez, Sabrina Jones, Peter Kuper, Mac McGill, Rebecca Migdal, Kevin Pyle, Nicole Schulman, and Chuck

Sperry—may be better known, but Seth Tobocman has been *World War 3 Illustrated*'s most dogged promoter and organizer.

After our conversation in the van I visited Seth's *Understanding the Crash* Amazon page. I was shocked by the *Publishers Weekly* review I saw there:

> Most of us could certainly use a primer on the causes of today's disastrous economic climate and the dizzying world of credit default swaps, collateralized mortgage obligations, and derivatives. Those without degrees in finance (or at least a subscription to the *Wall Street Journal*) are often left scratching their heads amid this morass of jargon. Despite the promise of its title, Tobocman and Laursen's quasi-incendiary tract will do little to untangle that confusion. With its remedial tone and message of grassroots empowerment, their book could be useful for instructing some community and labor organizers, but beyond that it's hard to imagine just who this book's target readership might be. Tobocman's crude, woodblock-like inks do little to enliven his painfully unimaginative imagery; such grim subject matter is no excuse for the book's utter lack of wit or style, and the depiction of bankers and brokers as piranhas, sharks, and the like is a shopworn metaphorical device. The authors' progressive politics and fiercely anticorporate rhetoric is ill-served by such an obvious piece of work.
>

Seth Tobocman has an established market niche and coauthor Eric Laursen is a respected financial journalist. Were Seth's expressionist style and lifetime of political impact unknown to the book's reviewer?

What kind of bookstore attacks a book it is selling?

It was 1996. "Who is this Amazon company that's advertising in the *New York Times* every day?" the lady in the audience asked the panel. "How can they afford that?"

Up on the dais, the experts considered who should respond. Tim O'Reilly, the computer book publisher, tried first. "They're doing something different. It's not the kind of thing you're in a position to try." His effort to relax the questioner was not succeeding.

"How can they spend so much on advertising?" she repeated. "How am I expected to compete with that?"

Logos Bookstore owner Jay Weygandt went next. "Websites are great for your store's marketing campaign; concentrate on that. If some company wants to try really selling over the Internet, don't let that distract you. It's a different business idea. You have a bookstore already; don't get overwhelmed. For now, definitely set up a website to promote your business. It's important to get started right away."

This was a difficult sell. The conference room for the Internet marketing session at the 1996 Book Expo America convention was packed, and most of the booksellers were worried. They had no money to spare for making a website, and they hadn't been convinced by the panelists that it would help their stores survive the superstore onslaught anyway. You couldn't safely use a credit card on the Internet. Marketing was the benefit of a website, and most customers weren't on the web. Why waste valuable time and money to create a marketing campaign no one would see?

I felt the same way. Yet I too had noticed the tiny, daily ads at column-bottom on the front page of the *New York Times*. I was disappointed that the panelists seemed to have nothing to say that would help me understand this odd new company, Amazon.com.

It has remained hard to understand Amazon because they use a counterintuitive practice of creative destruction. This strategy isn't about convincing more people to read more books; it's about inflicting damage on the book industry, then profiting from the ensuing chaos.

For instance, while capitalizing their business during the nineties dot-com bubble Amazon captured market share by heavily discounting trade books. Underpricing storefront bookstores, they absorbed annual losses of hundreds of millions of dollars. This was a monopolistic tactic none of their bookselling competitors could match, since indie and chain bookstores didn't have access to the massive amount of venture capital sloshing around the computer business. This was the first time Amazon damaged an existing industry: retail bookselling.

Then in 1999—inspired by their competitor Half.com— Amazon attacked their own trade book business by inviting used-book dealers to conduct sales on Amazon book pages, placing low-priced used copies in direct competition with higher-priced new copies of the same books. As publishers feared, while used-book sales on Amazon grew (to nearly 30 percent of transactions), new book sales growth halted. This was the second time Amazon inflicted damage on an existing industry: publishing.

In a confused rush, the nation's used-book dealers had posted their massive, hand-built inventories onto the Amazon website. Between 1999 and 2002, many dealers did well. But as hundreds of thousands of amateurs posted tens of millions of personal books on Amazon, looking to generate spare household income—and willing to accept low prices—the overall accepted value of used books plummeted. Many professional dealers who had originally been thrilled with the Amazon sales opportunity became disillusioned as their inventories lost value amid the glut of online book listings. Thousands of storefront used bookstores closed as dealers could no longer justify paying rent; neighborhoods were stripped of a type of business that has long anchored community life. On the plus side, people wanting to cull home libraries could no longer sell to neighborhood stores, so book donations to charities increased sharply. Some Friends of Libraries groups launched used bookstores inside libraries, while innovators like More Than Words in Waltham, Massachusetts, employed donated books to create bookstores that provide job-training for at-risk youth. But such projects did not approach replacing the enormous number of used bookstores lost. This was the third time Amazon inflicted damage on an existing industry: storefront used bookselling.

By 2003 nearly a million people were signed up to sell used books on Amazon. Benefiting from used-bookselling fees and commissions, Amazon was finally able to satisfy its investors by posting hundreds of millions of dollars in profits annually, meanwhile happily walking away from what would have been money-losing—because heavily discounted—new-book sales.

Amazon had developed a viable income model, but lost money whenever selling new books produced by trade publishers (though Amazon did mitigate these losses by strong-arming publishers into both buying ads and giving high wholesale discounts). So, like every bookseller Amazon had to act on their understanding that the real profit is in the sidelines. Their long-term goal became to use books as bait to attract customers who would be diverted into buying household goods, computers, gardening products—a Walmart's-worth of merchandise. They achieved a key target when, in 2010, nonbook merchandise exceeded book sales volume.

Meanwhile, back in 2007, Amazon had once again attacked the book industry—including their own systems and those of their affiliated used-book dealers. This time e-books were their weapon of choice. A publicity juggernaut promoting tech gadgets convinced millions of customers to buy limited access to remote-control texts via electronic screens. The result is certainly an ever-greater concentration of reading in bestselling titles, since publishers can justify buying Amazon book-recommendation advertising for only a limited number of titles. Result: everyone notices and reads the same books.

Most readers say they like Amazon, and Amazon's market share has certainly increased steadily over the past several years, mostly at the expense of superstore chains. But the American Association of Publishers reports that the new book market has remained stuck at $25 billion annually for the past decade, which proves that Amazon has failed to attract more people to books.

Amazon can never be the solution for distributing Seth Tobocman's books, but Seth's strength is his reputation and on his side he has something more powerful than Amazon: an informal network of çollective bookstores dedicated to changing the power structure in an era when communications are dominated by growth-hungry corporations. On tour, with his larger than life persona, Seth is a popular Jeremiah; his readers identify the bookstores with the author, and the author with the ideas, and the readers believe in the ideas.

The Wooden Shoe looked different. Front windows seemed larger, space inside less cramped, the display of handmade zines had tripled in size (try finding *those* in Amazon's "everything" database). I didn't remember the restaurants nearby either—the neighborhood seemed to have changed since two years before.

"Did you guys remodel?" I asked, as we carried in my horns and Eric's drums.

"We moved last year," the bookseller answered. "This space is twice the size of our old store."

"You must be doing great."

"We have a supportive community, yes," she said.

We had arrived at eight-thirty: bad, because the show had been scheduled for seven. Our escape from Brooklyn had been tough, and by the time we reached New Jersey we were very late. We'd phoned Philly; The Wooden Shoe bookseller was reassuring.

As we set up, the audience who'd been there at seven trickled back; most had gotten dinner. I was amazed these customers were so patient. Better, some had seen our show in 2008 and were back for more, bringing friends.

Two years before had been my first time on tour with Seth Tobocman. His graphic novel *Disaster and Resistance*, published by AK Press, told stories of activists defying government in the wake of Hurricane Katrina when public housing residents were denied the right to return home. After that show I had ventured to ask one of The Wooden Shoe's collective members, James Generic, if he would consider stocking my book *Rebel Bookseller* at The Shoe.

He answered, "We carry it. I used it to design my events program."

I was perplexed. "You've read it?"

"It inspired me to start this author series." He was smiling.

Now I was amazed. "I'm performing in a series that was inspired by my book?"

"Would you like to read the book I wrote about The Shoe?" He handed it to me: a history of The Wooden Shoe, which had been founded thirty years before.

That night, our six-person troupe separated to spend the night at the homes of Shoe friends. James took Eric and Valerie Blitz and Steve Wishnia, while Seth Tobocman, Rebecca Migdal, and I went with Sachio Ko-Yin.

Sachio had gotten involved with bookselling after his release from a thirty-month federal prison term. He'd carried out a Plowshares antinuclear action in Colorado, banging on a missile silo with a hammer. Sachio's apartment was floor to ceiling books, mostly philosophy, poetry, and history. We talked for hours. His commitment to nonviolent direct action had profound roots.

It was nine o'clock and our delayed *Understanding the Crash* show was finally ready to begin. To our delight, our 2008 host Sachio Ko-Yin arrived just in time. He'd thought to try and catch us before we finished, but instead had arrived as we started.

After the show, Seth Tobocman asked the group to review *Understanding the Crash* on Amazon. When I considered the contrast between nonviolent peace-activist-cum-bookseller Sachio Ko-Yin and Wall Street shark-turned-dot-com-billionaire Jeff Bezos, I felt really glad to have had the chance to work with Sachio.

The East Coast tour lasted ten days—including shows at Red Emma's Bookstore Coffeehouse in Baltimore, Lucy Parsons Center in Boston, Black Sheep Books in Montpelier, and Food for Thought Books Collective in Amherst—then Seth Tobocman and Eric Laursen traveled in the Midwest and West for several more weeks without Eric Blitz and me. But my *Understanding the Crash* touring wasn't over. At Bluestockings in June a professor from Hofstra University had approached after the show. Cynthia Bogard ran a community outreach program called "Day of Dialogue" every October. She told Eric Laursen our show would be just the thing to get students thinking. So four months later, in the two-hundred-seat auditorium of the Hofstra library we performed for a hundred students clustered in the back rows. We did not hold back, giving a full-on, shouting, banging, and screeching show.

We asked for questions. One student politely inquired, "Are you Marxists?" Another suggested, "Don't you think you should be more pragmatic? Don't Democrats and Republicans need to work together?" A third said, "My uncle and aunt took a mortgage they couldn't afford. Now they've borrowed thousands of dollars from my parents. My parents can't help them anymore. Why do you say this is the banks' fault? If people make bad decisions, aren't they responsible?"

I had let Seth and the two Erics respond to the first questions but this one hit home: in my life I'd taken big risks and suffered losses. I said, "Money is not metaphysically real. It's not a sin to make a financial misjudgment. When you read *David Copperfield* you learn about debtors' prison. That's what used to happen if you made a mistake with money; you got stuck in prison until somebody paid. The bankruptcy laws of the 1930s were a huge reform, letting people wipe the slate clean. Society benefits when people get a chance to start fresh. You never know what will happen in your life."

As we packed up, a student darted over and whispered, "That was awesome."

Our touring paid off: *Understanding the Crash* sold through its print run. With our bookstore allies we side-stepped Amazon's automated attack and distributed our honest ideas about how Americans should fight back against corporate control of our lives.

The struggle continues. Collaborative building of social capital is the way forward. Success is in our hands.

AN APPRECIATION OF REBEL BOOKSELLERS

By Bill Ayers

On September 11, 2001, the world cracked open, and everything before seemed suddenly far away and long ago, everything after broken or brittle, frighteningly off balance for a time. We'd already been living in a post-Holocaust, post-Hiroshima, post-Vietnam world—each a marker of mass terror perpetrated on innocents—and now this—the horror of commercial airliners turned into giant missiles piloted by fundamentalist suicide bombers slamming into buildings—a post–Holy War world. Those images of planes slicing into office towers, of falling buildings and falling bodies, playing over and over, cutting deeper and deeper, had their toxic effect, dulling and sickening, less and less illuminating as time passed, until they became pure poison.

As it happened *Fugitive Days*, my memoir of the mad and ecstatic years of resistance and mass rebellion, was first published in early September, just days before the horrifying events of the eleventh. The coincidence of timing forced some hard questions onto the book—why did you do this or that and not something else? Was it the correct thing to do politically or the right thing ethically? Did you cross some lines you wish you hadn't?—and some fundamental questions about our country and politics: What role does the US play in the world? What should that role be? What is our responsibility as citizens? What are the limits of protest?

I had read at an independent book store in Michigan on September 10, and I was in Ann Arbor the morning of the disaster, scheduled for Shaman Drum that night. The *New York Times* had run a front-page story on the book in the Arts Section that morning with the inaccurate and unfortunate title "No regrets for a lifetime love of explosives," but since this was to be the start of a thirty-five-city book tour, everything was looking up for the book. Well, a lot reversed course on September 11, including the fate of many books and other projects for many people, but of course the fate of a book is a fairly trivial matter on the scale of suffering and horror released that day.

Then again, the fate of the book is never trivial to some (and that's worth noting), never to the rebel booksellers, for example, and never to their mild-mannered, militant soul mates, the librarians (one of my other favorite groups of freedom fighters), who stand shoulder to shoulder with them in defense of thought, inquiry, enlightenment, liberation. Talking to the rebel booksellers I knew and admired, including Andy Laties, I resolved to travel to every city and read at every venue as soon as we could regroup.

The book tour was delayed, of course, and disrupted: my appearances were canceled at three universities (including Harvard!), one large bookstore chain (to remain nameless—and heartless), and the Illinois Humanities Festival (under pressure from its major corporate sponsor, American Airlines). Some said that security could not be guaranteed (I responded that I neither wanted nor needed "security"), others that I was promoting a toxic book (I said, it's a book for goodness sakes).

It seemed to me then, as it does now, that the major story of this extraordinary moment was not the cancellations, not the attacks, but rather that every independent bookstore and every rebel bookseller welcomed the events whole-heartedly, not as an endorsement of me or my book, but as a statement about BOOKS, the big metaphor for ideas and debate and the freedom to think at all. Each embraced the opportunity to uncover, discover, create, and recreate the public square, and then to make conversation in that magical, expansive place as an act of affirmation in a time when the public itself was in retreat and under attack.

Everywhere I went large crowds came out, and I found myself participating in a wild and rolling teach-in on the times of our lives, the dangers, the possibilities. I was not leading the teach-in so much as providing a reason to engage, and everywhere people were hungry simply to talk, to question, to wonder. Each of us feeling raw and aggrieved, we tried to be kinder, more caring, allowing multiple expressions of strong feeling, but resisting as best we could any gesture toward self-righteousness, replacing it with compassion, generosity, and imagination. We created a space in each venue for inquiry, truth-seeking, and soul-searching. And at every stop I urged people to buy a book—not my book necessarily, but any book—as a gesture and a concrete act of solidarity and support for the rebel booksellers and their independent bookstores, places in frightened and barricaded America where we could still have a public gathering, face one another as authentic and irreducible, debate ideas, and live the dream of democracy.

A particularly precious moment came in late September in Milwaukee, where David Schwartz of Schwartz's Bookstore was under intense pressure and an organized campaign to cancel my reading. There were threats to boycott the store, burn it to the ground, and physically hurt his employees. David never wavered. He wrote a brilliant edi-torial in the local paper defending speech and the First Amendment, and in his introduction of me, outlined pre-cisely why it was unpopular ideas in difficult times that tested our understandings of basic freedoms. He noted that what was actually at stake was a willingness to challenge orthodoxy, dogma, and mindless complacency, to be skep-tical of authoritative claims, to interrogate and trouble the given and the taken-for-granted, and he explained why the growth of knowledge, insight, and understanding depends on that kind of effort—the inevitable clash of ideas that fol-lows must be nourished and not crushed. This is the primary work of Schwartz's, he said, and he evoked the memory of his father, Harry, who founded the store, and said that he, too, would have stood up that night. Schwartz's has since closed (that's another dramatic and serious story) and David passed away, but he was on fire that night, passionate, com-mitted, courageous as he reminded us all of the power of the book. This is precisely why we need more rebel booksellers and more independent bookstores.

In this era when the independents are on the endangered species list, we need them more than ever, and the power of *Rebel Bookseller* is that Andy Laties offers evidence and argument for grassroots initiatives to create them in large numbers. It seems counterintuitive and paradoxical at first, but now is the best time for folks of courage and goodwill to create a movement of rebel booksellers and to open addi-tional independents. The forms will vary, and the venues will be far-flung, but don't believe the bullshit: as the death of the book and the independents is proclaimed from on high, an explosion can begin brewing underground.

Anyone can take up the task, and *Rebel Bookseller* offers

insight toward getting started—the difficulties, barricades, and obstacles, but also the lasting rewards that come from caring in a time of carelessness and fighting for thought in a time of thoughtlessness. *Rebel Bookseller* is a guide and a manifesto to motivate folks to get busy. Here Andy Laties is a cartographer of hope: he maps the geography of possibility.

In Brecht's play *Galileo* the great astronomer set forth into a world dominated by a mighty church and an authoritarian power: "The cities are narrow and so are the brains," he declared recklessly. Intoxicated with his own insights, Galileo found himself propelled toward revolution. Not only did his radical discoveries about the movement of the stars free them from the "crystal vault" that received truth insistently claimed fastened them to the sky, but his insights suggested something even more dangerous: that we, too, are embarked on a great voyage, that we are free and without the easy support that dogma provides. Here Galileo raised the stakes and risked taking on the establishment in the realm of its own authority, and it struck back fiercely. Forced to renounce his life's work under the exquisite pressure of the Inquisition, he denounced what he knew to be true, and was welcomed back into the church and the ranks of the faithful, but exiled from humanity—by his own word. A former student confronted him in the street then: "Many on all sides followed you . . . believing that you stood, not only for a particular view of the movement of the stars, but even more for the liberty of teaching—in all fields. Not then for any particular thoughts, but for the right to think at all. Which is in dispute."

This is surely in play today: the right to talk to whomever you please, the right to read and wonder, the right to pursue an argument into uncharted spaces, the right to challenge the state or the church and its orthodoxy in the public square. The right to think at all.

SHOWCASING YOUR STORE

It's unconventional and probably unwise for businesspeople to publish trade secrets. But my dad edits scientific journals: I learned as a child that good researchers share their findings. In 1987, at age twenty-eight, it never occurred to me that my wife Christine Bluhm and I shouldn't work hard to popularize our two-year-old bookstore's discoveries and inventions.

We succeeded. My *American Bookseller* magazine articles entitled "Showcasing Your Store," were distributed, in reprint form, over a ten-year period, to thousands of prospective booksellers by mail, and to thousands more at dozens of booksellers schools.

Some material in the articles is outdated now: that's one reason I wrote this book. Not outdated is the presumption that verbal and visual human contact among flesh-and-blood people trumps the disembodied virtual life every living moment. So while indie booksellers must create websites, we should never rely on them. Similarly, activist booksellers should avoid exclusive dependence on e-mailed newsletters and social media. Our power is physical presence among neighbors; we should continue to use snail mail to engage customers and befriend local reporters and editors, also phoning regularly, our objective being to establish ourselves as trusted sources, columnists, personae.

Community indies can rise above our chain-store and

digital competitors by selling books in audibly passionate, analog voices.

SHOWCASING YOUR STORE, PART ONE

Reprinted from *American Bookseller*, February 1988.

A children's bookseller with an in-store theater company shares his experience with creating lively events that attract both the public and the media.

I am two weeks behind on my computer work and book-keeping, I don't spend enough time on the sales floor, and I'm always tired. At times like this, I often ask myself why I'm spending five to twenty hours a week designing and pushing through ever-more-elaborate in-store programs and publicity campaigns. Shouldn't I be running the store?

It's strange to think how this question has changed in my mind. Two years ago, when Christine Bluhm and I had finally gotten our store open, and I found myself in this same overworked condition, I was asking myself why I had turned from full-time theater and music work to running a bookstore.

As an actor, musician, and producer in several touring children's theaters and jazz bands, I had often talked with friends about opening a small performing-arts space. Meanwhile, Chris was working in her umpteenth bookstore job and dreaming of one day opening her own bookstore. The possible combination of our interests finally dawned on us, and The Children's Bookstore was born.

We saw the possibility of creating a bookstore that would also be a vigorous community institution, comparable to museums, public libraries, or gallery-performance spaces.

Our plan was to put together a top-notch children's book inventory, covering all subjects, but especially strong in science and the arts. By merchandising unusual science toys and learning materials with the books, we would give the store a museum-shop feel. We would provide a constantly shifting array of free programs for the community that would bring in so much traffic that they would generate their own income through extra book sales. My performance experience had taught me that we would be able to pack at least 400 kids into our 1,150-square-foot sales space. In fact, our most packed house so far, 230 people, was pulled by folksinger Tom Paxton, and lots of space was wasted on bulky adults.

So, no, I should not be spending more time running the store. That's more Chris's job. My job is to get these programs to pay for themselves better! Then I'll be able to keep our staff levels up, and I won't feel overworked.

It is a constant challenge to keep our programs in the black. The first year, we did it. This second year has been a struggle—the public seems to take us more and more for granted—so I'm constantly trying new programs out, testing new publicity routes, reassessing my costs, and redefining my goals. Certain goals, however, remain unchanged.

First and foremost, I try not to run a bookstore promotional program. I run a children's theater production company, financed by a bookstore. My staff consists of myself, and one bookstore employee. We have preassigned part-time hours to work on program design, coordination, and publicity. We have an annual budget that is independent of the store's advertising budget and that includes part of our salaries. For the past two years the total production budget has been about $16K per year.

Our events are designed with two goals in mind: first, to

delight, enlighten, and educate all who attend, and second, to pay for themselves by attracting bookstore customers and media attention. I don't care if our events relate to books or reading in a narrow sense. Books have to do with everything! It's impossible to program something that doesn't relate to books.

I've worked with children long enough to have strong views on what's interesting and what's boring. I want the children involved in our programs to remember them for a long time and to take away valuable impressions. So I like our programs to be unique and to have unusual twists to them.

I prefer to be the only venue in town for our events. Exceptions are such popular programs as preschool story hours, or programs that have an admission fee elsewhere but which we can provide for free, like shows by professional children's performers. Incidentally, we pay all storytellers and performers a solid wage. Our storytellers, who are usually bookstore employees, earn $20 per story hour; professional performers have earned from $50 to $600 working in the store. Paying properly ensures a high level of performance.

Strong programming, when provided for free to the public, is expensive. But I believe that, properly designed, it can pay for itself. If an event costs $100 to produce from beginning to end, I feel it must generate at least $500 in otherwise unanticipated sales. Since programs almost never pay for themselves through same-day audience book buying, annual sales increases are the only way to measure success. Even seasonal figures will not tell you about the success of your promotions. Well-publicized programs held in April may only pay for themselves in December, via improved public awareness that translates into sales those many months afterward.

Our programs cost $16K in 1986, so I set a target of $80K of otherwise unanticipated business that year. We had a $400K first year in an 1,150-square-foot sales space, so I felt we had succeeded. In 1987 we again will have spent $16K, and at this writing (December 1987) it looks like our gross will be $480K, or a 20 percent increase. I think we should have increased 25 percent, but I'm certainly pleased with 20 percent. Now if we can hold our production expenses at $16K per year, 15 to 20 percent annual increases for another two years will render that figure a much smaller proportion of the annual gross.

By the way, please note that our high gross per square foot does not currently mean much in the way of net profitability. A lot of cash is drained directly into programming and publicity costs! But I would rather make a two percent profit on sales of $500K than a five percent profit on sales of $200K. The higher gross means faster turnover, a larger inventory on-hand, a larger margin for error, and prominence in an increasingly competitive children's book marketplace. It also holds the promise of better profits long-term.

Though it is one way to raise money, I don't like to charge admission to programs, since this keeps nonaudience customers out who could be shopping in another part of the store. Free programs also set us apart from other professional children's promoters and make our activities a more widely accessible public service. And it's our public-service image that convinces media people that it's legitimate to give us free publicity.

Since the public almost never buys enough books on the

day of an event to finance that event, free publicity is the main medium of repayment for our expenses. This publicity should, over the long term, generate sales, attract new customers, and build customer loyalty. And generating publicity is so much cheaper than buying comparable advertising! So programming with the media in mind is essential. Does this mean corrupting your programs to grab the media spotlight? No. In fact, blatantly courting the media almost always backfires. The framing and presentation of programs to the media is essentially an organizational technique.

Media people deal constantly with ingenious publicity campaigns orchestrated by professional publicity firms for major corporations. These businesses stick to campaigns that promote their own interests. Journalists try to be scrupulous. They want to serve primarily the public, not businesses. Bookstores that provide some services with no apparent link to book sales are more credible as public-interest programmers since there is little profit to be gained directly from such programs. If you want coverage, it is in your own best interest to design programs that really are unusual, and that clearly and truly benefit the public. And these are the only kinds of programs worth putting together anyway.

We run five free public series of special Saturday events each year. We also run free nonpublic series for any institutions that request them. All of these events take place in the store. Most series consist of eight events.

My goal is to generate advance newspaper and radio announcements for at least half of our special events, and news coverage for one out of every eight events. In the past two years we have sent out over 25,000 press releases and have received coverage many times on television and radio and in newspapers and magazines.

Basic publicity work is very simple. It only requires good writing skills, a pleasant telephone personality, and time. Your most important tool is your own press mailing list. To compile one, either get a copy of your local press club's book of media contacts and choose names from it carefully or call every newspaper, magazine, radio station, and television station in the Yellow Pages and ask for the names of the people who cover entertainment listings, education, shopping news, features, children's specialty items, community relations, and news assignment. For each series of events, you must mail packets of descriptive but brief press releases to all those people, at each media source.

Our press list is currently up to 300 names, including several of the top local media personalities. Though all of these people may not seem relevant to each event, our frequent releases have helped establish our credibility as public-interest presenters. In the future, when an event is right for a contact who has never before seemed completely appropriate, he or she will know who we are.

I do at least five mailings to my press list each year, one mailing for each major series. Each contact receives a press packet containing a cover letter listing all the events in the series, eight individual press releases, one per event, and one release announcing the renewal of our Monday–Friday preschool story hour program.

My press releases run one page in length, double-spaced. At the top is a headline describing the event. The next line gives a dated period for release of the information, plus the statement "For Editorial Consideration." The dated period usually starts one week (or one month, for magazines) before the event. This information ensures that the release will be put into the right file, where it will wait until its time has come. The "For Editorial Consideration" assures the media contact that we are happy to help them turn the event into a news or a feature story.

The body of the release is made up of three paragraphs. The first paragraph reads like a radio announcement of the event. It's clear, brief, and includes all the essential descriptive information, including our address and telephone number. I want this paragraph to be read verbatim on the air. The second paragraph contains background information on the performer/performance, author/book, or event. I want this paragraph to lead a reporter to cover the event. The third paragraph is about what kind of series the store is running currently, and it notes how many events we've run during the past year. I want reporters to read this paragraph and decide to use the event as an angle for covering the store. I put my name and telephone number at the bottom of the page as the press contact. This is just one of the many possible press release formats. The only hard-and-fast rules are to be clear, brief, and consistent.

Several weeks after the mailing, I make follow-up calls to media contacts whom I think will be seriously interested in listing or covering an event. I call just before their deadlines for listing or coverage. If I don't know their deadlines, I call and ask. The problem here is that you can never know if any particular contact really will be interested in a given story or listing. But although you don't want to call someone if an event is not likely to interest them, you can't be timid either and think you'll irritate them by calling. Professional journalists take hundreds of calls each week, and if your

event does turn out to interest them, they'll be glad you
called. Just try to imagine their position: Is your event a
worthwhile listing or is it real news?

When you do call, don't badger. Be cheerful, quick and
informative. If they've lost the release, mail or messenger
another immediately. Ask them who else might be interested. It may be necessary to speak to several people at
each media source before you find the person who can use
your event. Later, you can add these new contacts to your
press lists. Always be polite. You are meeting people you
may work with and depend on for years. You are asking
these people to depend on you to provide solid information
and a good program. Plus, you are making customers—
many local journalists now shop regularly at our store.

Each event lends itself to different publicity expectations.
A free concert or reading may generate advance listings in
newspapers, or radio and television announcements by community service directors, but no feature or news coverage.
This is because the media feel the public needs to have the
opportunity to attend such an event, but that this same
public will not consider the performance interesting as
news.

Many of our free concerts, children's theater shows, or
storytellers get recommended in "What's-Doing-This-Week-
for-Kids" columns. For one famous storyteller, Jackie
Torrence, I was asked to come on an afternoon television
show to talk about the upcoming event. It cost us $600 to
hire Jackie Torrence, but her appearance generated that television spot, plus a radio spot and full-scale write-ups in
the two major newspapers' kids' events columns.

The only post-event coverage we've ever received for a

straightforward performance has been for our Monday–Friday story hours. Since these run every week, a wide variety of media have covered them. Thus our simplest program has pulled the most coverage, simply because it is a reliable option for the public—and the media—anytime during the year.

One Thursday afternoon I received a phone call from a harried producer, asking if we would be having a story hour that day. She needed to fill five minutes of airtime on an "Entertainment This Week" TV show. She had found our press release in her "ongoing" file. I offered to set a story hour up; she said the minicams would be in the store at three o'clock. I called up Debbi Welch, one of our regular story-tellers, and several regular customers who have preschool-age children. We staged the story hour successfully, and Debbi's entire reading of Jill Murphy's Five Minute's Peace, inter-spersed with lovely shots of kids against a backdrop of bookcases, was broadcast twice on WMAQ-TV/Channel 5. To think I didn't ask Putnam for co-op!

A short-notice event with a politician or celebrity may be difficult to get announced ahead of time. Such advance announcements get suppressed not only because of early deadlines for newspaper and magazine listings, but also because the press may expect a busy public figure to cancel at the last minute. Still, you can often get at least some advance radio announcements with vigorous last-minute telephoning, to reassure the community relations directors that the celebrity will indeed be there.

But while pre-event publicity is iffy for these public fig-ures, news coverage is practically guaranteed because many are followed everywhere by a press entourage. We ran a series of story hours with the candidates in Chicago's recent mayoral elections. We had trouble with the advance announcements for Mayor Washington's story hour, since his campaign aides refused to definitely confirm the appearance until two days before the tentatively announced date. Nevertheless, all the major media attended, simply because they went everywhere Mayor Washington went, and we made the evening television news, a few newspapers, and some radio shows.

Former Mayor Jane Byrne set her story hour date well in advance, and then canceled literally at the last minute, after we had successfully publicized her appearance on radio and in the newspapers. We had 40 parents and children in the store waiting for her, and her press secretary called to cancel 10 minutes after the event was scheduled to begin. After my assistant, Laura McVey, lectured him on the political importance of our clientele, he agreed to send Byrne's daughter to run the event. While we waited, I ran a discussion with the children about the nature of political campaigns, and when Kathy Byrne arrived, she did a very nice job. (Still, I think Jane Byrne lost some votes that day.) Since the media were following Mayor Byrne around, they never made it to the bookstore. Despite this, the story hour was successful as a publicity event, since many people heard about it in advance and never learned that it didn't actually take place.

Our most recent political event, with presidential candidate Paul Simon, went very well, pulling a large crowd and generating both preevent announcements and postevent coverage. Senator Simon's campaign is extremely well organized. The children who participated had a truly memorable experience. Simon for President!

An unusual contest may generate both advance notices

and coverage at the time the contest winners are announced. For our first writing contest, we planned for the work of the winners to be performed in the store by the Child's Play Touring Theatre. This unusual twist resulted in an article in the *Chicago Tribune,* describing the program in detail, with much attention to the theater company, and little mention of the bookstore. This was just fine. After all, everyone interested in the theater company came to the bookstore to see them! Many schoolteachers saw the article and had their classes write a contest entry. The two performances and the awards ceremony were well attended, and the local public radio children's show, *Zoo Party,* ran a remote broadcast from the store the following week, during which several of the winning pieces were performed.

Similar events, however, failed miserably at generating either audience attendance or coverage. The Republican mayoral candidate attracted only fifteen people, and no media, to his story hour. (That's Chicago for you!) On several occasions we have run expensive concerts and performances, only to have a handful of people attend. This is disheartening. However, even when this happens, with proper publicity work, at least you will have received free advance listings for the event, so people throughout your community will have read or heard about your program and have been reminded of your store.

SHOWCASING YOUR STORE, PART TWO: IN-STORE EVENTS

Reprinted from *American Bookseller,* March 1988.

From mayoral story hours to presidential primaries and children's lit classes for parents, a children's bookseller shares his experience in programming fifteen different kinds of in-store events.

Attracting enough media attention for events to ensure that they pay for themselves is one task, discussed at length in last month's article. But what about the events themselves? First I'll describe briefly some events and series that we have run at The Children's Bookstore in Chicago, then elaborate on the guidelines we've followed in developing them.

Our basic concept is that we do not run a bookstore promotional program, but a children's production company, financed by a bookstore. Our events are designed first to delight all who attend and, second, to pay for themselves by attracting bookstore customers and media attention. We prefer to be the only venue for our events and try to maintain a high level of programming; the programs are almost always provided free to the public. Please keep in mind the essential motto developed by master grant-writer Alvin Reiss, "Adapt, Don't Adopt." What works for me in my community will not necessarily work for you. But the styles of brainstorming, planning, and follow-through can lead you to your own best programs and publicity campaigns.

Children's Mayoral Election & Mayoral Story Hours

Three mayoral candidates came to the store and read children's books with themes pertinent to their campaigns. They expounded on these themes and then took questions from the children in the audience. Two days before the actual election, we conducted a mock Mayoral Election for children.

Organizing the story hours required some rather crafty telephoning by my assistant Laura McVey. First she called each candidate's campaign office. Since none of them declined to participate outright, Laura was able to call them all back later and tell them that the other campaigns were "interested." Meanwhile Laura called some major media contacts, who also said they would be interested if all three candidates were involved. Laura's urgent-sounding daily phone calls finally swung the candidates into line, one by one, since none wanted to be left out.

The Children's Bookstore Mayoral Election generated as much coverage as our story hours and was far easier to put together. We simply publicized via press release and in-store fliers that children of all ages could cast their ballots in the store on the Saturday before the election. We did our standard publicity work, and the press, which was swarming all over town looking for unusual election stories, showed up in numbers. Fifty children voted, and their preferences were reported on radio and TV. WBEZ-FM even did a few remote broadcasts during the day to report on the voting.

Children's Presidential Press Conferences

Through the local public school administration and an after-school tutoring program, we selected sixteen children, ages 10–14. We organized two journalism workshops for them with prominent Chicago journalists from WBBM-TV and WBEZ-FM. The children then met Senator Paul Simon for a fifteen-minute news conference and posed their questions. As of this writing, Jesse Jackson is scheduled to hold a children's press conference sometime in March, the Dukakis staff has expressed interest, and we're working on several other candidates.

This program has taken time to organize, but is not really too complicated. We wrote letters detailing our past programs, and proposing the press conferences, to twelve presidential campaign headquarters. Since "children's issues" such as education, the day-care crisis, and teen pregnancy are hot in this election, we felt that several candidates might be interested in this sort of press conference.

The Simon and Jackson campaigns, both of which have strong Chicago bases, were the first to become interested. My assistant Judy Zartman developed several contacts at the Simon campaign, and called them every few days for a period of three months, following through and urging them to commit. She was successful. Meanwhile we organized the children's journalism workshops through community relations directors at the TV and radio stations. One radio producer became very intrigued with the project and helped us every step of the way. The event itself went off like clockwork.

Senator Simon was so pleased with the successful outcome that he said he wanted to take part in children's press conferences in bookstores in Iowa and New Hampshire! While it may be too late for that, I think many bookstores could run successful children's press conferences with their local and state candidates during the 1988 election. This month we also plan to sponsor our own presidential primary, with seventh- and eighth-graders from twenty-five different schools casting ballots. We've even prepared special packets for each classroom, including a "Hail to the Chief " board game.

One cautionary note here: A good track record is essential to carry off this type of program. All politicians are wary of improper or preferential business affiliations or endorsements. The Simon campaign found proof of the altruistic nature of our store in our book giveaways and special programs for low-income children. Our recent winning of the Lucile Micheels Pannell Award was another stamp of approval. In addition, the

Simon campaign was persuaded of our ability to engineer the press conference by our success in staging the Mayoral Story Hours. One program builds upon another.

Writing/Drama Workshops and Book Giveaways to Children from a Low-Income Housing Project

For each political event, we set aside a percentage of that day's earnings to be donated in books and programs to a literacy program at a low-income housing project. We turned this giveaway into a series of events. One hundred and fifty children visited the store twelve times for group writing/drama workshops, plus a magic performance/workshop, a dance/percussion workshop, and several free-book selection sessions. About $1,450 in books have been given away so far. We gave the series a full publicity push and received nine "here's-an-unusually-public-spirited business" announcements on a late-night community-service TV show.

Bilingual Story Hours

To date, about 150 children have attended six story hours featuring simultaneous English/foreign language readings of popular children's books. These events have also generated advance listings and magazine coverage.

We find that bilingual story hours are best presented with two storytellers reading almost simultaneously, like a speaker and interpreter. This type of event seems to need an additional hook to pull a reasonable crowd. So, for instance, we borrowed a Babar costume from a touring children's theater and ran a story hour advertised as *"Babar!* A Story Hour in French and English with a Visit from Babar Himself."* This event pulled a much better house than our earlier "Read-Around-The-World French/English Story Hour."

Live Radio Broadcasts

Our constant press releases about our events to many journalists at the local public radio station have resulted in six live story hours, three remote broadcasts of events happening in the store, and several feature spots on store events.

Writing Contest with Performance of Children's Work

We are currently running our third of this type of series. I present writing/drama workshops at a low-income housing project. The children write stories and poems, and the best material is adapted for the stage, using these same children as actors. The program culminates in a performance and bookfair at their housing project, with the books (remainders) at the fair sold at our wholesale cost. This event not only benefits the children and distributes many books to people who could not normally afford them, but also is a guaranteed publicity bonanza.

Dance/Percussion Workshop Series

Judy Zartman, a staff member who is a dancer, has worked with several professional percussionists to present movement workshops for children. After a series of warm-up exercises, the dozen or so children each got to play one percussion instrument, then they all participated in movement choreographed by Zartman.

Professional Performers

We have sponsored free performances by storytellers, musicians, puppeteers, theater groups, clowns, magicians, and dancers. I am careful about the people I hire, preferring them to come recommended by someone I trust: the quality of performers for children is very uneven. Perform-ance-workshops are a good format for children.

Frequent Free Story Hours

Aside from our regular twice-a-week series, we provide free thematic story hours for any organization requesting them. Such groups have included a school for the mentally handi-capped, day-care centers, and local elementary schools. For example, for a second-grade class studying a unit on Japan, we read Japanese folktales and I played the Japanese flute.

Adult Classes in Children's Literature

Kathy Larkin and Arthur Livingston, bookstore employees who are experts in children's literature, have provided free in-store classes for graduate students from local universities. I paid Kathy and Arthur each $50 for the presentations. The students, who were classroom teachers, bought many books after the classes.

Booktalks for Parent Groups

These are similar to the above-mentioned classes, but are geared to the needs of new parents. Again, I pay $50 to the employee who conducts the class, an amount easily recouped by the parents' book purchases. Typically, the ses-sions involve presentations of concept books, alphabet and counting books, board books, bath books, and a few classics for three- to five-year-olds.

Language Development Workshops for Toddlers

Debbi Welch, a professional language-development con-sultant and one of our regular storytellers, conducts a series of memory-games workshops each year.

Children's Small-Pet Show-and-Tell

In honor of a visit from Stephen Kellogg, we ran a series of pet events. At the show for small pets, children brought in and told about their pets (an iguana, a guinea pig, a rabbit, a parrot, etc.) and were counseled on pet care by a representative of the local SPCA. Every pet got an award, with the children deciding the winning attribute—the rabbit won for longest ears. Related activities have included a "pet pottery workshop" and a visit from a naturalist.

Author Appearances

The caliber of authors offered us by publishers has clearly been affected by their view of us as reliable publicists. This year Steve Allen and Jayne Meadows, Norman Bridwell, Peter Spier, and Stephen Kellogg have made presentations in the store. Though we are located in a major book market, that alone did not ensure these authors visiting us in the past; they were usually offered to other, larger bookstores before we came along with a vigorous events/publicity program.

Child-Development Workshops for Parents

These workshops, presented by local child care professionals, cover language therapy, baby sleep habits, toddler discipline, and early childhood conceptual development. Attendance at these events is not high, but the parents who attend find them informative. The media are sometimes interested, especially reporters on the health beat. The professionals who run these programs are not paid. Usually they approach us asking to run a sample session in the store, in hopes of garnering some new clients; in addition, they are attracted by the prospect of our doing publicity work on their behalf.

Here are some rules I try to follow in designing events and series:

Be theatrical. Think about plot, theme, narrative flow, strong beginning-middle-end structure, prospective audience, use of space, and financing. Designing a good program or series of programs is like writing a play or short story.

Never settle for the simplest form of an event. For instance, avoid run-of-the-mill author autographings. If the author will not present a reading or workshop, hire someone to run an event immediately before the author arrives. When Salem House wanted to send Kate MacDonald, author of *The Anne of Green Gables Cookbook,* but she didn't have time to stage an event, I hired an actress to present a professional reading of the chapter in *Anne of Green Gables* in which Anne puts anodyne liniment in a cake. Laura McVey baked the correct version of the cake from the recipe in the cookbook. The combined reading, taste test, and signing was much more exciting than a simple autographing, and was also easier to promote. It drew a healthy crowd.

Be aware of local tie-in issues. Always look for a good conceptual hook for your programming. Such hooks can be current events (such as an election), long-term issues (the existence of widespread illiteracy), or seasonal (science-fair time in the schools).

Work backwards and forwards simultaneously. Often your best ideas will come from imagining a desired end result— providing hundreds of free books to children—or getting on TV. Think about that end result, and then figure out how to make it happen.

Be eclectic. If you stay with the same programmatic themes season after season, your clientele will become stagnant, and you won't discover many new customers. Eclecticism in programming is like buying books for many sections of your store, to please many customers. Program something for everyone.

Think constantly about new programming possibilities, and encourage employees to discuss their ideas actively. When you are zeroing in on a new or large-scale idea, get everyone in the store involved. Consult media people who might be interested in covering such a program. The more people involved, the richer the result. The final program should, however, be edited down by one to two people, to guarantee its coherence.

Plan well ahead of time. In 1987, I structured the five major seasons of events in January, and budgeted for the whole year then. Many things changed, but I stuck to the broad outlines of my plan and budget. A good framework provides perspective: You know if you're overspending or underspending. Moreover, it allows you to set gross earnings goals a certain number of percentage points above what you would otherwise project for the year. Advance planning is essential if you intend to mount properly organized publicity campaigns and send regular mailings.

I hope I haven't made this all sound too difficult. The key is to find out exactly what size production company you can feasibly operate out of your store. If you are doing the right amount of programming, you should be able to buy back your own time to do the production work.

Producing public events is a challenge, and is often exhausting. But seeing children and parents become excited by an unusual program provides new energy. The secret is to get organized and get going.

ACKNOWLEDGMENTS

I thank the hundreds of professionals who sold books alongside me, the thousands of authors who created the books we sold, and the millions of readers who gave our work meaning.

John Milton says, "When a man writes to the world, he summons up all his reason and deliberation to assist him: he searches, meditates, is industrious, and likely consults and confers with his judicious friends; after all which done he takes himself to be informed in what he writes, as well as any that wrote before him." In my case, several dozen friends, acquaintances, agents and editors received manuscripts from me over the years: many helped me understand what I could say and how best to approach saying it. None bears responsibility for the ungentle outcome of their gentle suggestions; all helped me learn to echo Stefan Zweig: "If I am aware of any art of my own it is that of being able to forego, for I make no complaint if of a thousand manuscript pages eight hundred make their way into the waste basket and only two hundred—the essence—survive the sifting." For assistance, support, and forbearance, to Mitch Ahern, Bill Ayers, Jessica Stockton Bagnulo, Eric Blitz, Eliza Brown, Bobbie Carle, Eric Carle, Nick Clark, Esmé Codell, Dan Cullen, Chris Doeblin, Tom Ehrenfeld, Rebecca Fitting, Janet Ginsburg, Norton Juster, Alix Kennedy, Rita Marshall, Sally McConnell-Ginet, Terry McCoy, Ava Morgenstern, Ed Morrow, Dawn Orluske, Mary Phelan, Daniel Pinkwater, Art Plotnik, June Podagrosi, Andrea Powers, Bernie Rath, Ellen Reeves, David M. Seager, Doug Smith, Carol Stigger, Nolen Strals, Lance Tilford, Seth Tobocman, Lillian Weir, Lauren Wohl, and Glenn Wolin, I owe unreserved appreciation.

The courageously defiant publishers of this book's first edition, Holley Anderson and Sander Hicks, were enormously encouraging. To them and their colleagues at SCB Distributors I am most grateful, as I was creating what I believed might be an unpublishable, undistributable book.

This second edition's Seven Stories Press team has drawn me out even more. I am very fortunate that publisher Dan Simon offered me this chance to stay engaged in the industry's ongoing, essential transformation. I'm thankful to my editor Veronica Liu for her insight, engagement, and persistence in helping me expand my ideas and sharpen my thinking. Thanks also to Jon Gilbert, Anne Rumberger, Ruth Weiner, and Crystal Yakacki for terrific design and marketing work.

For collegial support throughout my bookselling career I thank the American Booksellers Association's staff and entire membership. In particular, thanks to Oren Teicher for his wise counsel that this second edition be updated to address the challenges of the twenty-first century.

For love throughout my life and unflagging assistance creating this book I thank my parents, Martha and Victor, and my sisters, Nancy and Claire. For patience, tolerance, and collaborative thought amid the turmoil of my inept attempts to be a decent father, husband, and business partner, I thank Samuel and Sarah Laties, and Christine Bluhm.

My spirit has been renewed after a time of sorrow by Rebecca Migdal, to whom I cannot express enough love and gratitude.

As poet Laura Riding writes, "Whole is by breaking and by mending."

NOTES & SOURCES

Page 7. "Books are not absolutely dead things"
John Milton, *Areopagitica* (1644). Quoted in Anne Lyon Haight, *Banned Books, 387 B.C. to 1978 A.D.*, 4th Ed., updated and enlarged by Chandler B. Grannis (New York: Bowker, 1978), 123.

Page 7. "Insane generosity is the generosity of rebellion"
Albert Camus, *The Rebel: An Essay on Man in Revolt*, trans. Anthony Bower ([1951] New York: Alfred A. Knopf, 1956).

FOREWORD

Page 16. "electronically repossessed the copies of Orwell's *1984*"
Brad Stone, "Amazon Erases Orwell Books From Kindle," *New York Times* (July 17, 2009).

INTRODUCTION

Page 22. "Vox Pop, a hybrid company just being launched"
Vox Pop published five books, and the café lasted six years. For a nice obituary see: Richard Nieva, "State Seizes Vox Pop, but not its Spirit," *Brooklyn Ink*, October 7, 2010, http://thebrooklynink.com/2010/10/07/15254-state-seizes-vox-pop-but-not-its-spirit/.

Page 23. "A situation like back in say 1991"
For a terrific quantitative analysis of the indie bookstore boom, see Richard Howorth, "Independent Bookselling & *True* Market Expansion," *BookWeb*, January 1999, http://web.archive.org/web/19990822110434/http:/www.bookweb.org/news/btw/1932.html.

Page 24-5. "a new educationally oriented industry gathering"
American Booksellers Association, "Winter Institute," *BookWeb*, www.bookweb.org/events/institute.html.

Page 25. "the best academic bookstore in the country"
A celebratory article that mentions the Co-op's role in Labyrinth's development: Josh Shonwald, "After 40 Years, Seminary Co-op's inventory continues to lure," *University of Chicago Chronicle*, October 4, 2001, http://chronicle.uchicago.edu/011004/bookstore.shtml.

Page 26. "St. Mark's Bookshop"
History: Nomi Schwartz, "St. Mark's Bookshop—An Award-Winning Environment for Discriminating Readers," *BookWeb*, July 24, 2003, http://news.bookweb.org/news/st-marks-bookshop-award-winning-environment-discriminating-readers

Page 26. "thousands of neighborhoods"
For instance, Jack McKeown's extensive research shows that lack of proximity to an indie bookstore is a major reason many readers don't shop at one. Judith Rosen, "Converting Mindshare to Market Share: Survey Points to Ways Indies Can Win Over Customers," *Publishers Weekly*, June 21, 2010, http://www.publishersweekly.com/pw/by-topic/industry-news/bookselling/article/43568-converting-mindshare-to-market-share.html.

Page 27. "bookstore-locator website"
The map can be accessed from: *Independent Booksellers of New York City*, http://ibnyc.wordpress.com. "This map is a guide to the Independent Booksellers of New York City. The IBNYC is an alliance of independent booksellers working together to promote the cultural, literary and economic benefits of shopping at the city's diverse collection of bookstores. We are united in our goal to keep indie bookstores thriving and raise awareness of the vital contributions that these local businesses make to New York City's rich tradition as a center of publishing and bookselling."

Page 28. "Houston bookselling collective whose store was set on fire in 2007"
A founder's account: Katie, "Sedition Books Burns," *Houston Indymedia*, February 26, 2007, http://houston.indymedia.org/news/2007/02/56533.php.

Page 28. "ABA's new buy-local initiative, IndieBound"
"Why shop Indie? When you shop at an independently owned business, your entire community benefits:
The Economy
• Spend $100 at a local and $68 of that stays in your community. Spend the same $100 at a national chain, and your community only sees $43.
• Local businesses create higher-paying jobs for our neighbors.

• More of your taxes are reinvested in your community—where they belong.

The Environment

• Buying local means less packaging, less transportation, and a smaller carbon footprint.

• Shopping in a local business district means less infrastructure, less maintenance, and more money to beautify your community.

The Community

• Local retailers are your friends and neighbors—support them and they'll support you.

• Local businesses donate to charities at more than twice the rate of national chains.

• More independents means more choice, more diversity, and a truly unique community.

• Now is the time to stand up and join your fellow individuals in the IndieBound mission supporting local businesses and celebrating independents."

Indiebound, www.indiebound.org.

Page 29. "anti-chain movement"
For a superb comparison of the anti-chain movements of the 1930s and the 2000s, see: Daniel Scroop, "The Anti-chain Store Movement and the Politics of Consumption," *American Quarterly*, 60 (4), (2008): 925-949. The article can be downloaded from White Rose Research Online, http://eprints.whiterose.ac.uk/11017.

Print 29. "Today's buy-local movement cites analyses"
The Andersonville Study of Retail Economics, www.andersonvillestudy.com.

Page 30. "She won the $15,000 first prize"
See: Joyce Shelby, "Plan for Independent Store Nets Prize," *New York Daily News*, January 28, 2008, www.nydailynews.com/ny_local/brooklyn/2008/01/29/2008-01-29_plan_for_independen _store_nets_prize.html.

Page 31. "A Brooklyn neighborhood organization had found"
"In the 'retail' category, 74 percent of respondents said they wanted, above all else, a bookstore—something Sachs attributes to the 'artistic and eclectic feel' of the neighborhood." Community Newspaper Group, "What You're Looking for: Fort Greene Retail Survey Shows Big Needs," *Brooklyn Paper*, March 22, 2008, www.brooklynpaper.com/stories/31/12/31_12_what_youre_looking_for.html.

Page 32. "Financial data provided"
Joe Keohane, "Indie Bookstores Rising—An Inside Look at Greenlight Book's Monthly Ledgers," *New York Magazine*, August 1, 2010, http://nymag.com/arts/books/features/67395/.

Page 33. The end of books?
The end of books? Thesis: "Publishers are facing a new kind of reader, one who absorbs information from multiple sources simultaneously. As we move from the 'don't bother me, I'm reading the newspaper' generation to the 'yeah, got it' sound-bite generation, publishers will have to adapt to a multimedia culture bombarded with information but lacking in knowledge. . . . As empowered members of an increasingly multitasking interactive generation that lives in electronic communities, audiences are expecting unprecedented form and delivery of content and services. Only time will tell if the traditional publishing companies are up to the challenge." Chuck Martin, "The Nine Dynamics of Future Publishing," *Blueprint to the Digital Economy: Creating Wealth in the Era of E-Business*, ed. Don Tapscott, Alex Lowy, and David Ticoll (New York: McGraw-Hill, 1998), 154–155.

The end of books? Antithesis: "It is interesting to note how often a technological development—such as Gutenberg's—promotes rather than eliminates that which it is supposed to supersede, making us aware of old-fashioned virtues we might otherwise have either overlooked or dismissed as of negligible importance. In our day, computer technology and the proliferation of books on CD-ROM have not affected—as far as statistics show—the production and sale of books in their old-fashioned codex form. Those who see computer development as the devil incarnate (as Sven Birkerts portrays it in his dramatically titled *Gutenberg Elegies*) allow nostalgia to hold sway over experience. For example, 359,437 new books (not counting pamphlets, magazines and periodicals), were added in 1995 to the already vast collections of the Library of Congress." Alberto Manguel, *A History of Reading* (New York: Penguin, 1996), 135.

The end of books? Synthesis (and new Thesis): "In *The Gutenberg Elegies: The Fate of Reading in an Electronic Age*, Sven Birkerts warns that increasing multimedia experiences at the expense of written text risks 'language erosion,' decline of analytic and logical thought, 'flattening of historical perspectives,' and 'the waning of the private self.' Texts viewed as 'difficult,' predicts Birkerts, will increasingly be glossed over (which is, in fact, happening as students are both unwilling and unable to grasp the more subtle meanings or attend long enough to read them). As we forget or ignore the complexities of history's lessons, a bland 'electronic collectivization' will render us ripe for political totalitarianism." Jane M. Healy, *Failure to Connect: How Computers Affect Our Children's Minds— and What We Can Do About It* (New York: Simon & Schuster, 1998), 150. Sven Birkerts, *The Gutenberg Elegies: The Fate of Reading in an Electronic Age* (New York: Fawcett Columbine, 1994), 128–130.

New antithesis: "In his book *The Religion of Technology*, [science historian David] Noble traces the interweaving of the technical arts with the millenarian spirit and shows that from the twelfth century on, technology has been perceived as a tool for precipitating the promised time of perfection. On the eve of the scientific revolution, Johann Andreae, Tommaso Campanella, Francis Bacon, and Thomas More each envisioned a manmade New Jerusalem—a fictitious city in which technology would play a key role. Andreae's *Christianopolis* [1619], Campanella's *City of the Sun* [1602], Bacon's *New Atlantis* [1626], and More's *Utopia* [1516] were all versions of idealized Christian communities notable for their use of technology. Today too, champions of cyberspace suggest that their technology will create a new utopia—a better, brighter, more 'heavenly' world for all. With contemporary cyber-utopianism, the . . . technology is digital rather than mechanical, but the dream remains the same." Margaret Wertheim, *The Pearly Gates of Cyberspace* (New York: Norton, 1999), 42–43. David Noble, *The Religion of Technology: The Divinity of Man and the Spirit of Invention* (New York: Knopf, 1997), 5.

All these, trumped by NEW SYNTHESIS: "Of man only the brain would remain, beautifully encased in a duroplast: a globe equipped with sockets, plugs and clasps. . . . The brain case could be connected to any number of appendages, apparatuses, machines, vehicles. . . . Then . . . transcepting would do away with crowds and congestion, the consequence of over-population. Channels of interbrain communication, whether by cable or radio, would make pointless all gatherings and get-togethers, excursions and journeys to attend conferences, and therefore all personal locomotion to whatever location, for every living being could avail itself of sensors and scanners situated over the whole expanse of human habitation. . . . At this point I stopped and remarked that the authors of these papers were surely deranged. Trottelreiner replied coldly that I was a bit hasty in my judgments . . . the criterion of common sense was never applicable to the history of the human race." Stanislaw Lem, *The Futurological Congress*, trans. Michael Kandel ([1971] New York: Continuum, 1974), 135–136.

PRELUDE: MEET THE AUTHOR

Page 35. "list of the ones I needed"
Mervyn Peake, *Titus Alone* (1959), reprinted in *The Gormenghast Novels* (Woodstock, NY: Overlook, 1995); *Ursonate* (1922–1932) is reprinted in Kurt Schwitters, *Pppppp: Kurt Schwitters Poems, Performance, Pieces, Proses, Plays, Poetics*, trans. Jerome Rothenberg and Pierre Joris (Philadelphia, PA: Temple University Press, 1994); Stanislaw Lem, *Memoirs Found in a Bathtub*, trans. Michael Kandel and Christine Rose ([1971] New York: Seabury, 1973).

Page 37. "way before, way behind, way beyond"
"'And *"the wabe"* is the grass-plot round a sundial, I suppose?' said Alice, surprised at her own ingenuity. 'Of course it is,' [said Humpty Dumpty]. 'It's called *"wabe,"* you know, because it goes a long way before it, and a long way behind it—' 'And a long way beyond it on each side,' Alice added." Lewis Carroll, *The Annotated Alice*, Updated Edition, ed. Martin Gardner ([1960] New York: Norton, 1999).

Page 37. "I thread through the crowd announcing"
Mary Elise Monsell, *The Mysterious Cases of Mr. Pin* (New York: Macmillan, 1989). Recent work: Shanta Nurullah, *Shanta, Live in China* (Boom Video Productions, 2000), Videocasette (VHS); Marc Weissbluth, *Healthy Sleep Habits, Happy Child*, Revised Edition (New York: Ballantine, 1999); Eric Carle, *The Very Hungry Caterpillar* (New York: Putnam, 1969); Ralph Steadman, *That's My Dad* (London: Anderson, 1986).

Page 38. "National Public Radio commentaries"
"Writing books for kids is a pleasure, but the business side of it leaves a lot to be desired. So I was pretty excited when I was approached by a public relations firm. . . . I was supposed to . . . speak in behalf of . . . literacy . . . and pudding. . . . I figured out what I'd say: Good evening ladies and gentlemen. Eat pudding. Books are good. Eat pudding. If kids read a lot. Eat pudding. They'll get so they can think clearly. Eat pudding. And if enough kids read and think. Eat pudding. We will have world peace. Eat pudding." Daniel Pinkwater, "Add Cold Water and Read," *Fish Whistle: Commentaries, Uncommontaries and Vulgar Excesses* (Reading, MA: Addison-Wesley, 1989), 3–4.

Page 39. "America's Viking discoverer"
Ingri and Parin D'Aulaire, *Leif The Lucky* ([1936] Sandwich, MA: Beautiful Feet Books, 1984).

I make no distinction among dealers in new, second-hand, and rare books. The varieties of expertise form a continuum. In order to successfully buy and sell the right book at the right time, "It is important . . . to grow constantly in book knowledge—knowledge of prices, trends, bibliography . . . authors, and presses. Nowhere does the axiom 'Knowledge is power' prove itself more directly. . . . Truly, you can never know enough about books." Jack Matthews, *Collecting Rare Books for Pleasure & Profit* (Athens, OH: Ohio University Press, 1981), 244. (The author is referring both to dealers and collectors.)

FIRST RANT: DEATH ENERGY

Page 43. "what Buddhists call death energy"
The wisdom of Suzuki Shosan: "In the spring of the fourth year of Keian (1651), the Master said: 'Rather than carrying around your own views, it's better to rouse death-energy. . . . I adopt the mind of one about to have his throat cut. . . . When I hear of all the people who die, I receive death's vital energy just like that. . . . I never seem to be without it. . . . It even shows me how to reason. . . . I believe this death-energy can be the beginning of freedom from birth and death.'" *Warrior of Zen: The Diamond-hard Wisdom Mind of Suzuki Shosan,* trans. Arthur Braverman (New York: Kodansha America, 1994), 30–31.

CHAPTER ONE: BREAKING THE ICE

Page 45. "she'd had to fire her previous receiving clerk"
For a brilliant evocation of life in a chain, read *Bookstore:* "It's 9:05 AM, the beginning of a beautiful, sunny, mild spring day, and the first dumb bitch in the door asks the question: 'Do you work here?' My first thought is, No, lady, I'm standing behind this register just to fool you. But I say, 'Yes, Ma'am.'" Kitrell Andis, *Bookstore* (Indianapolis, IN: GeekSpeak Unique Press, 1996), 13–14.

Page 46. "known for promoting Chicago authors"
Stuart Brent, *Seven Stairs: An Adventure of the Heart* ([1962] New York: Simon & Schuster, 1989).

Page 46. "legendary *New York Times* reporter"
Harrison E. Salisbury, *Travels Around America* (New York: Walker, 1976).

SECOND RANT: THOUSANDS OF BOSSES

Page 48. "Nature arms each man"
Ralph Waldo Emerson, "Wealth," *Conduct of Life* (Boston: Houghton Mifflin, 1860), 91.

CHAPTER 2: OPENING MINDS

Page 51–2. "working as an actor"
Child's Play Touring Theatre, 2518 West Armitage Avenue, Chicago, IL, 60645. (773) 235-8911.

Page 52. "we'd strengthen the street he'd invested in"
Howard Cohen essentially assembled the collection of bookstores on Lincoln Avenue by encouraging existing and prospective booksellers to locate near his own store, to our mutual benefit.

Page 54. "ABACUS Financial Profile"
The results of ABA's annual ABACUS Survey are supplied for free—with customized analysis—to those bookstores that have participated by supplying financial data. Non-participating ABA bookstores can receive the ABACUS Survey for a fee.

Page 55. "helped lead a young bookseller revolt"
"By the early 1980s, with many of its member stores fighting for survival because of the recession and competition from three rapidly expanded national chains, the ABA faced one of its most important challenges. . . . Out of despair at effecting any positive change, the general membership rose up in near rebellion, and at a series of emergency sessions around the country, communicated their unhappiness. . . . Beginning in the spring of 1984, a more democratic and aggressive ABA began to take shape with the election . . . of four out of five members of an alternative slate. It was clear that the membership was impatient . . . with the ABA's apparent inability to address perceived price discrimination." *A Guide For Volunteer Board & Committee Members* (New York: American Booksellers Association, 1985), 2–3.

Page 55. "chain stores swamped hundreds of independents"
"In 1958, one-store book firms accounted for nearly 80 percent of book sales; by 1982 that figure had fallen to 26 percent . . ." Jon Bekken, "Feeding the Dinosaurs: Economic Concentration in the Retail Book Industry." *Publishing Research Quarterly* (1997): Volume 13, no. 4, 3–26.

Page 57. "'read my book'"
"Book lovers young and old know that there is no pleasure exactly like the moment when book and reader meet and are just right for each other." Zena Sutherland, *Children and Books,* 9th ed. (New York: Addison Wesley Longman, 1997), 4.

Page 58. "Booklog inventory management software"
"Booklog is the first true 32-bit Windows point-of-sale and inventory management system designed specifically for booksellers. With over 1,400 systems sold since 1983, Booklog continues to be an industry leader, providing reliable and affordable software solutions to successful retailers around the world." Booklog, http://www.booklog.com/standard/index.html.

THIRD RANT: STEAL THIS TECHNIQUE

Page 61. "there *will* be a next generation"
"In industries that depend on individually created products that appear sporadically, that do not have sizable sunk-costs (capital investments that cannot easily be changed) in plant equipment or product development, and that face highly unpredictable markets, mergers and concentration trends are neither permanent nor irrevocable. Research on the popular music industry by sociologists Richard A. Peterson and David Berger suggests that industries involved in popular culture alternate between periods of competition and oligopoly." Lewis A. Coser, Charles Kadushin, and Walter W. Powell, *Books: The Culture and Commerce of Publishing* (New York: Basic Books, 1982), 23; Richard A. Peterson and David Berger, "Cycles in Symbol Production: The Case of Popular Music," *American Sociological Review* 40 (April 1975), 158–173.

Page 62. "Adapt, Don't Adopt"
My favorite business mantra is from Alvin Reiss, *Cash In!: Funding and Promoting the Arts* (Backinprint.com, 2000).

Page 63. "'Nature loves analogy'"
Charles Ives, "Emerson," *Essays Before a Sonata* (New York: Knickerbocker Press, 1920).

Page 63. "'If . . . individuality were to be extinguished'"
P. B. Medawar, *The Uniqueness of the Individual* (London: Methuen,

1957), 155.

CHAPTER 3: BECOMING THE BOOKSTORE

Page 65. "our paths had never crossed"
Ella Jenkins, *Songs Children Love To Sing* (Washington, DC: Smithsonian Folkways, 1996): CD.

Page 66. "reading his catalog"
Huddie Ledbetter, *Lead Belly Sings for Children*, released 1999, SFW CD 45047, compact disc; Various Artists, *Skip Rope Games*, recorded 1955, SFW CD 07029, compact disc.; Charles Bogert et al, *Sounds of North American Frogs: The Biological Significance of Voice in Frogs*, recorded 1998, SFW CD 45060, compact disc; Pete Seeger, *Abiyoyo and Other Story Songs*, recorded 1989, SFW CD 45001, compact disc; Woody Guthrie, *Songs to Grow On for Mother and Child*, SFW CD 45035, compact disc.

Page 67. "'You can get publicity'"
"Selective fictiveness is . . . what we experience every day when we read the newspapers, which are nothing more than books on a colossal scale, what [Benedict] Anderson [in *Imagined Communities*] terms 'one-day best-sellers.' For they link together unrelated events worldwide through our imaginations in two ways: by subsuming them under a single calendrical date and by ensuring that they are simultaneously read at specific moments of each day by masses of people who are part of the same print-language community. More than anything else, the newspaper and its market reassures us that 'the imagined world is visibly rooted in everyday life.'" Anthony D. Smith, *Nationalism and Modernism* (London: Routledge, 1998), 134; Benedict Anderson, *Imagined Communities: Reflections on the Origins and Spread of Nationalism*, 2nd ed. (London: Verso, 1991), 36.

Page 68. "performers who were friends"
More recent work: Ed Wilkerson and 8 Bold Souls, *Last Option*, released 2000, thrill 071 2000, compact disc. Howard Levy, Mark Nauseef, and Miroslav Tadic, *The Old Country*, recorded 1994, M029A, compact disc; Jamie O'Reilly and Michael Smith, *Pasiones: Songs of the Spanish Civil War 1936–1939*, released 1997, Bird Avenue, compact disc.

Page 68. "editor at Harper"

Margaret Wise Brown, *Goodnight Moon*, Illustrated by Clement Hurd (New York: Harper, 1947); E. B. White, *Charlotte's Web*, Illustrated by Garth Williams (New York: Harper, 1952); Maurice Sendak, *Where The Wild Things Are* (New York, Harper, 1963).

Page 69. "local legend"
Kathy Larkin's innovation was to apply rare-bookselling techniques to trade bookstore settings: she helped her many devoted clients invest in just-released books. Kathy's model customer: "A person of taste and cultivation. . . . For twenty years he has been buying books—first editions, but he has been buying them as new books, making his own forecast of the judgment which time would make of their authors. He has made few erroneous decisions—and so many accurate ones that I know of at least one dealer who would be glad to pay him a handsome sum for his collection." John T. Winterich, *A Primer of Book Collecting* (New York: Greenberg, 1926), 195.

Page 71. "Our reputation spread nationally"
A sampling: Sonja Bolle, "Chicago's Children's Bookstore: Imaginative Owners Combine Retail and Theatrical Talents in an Award-winning Business," *Publishers Weekly* (February 26, 1988): 164–166; Ed White, "Kids Would Run the Oval Office Differently," *Associated Press* (November 7, 1988) (this AP piece ran in many newspapers—we got calls from friends in Chattanooga and Honolulu); "Despite Bustle, Holiday Sales Start Slow," *Wall Street Journal* (November 28, 1988); Deirdre Donahue, "A Storybook Tale: Children's Publishing Enjoys a Growth Spurt," *USA TODAY* (August 27, 1990); Carol Lawson, "Once Upon a Time in the Land of Bibliotherapy," *New York Times* (November 8, 1990); Nina Barrett, "Should Our Children Be Told?" *Los Angeles Times* (March 31, 1991); Deirdre Donahue, "Shaking Up the Art of Kids' Storytelling," *USA TODAY* (November 29, 1991). Many articles about The Children's Bookstore are posted in the online archives of *The Chicago Tribune* (http://pqasb.pqarchiver.com/chicagotribune/) and *Chicago Sun-Times* (www.suntimes.com/archives).

Page 72. "one book he recommended"
William Steig, *Abel's Island* (New York: Farrar, Strauss, 1976).

Page 72. "the first Pannell"
Rafe Martin, *The Hungry Tigress and Other Traditional Asian Tales* (Boulder, CO: Shambala, 1984).

Page 77. "We have met the customer and he is us"
Walt Kelly first used the famous phrase, "We have met the enemy and he is us" on a 1970 poster for Earth Day.

FOURTH RANT: DAMNED BENCHMARKS

Page 81. "I don't believe in money"
"'It has long been known that the first markets were sacred markets, the first banks were temples, the first to issue money were priests or priest-kings.' (Norman Brown). . . . The English word derives from the first Roman mint, in 269 B.C., in the temple of Juno Moneta, whose coins carried her effigy. The first coins were minted and distributed by temples because they were medallions inscribed with the god's image and embodying the god's protective power. Containing such mana, they were naturally in demand, not because you could buy things with them but vice versa: since they were popular you could exchange them for other things. The consequence of this was that (as Becker puts it) 'now the cosmic powers could be the property of everyman, without even the need to visit temples; you could now traffic in immortality in the marketplace.'"
David Loy, *A Buddhist History of the West* (Albany, NY: State University of New York Press, 2002), 78–79; Norman Brown, *Life Against Death: The Psychoanalytic Meaning of History* (New York: Vintage, 1961), 246; Ernest Becker, *The Birth and Death of Meaning*, 2nd ed. (New York: The Free Press, 1971).

Page 81. "some standard model"
"Like ocean navigation or printing, money and credit are techniques, which can be reproduced and perpetuated. They make up a single language, which every society speaks after its fashion, and which every individual is obliged to learn." Fernand Braudel, *The Structures of Everyday Life, Civilization & Capitalism, 15th–18th Century*, vol. 1 (New York: Harper & Row, 1981): 477.

Page 86. "Meanwhile, over the Internet"
The Eric Carle Museum Bookstore online, www.carlemuseum.org/Shop_Home.

CHAPTER 4: HOLDING ONTO SHORTS

Page 87. "we must become a nation of readers"

Caravette Productions, *The Art of Selling Children's Books* (Tarrytown, NY: American Booksellers Association, 1992), Videocassette (VHS).

Page 87. "two ways to run a race"
"'The ABA?' says Riggio. 'Them again? You know, there are two ways to run a race. One way is, you try to run faster. The other way is, you try to hold on to someone else's shorts. . . . Not only am I running fast, I am running on a different track. Nobody is grabbing my shorts, and I sure as hell am not grabbing theirs.'" David D. Kirkpatrick, "Barnes & Noble's Jekyll and Hyde," *New York Magazine* (July 19, 1999). '

Bookseller Wallace Kuralt offers evidence to the contrary: "Chains [use] their 'buying power,' or 'muscle,' to force extra discounts, fees, rebates, terms, free goods, special advertising allowances and 'slotting fees,' much of it in violation of the antitrust provisions of the Robinson-Patman Act. In papers recently filed in federal court in New York, it can be seen that the national chain bookstores are receiving discriminatory prices. . . . These . . . permit the chains simply to expand at will and over-whelm any smaller competition." Wallace H. Kuralt, "Allegations and Proposed Reform by Wallace H. Kuralt, Owner of the Famous, 40-Year-Old, But Now-Failed Bookstore Chain," *Lawmall.com,* March 14, 2002, www.lawmall.com/rpa/rpa_whk1.html.

Page 87. "in dramatic decline"
"'This report documents a national crisis,' [NEA Chairman Dana] Gioia said. 'Reading develops a capacity for focused attention and imaginative growth that enriches both private and public life. The decline in reading among every segment of the adult population reflects a general collapse in advanced literacy." Garrick Davis, "Literary Reading in Dramatic Decline, According to National Endowment for the Arts Survey," *National Endowment for the Arts*, July 8, 2004, www.nea.gov/news/news04/ReadingAtRisk.html.

Page 88. "chain stores were slaughtering independents"
Dayton-Hudson Corporation stores have included Dayton's, Mervyn's, Marshall Field, and Target. Carter-Hawley-Hale ran Nieman-Marcus, Bergdorf-Goodman, and other apparel chains.

Page 88. "American Booksellers Association stalwart"
Eliot Leonard, *Operating a Bookstore: Practical Details for Improving Profit* (Tarrytown, NY: Booksellers House, 1992).

Page 89. "'*greed is good*'"
The phrase was made infamous by actor Michael Douglas playing a corporate raider (named Gordon Gekko) in the Oliver Stone film *Wall Street*. Supposedly the words were actually used by raider Ivan Boesky. Len Riggio: "It was the go-go eighties . . . there were a lot of sharks swimming in shallow water." David D. Kirkpatrick, "Barnes & Noble's Jekyll and Hyde," *New York Magazine*, July 19, 1999.

Page 90. "financial info, handbooks"
For instance, *A Manual of Bookselling*, 4th ed., ed. Robert Hale (New York: Harmony Books, 1987).

Page 92. "publisher at the American Library Association"
Arthur Plotnik, *The Elements of Editing* (New York: Macmillan, 1982).

Page 92. "*Colombia, where the pop-ups come from*"
The reference is to the years when most pop-up books were manufactured in Cali, Colombia, for industry leader Intervisual Communications.

Page 94. "the new chain superstores"
How the change came to Borders: "[In 1973] Borders Book Shop was a new business in town, run by two young brothers from Kentucky. They had burst through one storefront and were opening in a larger place on State Street. They recognized me as a browser . . . and I was hired. . . . Borders was all hustle and crackling fluorescents. The brothers kept the staff in motion all day long, unpacking boxes, stocking shelves, sorting backstock, and working the cash registers. We were expected to know titles and references. . . . I felt as if everyone were just waking up to books as I was. Suddenly there were thousands of serious readers in town. They thronged the aisles of the store, asked questions, placed orders. The books had an aura, an excitement about them. And just moving the titles back and forth, getting them onto the shelves and into the hands of customers, was an education. For the first time I caught a sense of what a genuine intellectual life might be like . . . I saw my role as quasi-priestly: I was channeling the nourishing word to the people who wanted it most." Sven Birkerts, *The Gutenberg Elegies: The Fate of Reading in an Electronic Age* (Boston: Faber & Faber, 1994), 51.

A decade and a half later: "A number of independent bookstores became 'superstores,' so successful, in fact, that the chains copied them or took them over. (Borders, the most successful of the independents, was acquired by Kmart.)" Richard J. Barnet and John Cavanagh, *Global*

Dreams: Imperial Corporations and the New World Order (New York, Simon & Schuster, 1994): 110. Kmart had purchased the Waldenbooks chain a few years earlier, and subsequently spun Borders/Walden off as an independent corporation.

Page 95. "bombshell announcement"
From the cited 1994 *Show Daily* article: "Among the examples of illegal practices mentioned in the suit . . . was Barnes & Noble's 'bestseller pricing' system which requires publishers to pay for their titles to be discounted as bestsellers—even though [sic] may never be true bestsellers—by having them pay fees of at least $18,000, terms that are not available to independents. . . . Association attorney [Jerald] Jacobs told PW that, after a year-long investigation into the situation, his law firm [Jenner & Block] 'learned that the industry is rife with secret payments and under-the-counter deals.'" John Mutter and Maureen O'Brien, "ABA Sues Five Publishers," *Publishers Weekly*, May 28, 1994, 1.

Page 96. "thousands of their books never achieved adequate representation"
See for instance this marvelous analysis from New Rules Project: "One might be tempted to think that the rise of giant chain bookstores has been a boon to authors. After all, the typical Barnes & Noble or Borders superstore stocks upwards of 150,000 titles, compared to an average of 20,000 for an independent. Not so, according to a new study written by David Kirkpatrick on behalf of the Authors Guild. Midlist titles—serious non-fiction and literary fiction books which typically sell fewer than 10,000 copies—are more available now than ever before. Publishers continue to turn them out. More and more shelf space is devoted to selling them. Yet, midlist titles are fast losing market share." "'The best explanation for the leveling off of midlist book sales in the 1990s is the rise of the superstores and other large chain booksellers,' concludes Kirkpatrick. A close look at sales data reveals that most of the titles stocked in a superstore 'serve essentially as wallpaper.' People buy a much narrower range of titles at chains that they buy at independents. Few in publishing believe this is the result of a change in readers' tastes, noting that popular interest in literary works as evidenced by the surprise success of books like Frank McCourt's *Angela's Ashes* and Charles Frazier's *Cold Moutain*, is higher that ever."

"The explanation lies in chain store marketing policies. The chains exact subsidies from publishers for promoting titles through prominent in-store placement and advertisements. A publisher might pay $10,000, for example, to have a title tabled at the front of the store for two weeks.

Only bestsellers, celebrity autobiographies, thrillers, and other big name books get this kind of promotion. This impacts midlist book sales in several ways. Publishers have fewer resources left over for marketing midlist books. Superstore customers are drawn to the prominent displays and give little notice to other books. Small presses can't afford to have any of their titles get the star treatment...." "Chain Bookstore Squeezing Out Midlist Titles," New Rules Project, August 1, 2000, http://www.newrules.org/retail/news/chain-bookstores-squeezing-outmidlist-titles; David Kirkpatrick, "Report to the Authors Guild Midlist Study Committee," Authors Guild, 2000.

Page 97. "Publishers needed chains *and* indies"
On the necessary coexistence of large and small enterprises: "'Capitalism (both past and present, with phases which are monopolistic to a greater or lesser degree) never entirely eliminates the free competition and market economy from which it has grown (and upon which it still draws) but continues to exist over and alongside them.' That is, I would maintain that the economy between the fifteenth and eighteenth century . . . had two levels: . . . monopolies, open or concealed, and free competition; in other words, capitalism as I have been seeking to define it, and the developing market economy." Fernand Braudel, *The Wheels of Commerce: Civilization & Capitalism 15th–18th Century*, vol. 2 (New York: Harper & Row, 1982), 577–578.

Similarly, Robert Heilbroner on trusts: "Surprisingly, the [1890s] merger movement never succeeded in wholly stamping out competition by other means. In fact, one of the most interesting findings about the trusts is that the shares of the market commanded by the great corporate giants steadily declined, as smaller and more aggressive firms stole business away from the large conservative monoliths, or as new firms were formed to enter the industry." Robert Heilbroner and Aaron Singer, *The Economic Transformation of America, 1600 to the Present*, 4th ed. (Fort Worth, TX: Harcourt Brace College, 1999), 202.

Page 99. "helped send paper prices higher"
For instance, this material, from a *Publishers Weekly* article about paper-price increases: "One production person"—in my own view, here overtly predicting reader resistance to spiking prices but subtly describing the over-ordering/paper-cost feedback loop—"expressed some relief that what he saw as wasteful 'over-production' on some less-than-notable titles would now have to go by the board." Jim Milliot and John Mutter, "Paper Crunch Presages Higher Book Prices," *Publishers Weekly*, May 1, 1995.

N.B. While *PW* is a fine magazine, no publisher can speak openly: chains are powerful customers, and their employees read *PW*! Reading and deciphering trade press is a skill like literary criticism or Kremlinology.

Page 99. "suggested retail prices"
The rise and rise of a benchmark multiple: I became alert to this inflationary mechanism during a 1995 ABA school slide show presented by the VP of a major publishing house. Her profit-and-loss statement for a typical book—the microeconomic perspective on publishing—showed that about 10% of this average title's suggested retail price should go to pay for its printing-paper-and-binding (PPB) expense. I took note because for a decade I'd been explaining to my own students in booksellers schools that the rough benchmark publishers used in establishing suggested retail prices for books was five times PPB—that is, PPB normally represented 20% of an average title's suggested retail price. Watching that VP's 1995 presentation, I suddenly understood that in the previous few years, with all the changes in the industry, the informal benchmark itself had changed.

I recalled that I had learned the five times PPB benchmark at the identical ABA school seminar in 1984, as taught by Edward Morrow (every ABA school included a session teaching the basics of the publishing process). In 1984 I'd seen a handout that showed a typical book's suggested retail price as a pie divided into five parts. One-fifth of the pie ordinarily went to pay for PPB. Two-fifths went for publisher operating costs (including author royalties) plus publisher profit. Two-fifths went for bookseller operating costs plus bookseller profit. The significance of the pie was that it demonstrated the rough income split between publisher and bookseller was fair: each player received about two-fifths of the suggested retail price. And now, in 1995, here I was listening to this VP teaching a ten times PPB target benchmark. I'd never realized a new informal benchmark was rationalizing higher prices—so much so that in later years, a business guru could confidently inform his readers, "A book costs about $2 to print and $20 in the store. A huge gulf! But most of that money disappears in advertising, shipping, and especially in the shredding of unsold books." Seth Godin, *Permission Marketing: Turning Strangers into Friends and Friends into Customers* (New York: Simon & Schuster, 1999), 68.

Page 100. "I was there. The excessive returns . . ."
For a terrific proof that excessive orders and returns caused the nineties-era price jumps, see Jeffrey Trachtenberg, "An Industry Gone Mad," *Wall Street Journal*, June 3, 2005.

Page 101. "book-buyers' provocative *suggestions*"

Art and oligopoly: "When the chains became bigger [companies] than the trade publishers . . . manuscripts were read with the requirements of the giant retail distributors in mind." Richard J. Barnet and John Cavanagh, *Global Dreams: Imperial Corporations and the New World Order* (New York: Simon & Schuster, 1994), 98, 99.

In other words: "Publishers [now] strive to produce books the national chains will buy. If the buyers for these chains, known as national accounts, turn down an individual title or declare lack of interest in a category, the book is in trouble. . . . Clark Kepler, owner of Kepler's Books & Magazines in Menlo Park, California, [says], 'This fight is about preserving what America is able to read. A network of healthy independent bookstores spurs publishers to produce a diversity of literature and to take risks with authors who are of less commercial but greater critical appeal.'" Olga Litowinsky, *It's a Bunny-Eat-Bunny World: A Writer's Guide to Surviving and Thriving in Today's Competitive Children's Book Market* (New York: Walker, 2001), 35–37.

In the largest sense, "What impact does market consolidation—that is, an industry in which a handful of firms dominate its products and sales—have on culture? Peterson and Berger's research showed that in the music industry, periods of high concentration were likely to be ones of creative stagnation. . . . Firms in concentrated industries, by virtue of their market power, feel no need to risk innovation even though consumers might be interested in new products." Lewis A. Coser, Charles Kadushin, and Walter W. Powell, *Books: The Culture and Commerce of Publishing* (New York: Basic Books, 1982), 23–24; Richard A. Peterson and David Berger, "Cycles in Symbol Production: The Case of Popular Music," *American Sociological Review* 40 (April 1975): 158–173. (While this passage refers to consolidation among publishers, it aptly applies to bookstores—in particular those that also publish.)

Art and oligopoly—the historical comparison: "The two-pronged control of severely limited numbers of [eighteenth-century London] theatre patents on the one hand, and of the censor on the other, had created a situation for playwrights—male or female—that posed extraordinary difficulties. . . . Whether a [theatre] manager chose to be encouraging or discouraging to a playwright . . . constituted a prodigious display of power. In economic terms, these men constituted an eighteenth-century version of an oligopoly, in which a few large suppliers predominate but cover their tracks by saturating the market with messages about product differentiation. But because they were not simply businessmen, although theatre certainly was a business, but also people whose decisions determined what the public would see in representation, we must also acknowledge that this was an artistic oligopoly. To the extent that it was uniformly dominated by the unconscious tastes and interests of a handful of white middle-class men, it was an oligopoly that had important implications for the way gender was constructed, challenged, or reinforced onstage. . . . Scholars have . . . argued that [theatre manager, director and actor David] Garrick had a profound effect on Mrs. [Elizabeth] Griffith's plays, and that in the end the energy and declarative power of her female characters were diluted in order to meet his requirements." Ellen Donkin, *Getting into the Act: Women Playwrights in London, 1776–1829* (London: Routledge, 1995), 97–98. Cited is the argument of Betty Rizzo, "Depressa Resurgam," *Curtain Calls,* eds. Mary Anne Schofield and Cecilia Macheski (Athens, OH: Ohio University Press, 1991), 120 ff.

Page 102. "few author royalties"
Barnes & Noble's massive displacement of books that pay royalties in favor of B&N-licensed royalty-free titles puts the entire royalty system in jeopardy. Embattled trade book publishers are implicitly challenged to match Barnes & Noble's pared cost structure. But it is the royalty system that permits authors to risk writing what they choose: authors sacrifice present income and aspire to future royalties. Economist Jacques Attali (through the lens of music composition): "A strange situation: a category of workers has . . . succeeded in preserving ownership of their labor. . . . If the remuneration of the molder [i.e., composer or author] is proportional to the number of sales, and not to the duration of his labor, then he can collect a rent and reduce the capitalist's profit. This is why it is in the interests of the capitalist process to [instead] incorporate molders as wage earners . . . *the specific remuneration of the composer has largely blocked the control of music by capital* [italics Attali's]; it has protected creativity and even today allows the relations of power between musicians and financiers to be reversed." Jacques Attali, *Noise,* trans. Brian Massumi ([1977] Minneapolis, MN: University of Minnesota Press, 1985), 40–41. The standard rejoinder that authors welcome republication of their out-of-print titles even if this requires that they settle for one-time flat fees is simply disingenuous. If royalty-based contracts weren't the best way to protect authors from exploitive underpayment by publishers then maintaining the royalty system wouldn't be such a battle. Count on Barnes & Noble to strike a deal in the best interest of Barnes & Noble.

Page 102. "it only cost him about $3 to print"

David D. Kirkpatrick, "Barnes & Noble's Jekyll and Hyde," *New York Magazine*, July 19, 1999.

Page 102. "'I am your master'"
Mary Wollstonecraft Shelley, *Frankenstein* (1816).

Page 103. "expand that percentage to 10 percent"
The article on B&N's expanded publishing program continues: "The company can place its own titles in strategically favorable locations, while relegating competing titles to out-of-the-way shelves, or refusing to buy them at all." Kristen French, "Barnes & Noble Flexing Publishing Muscle," *TheStreet.com* (February 16, 2002). Contrast this aggressive posture to Len Riggio's calming assurances to publishers sixteen years prior, at the time of B&N's purchase of B. Dalton (when B&N was relying even more heavily on vendor credit): "When one bookseller buys another . . . there is concern within the industry that the combination will restrict the number of authors that appear on bookshelves. . . . Mr. Riggio insisted that the purchase of B. Dalton was not 'connected' to his strategy at Barnes & Noble. The 'center of gravity' for B. Dalton, he said, 'will remain in Minneapolis; B&N's will remain in New York.'" Lisa Belkin, "Discounter Purchases B. Dalton: Barnes & Noble Adds 779 Units to Book Realm," *New York Times*, November 27, 1986, D1.

Page 103. "B&N had attained this 10 percent objective."
From the cited article: "they now self-publish 10% of their books." Eli Hoffmann, "Barnes and Noble: It's All in the Books," *Barron's Magazine*, October 22, 2006.

Page 103. "payments now required to ensure in-chain display"
A former self-publisher's voice: "I don't regret chances I've taken with independent bookstores. Without them, small press books like *Bomb the Suburbs* wouldn't exist. . . . Supporting independent bookstores becomes a matter of free speech. When was the last time you read a book criticizing Barnes & Noble, Borders, Crown, Waterstones, Ingram, or Baker & Taylor? . . . The most direct criticism I've seen appeared . . . in the untouchable *New York Times*. It reported major publishers pay chains in the millions to get their books displayed at the front of the store. How disgusting. I thought they put *Bomb the Suburbs* in the back as a matter of *taste*. Angry? Who me? No, I'm just a small business. I'm *friendly*. Nice chain bookstores. *Thank* you for carrying my book!" William Upski Wim-

satt, *No More Prisons* (New York: Soft Skull, 1999), 31–32; William Upski Wimsatt, *Bomb the Suburbs* (New York: Soft Skull, 1996).

Page 104. "employees were allegedly stealing"
My unprovable allegation of serious internal shrinkage at B. Dalton Bookseller in the early eighties will no doubt be disputed by that era's managers, but managers routinely hush up internal theft: my belief is based on employee gossip of a 1982 chainwide physical inventory with lockdown on store-to-store transfers that revealed a major discrepancy between computer records and on-hand inventory. Any unbiased retail expert will concur that a previously undocumented shortfall of this scale implies systematic employee theft.

Page 104. "a company whose own rapid growth"
I assert that Barnes & Noble and Borders have had an oligopolistic relationship: that is, I believe they have acted tacitly in concert. I don't believe they have maintained formal agreements on pricing. However they haven't appeared to me to have engaged in authentic price competition. In fact, since Barnes & Noble purchased so many other chains, but didn't purchase Borders, I would suggest B&N passively maintained Borders's independence so as to preempt antitrust action by the government. Thus, Borders served for years as an essential accomplice to Barnes & Noble in the overconcentration of the storefront bookselling industry.

Page 107. "'post their own reviews'"
John Hagel III and Arthur G. Armstrong, *Net Gain: Expanding Markets Through Virtual Communities* (Boston, MA: Harvard Business School Press, 1997), 30.

Page 107. "'no perfectly apt analogy'"
Evan I. Schwartz, "Let Affiliate Partners Do Your Marketing For You," *Digital Darwinism* (New York: Random House, 1999), 71–92. We actively promoted our pre-Amazon affiliate marketing innovations: "Mr. Laties has further capitalized on the [book-fair] niche by offering parents from book-fair schools a 10% discount as well as a 10% credit to their schools on store purchases year-round . . . earning Children's Bookstore both customer loyalty and the devotion of scores of school librarians." Joanne Cleaver, "3 R's: Reading, 'Riting, Raising Funds," *Crain's Chicago Business*, September 11, 1995, 45.

Page 108. "e-fairness legislation"
"ABA firmly believes it is the responsibility of state leaders to uniformly and fairly enforce sales tax laws by requiring all retailers—whether they operate online, in bricks-and-mortar stores, or a combination of both—to fulfill their obligation to collect sales tax. This is neither a new tax nor special treatment for independent bookstores—it is an equitable and uniform enforcement of existing state tax laws. Locally owned businesses have far greater positive economic impact on their communities and are largely responsible for our communities retaining their unique characteristics. To undercut them, by selectively deciding what laws to enforce and what laws to ignore, is simply wrong." "ABA Sales Tax Initiative," *BookWeb*, www.bookweb.org/advocacy/salestax.html.

Page 108. "'similar to a bookstore clerk'"
Amy Jo Kim, *Community Building on the Web: Secret Strategies for Successful Online Communities* (Berkeley, CA: Peachpit Press, 2000), 284.

Page 109. "'How could a virtual bookstore hope to compete'"
Patricia B. Seybold with Ronni T. Marshak, *Customers.com: How to Create a Profitable Business Strategy for the Internet and Beyond* (New York: Random House, 1998), 125.

FIFTH RANT: MAKE IT UP

Page 113. "Schwartz convinced publisher Alfred Knopf"
Harry W. Schwartz, *Fifty Years in My Bookstore: Or a Life With Books* (Tarrytown, NY: Booksellers Publishing, 1991).

Page 113. Consignment.
Sample consignment terms: Quimbys (www.quimbys.com/consignment.php); City Lights (www.citylights.com/info/?fa=text88); Amazon (www.amazon.com/advantage).

Page 113. "retailers rely on credit provided by their suppliers"
Publishers as piggy banks: "A recurrent problem that has exacerbated the returns problem this year is the tendency of some retailers and wholesalers to return large quantities of books when bills for them come due. . . . Mike Raymond of the distributors observed that 'If you explain this business to a banker, he'll say, "This is a consignment business."'
John Mutter and Michael Coffey, "Many Unhappy Returns: A Poor Holiday Season, Wholesalers Cleaning House and Cost-conscious Buyers

are Haunting Distributors and Small Presses," *Publishers Weekly,* July 17, 1996.

Rabelais (1546): "'But,' said Pantagruel, 'when will you be out of debt?' 'When we count by the Greek calendar,' answered Panurge, 'and when everyone in the world is happy. . . . May God keep me from being out of debt! . . . You've got to always owe something to someone. That way, there'll always be someone praying to God that He'll grant you a good, long, happy life—because he's terrified that he'll lose what you owe him. And wherever he goes, he'll always say good things about you, so you'll always be able to acquire new creditors, so you can borrow from them to pay him off and he can fill up his ditch with somebody else's dirt.'" Francois Rabelais, "Panurge's Eulogy of Debtors and Borrowers," *Gargantua and Pantagruel,* trans. Burton Raffel ([1534–1554] New York, Norton, 1990), 253–254.

Page 114. "tone of which attracted a demand"
The Wall Street Journal article that offended Len Riggio was Meg Cox, "Risky Plot: Barnes & Noble's Boss Has Big Growth Plans That Booksellers Fear," *Wall Street Journal,* September 11, 1992. While the Standard & Poor's "avoid" warning was well known before WSJ's article came out, and many insiders felt B&N was poorly positioned to go public, the failure of that offering was blamed by B&N on Meg Cox's article. This absurd public relations narrative was still in play several years later, as witness this version of the tale fed to *Crain's New York Business* in 1996: "Mr. Riggio decided to . . . sell a stake to the public in a $130-million initial public offering. But he met a cold reception. The Wall Street Journal shattered his plans with a story questioning the logic of opening so many superstores. . . . The IPO died." Phyllis Furman, "Profits, but Little Respect: Despite Stellar Rise, Barnes & Noble Exec Remains Outsider," *Crain's New York Business,* February 26, 1996.

Page 114. "play a little rough"
I've learned a lot from Barnes & Noble. Here's Fernand Braudel absolving Len Riggio and me: "I might be tempted to suggest that a major element in capitalist development was risk-taking and a taste for speculation. . . . The reader will have noticed that reference is often made to the underlying notion of gambling, risk-taking, cheating; the rule of the game was to invent a counter-game, to oppose the regular mechanisms and instruments of the market, in order to make it work differently—if not in the opposite direction. It might be fun to try and write the history of capitalism within the parameters of a special version of games theory. But the apparent simplicity of the word game (gaming, gambling) would

quickly turn out to cover a multitude of different and contradictory real-ities—forward gambling, playing by the rules, legitimate gambling, reverse gambling, playing with loaded dice." Fernand Braudel, *The Wheels of Commerce: Civilization & Capitalism 15th–18th Century,* vol. 2 (New York: Harper & Row, 1982), 578.

CHAPTER 5: SYMBIOTIC SOLUTION

Page 118. "helped us cheat"
On the sales rep's ambivalent perspective, here's legendary Berkeley book-seller Fred Cody, remembering the sixties: "One rep told of a New York publisher . . . who was especially delinquent in paying his commission travelers. Returning to New York after a long trip financed mainly from loans, the rep went to the offices of the publisher high in a Manhattan sky-scraper to collect the long-due commissions he had earned from an exhausting series of forays, covering the eleven Western states and Alaska. . . . After a prolonged argument, the publisher finally pulled a check book out of a drawer, opened it, and picked up his pen. 'Jesus,' said the publisher, glancing out of the window high above the city, 'I know I owe you the money but I swear to God I'd rather jump out that window than write this check.' 'Write the check,' said the rep, 'and then jump out the window.'" Pat and Fred Cody, *Cody's Books: The Life and Times of a Berkeley Bookstore, 1956 to 1977* (San Francisco: Chronicle Books, 1992), 144.

Page 119. "yielded essentially no profit"
Chicago Children's Museum's chief financial officer confirms "nominal" earnings from their previous gift shop and extols their new relationship with The Children's Bookstore in Joanne Cleaver, "Expanded Kids' Museum on Learning Curve; Copes with Lagging Contributions from Public," *Crain's Chicago Business,* November 11, 1995.

Page 120. "newly redeveloping Pier"
Navy Pier, 600 East Grand Avenue, Chicago, IL, 60611. Chicago's play-ground: A great place to visit but you wouldn't want to live there.

Page 122. "handle sales of the *Diary*"
Anne Frank, *Anne Frank: The Diary of a Young Girl* ([1947] New York: Doubleday, 1995).

Page 123. "children's holocaust literature"

Hana Volavkova, *I Never Saw Another Butterfly*, Revised Edition (New York: Schocken, 1994); Roberto Innocenti, *Rose Blanche* (Minneapolis, MN: Creative Editions, 1990).

Page 125. "so many personal statements"
For instance: Elie Wiesel, *Night*, Reissue Edition ([1955] New York, Bantam, 1982); Malcolm X with Alex Haley, *The Autobiography of Malcolm X*, Reissue Edition ([1963] New York: Ballantine, 1992); Richard Wright, *Black Boy* (New York: Harper, 1945).

Page 126. "contemplating an empty room"
Hannah Arendt, *Eichmann in Jerusalem: A Report on the Banality of Evil* (New York: Penguin, 1994); Alberto Moravia, *Boredom* ([1960] New York: New York Review of Books, 1999).

SIXTH RANT: HE WHO CANNOT, TEACHES

Page 131. "experts to give us all the answers"
"He who can, does. He who cannot, teaches." George Bernard Shaw, "Maxims for Revolutionists," *Man and Superman: A Comedy and a Philosophy* (London, 1903).

Page 132. "Good educators don't lead"
Educator Paolo Freire on mutual learning among teachers and students: "In the banking concept of education, knowledge is a gift bestowed by those who consider themselves knowledgeable upon those whom they consider to know nothing. Projecting an absolute ignorance onto others . . . the teacher presents himself to his students as their necessary opposite. . . . Problem-posing education is revolutionary futurity. . . . Hence, it affirms men as beings who transcend themselves . . . for whom looking at the past must only be a means of understanding more clearly what and who they are so that they can more wisely build the future. . . . The point of departure must always be with men in the 'here and now' . . . a deepened consciousness of their situation leads men to apprehend that situation as an historical reality susceptible of transformation. Resignation gives way to the drive for transformation and inquiry. . . ." Paolo Freire, *Pedagogy of the Oppressed*, trans. Myra Bergman Ramos (New York: Seabury, 1970), 58, 72–73.

Page 132. "'We learn through experience'"

Viola Spolin, *Improvisation for the Theater* (Evanston, IL: Northwestern University Press, 1963), 3–4.

CHAPTER 6: TRADING PLACES

Page 137. "dada poem, *Ursonate*"
"Schwitters survives, through a gramophone recording, as one of the most extraordinary performers of the century. When he read his "Primeval Sonata" *[Ursonate]*—a long poem made up entirely of wordless sounds— it was as if there had come into existence a completely new mode of human expression, by turns hilarious and terrifying, elemental and pre- cisely engineered. Others dreamed of reconciling art and language, music and speech, the living room and the cathedral, the stage and the unspoiled forest. Schwitters had the sweep of mind not only to dream of these things but to carry them out." John Russell, *An Alternative Art* (New York: Museum of Modern Art, 1975), 40.

Page 137. "predecessor of Schwitters"
Christian Morgenstern, *The Gallows Songs: Christian Morgenstern's Gal- genlieder,* trans. Max Knight (Berkeley, CA: University of California Press, 1963).

Page 138. "decade presenting the piece"
Lynn Book's and my duo performances of *Ursonate* were documented in Lynn Warren et al., *Art Chicago: 1945–1995* (New York: Thames & Hudson, 1996), and featured in the accompanying Museum of Contem- porary Art exhibition. Our *Ursonate* shows at The Children's Bookstore were described in Norman Mark, *Norman Mark's Chicago,* 4th ed. (Chicago: Chicago Review Press, 1993). The text for *Ursonate* [1922–32] can be found in Kurt Schwitters, *Pppppp: Kurt Schwitters Poems, Per- formance, Pieces, Proses, Plays, Poetics,* trans. Jerome Rothenberg and Pierre Joris (Philadelphia, PA: Temple University Press, 1994).

Page 138. "scholar compiled a comprehensive edition"
Krisjanis Barons, *Latvju Dainas* (compiled 1894–1914).

Page 138. "explaining our theories"
Malvina Reynolds, "Magic Penny," All rights reserved (Northern Music Co., copyright 1955, 1958, rights administered by MCA Music Pub- lishing, N.Y. N.Y.); Dave Mallett, "Garden Song," All rights reserved (Cherry Lane Music Publishing Co. Inc., copyright 1975, 1978). Both

songs' lyrics are reprinted in *Rise Up Singing: The Group Singing Songbook*, eds. Peter Blood and Annie Patterson (Bethlehem, PA: Sing Out, 1988, 1992), 240, 252.

SEVENTH RANT: PUKE APOTHEOSIS

Page 142. "'moral sense of man'"
Rabindranath Tagore, *Sadhana* (New York: Macmillan, 1913), 55.

Page 144. "dependent from the day we were born"
On dependence: "It is true that we are not conscious of our dependence, but by admitting our free will we arrive at absurdity, while by admitting our dependence on the external world, on time, and on cause, we arrive at laws." Leo Tolstoy, *War and Peace*, trans. Louise and Aylmer Maude ([1869] New York: Simon & Schuster, 1942), 1351.

CHAPTER 7: THE CONQUEST OF CHICAGO

Page 147. "'climate for bookselling'"
Barbara A. Brannon, "The Pioneering Journey of the Hampshire Bookshop: The First Ten Years," *Paradise Printed & Bound: Book Arts in Northampton & Beyond* (Northampton, MA: 350th Anniversary Committee, 2003), 26.

Page 148. "'tempting buyout offer'"
Andrew Malcolm, "Chicago's Largest Bookstore Chain Is Being Turned Over to Employees," *New York Times*, June 22, 1986.

Page 152. "presented our politicized essay"
Balanced: John Blades, "Staying Alive: The Children's Bookstore on Lincoln Avenue has shut down, possibly for good. But independent booksellers say they're not an endangered species, even if superstores rule the literary seas," *The Chicago Tribune* (March 20, 1996): Tempo. "When they found their bookshop outflanked by Barnes & Noble and other superstores, Laties counterattacked . . . starting up a second store in the Children's Museum on Navy Pier. . . . Before he closed the shop, Laties issued a bulletin to 'friends' of the store, urging them to patronize superstores 'as little as possible,' claiming . . . that their 'wasteful practices' are passed along to customers in the form of higher prices."

Page 152. "attacked our ideas"

"In a recent newsletter to customers, they bitterly blasted. . . . 'Book superstores are endangering the free flow of information in our society.' They are? What, by offering thousands of books at discounted prices? *Tricky.*" Irritated: Richard Roeper, "Bookstore's Owners Have Way With Words," *Chicago Sun-Times*, January 18, 1996.

Page 153. "his obituary column"
Tom Ehrenfeld, "Bookstore Owner Refuses to Grow, Pays Price: A Look At Why a Legendary, Community-Based Bookstore Failed After Years of Success," *Inc. Magazine*, October, 1996. Tom felt that our late-eighties decision not to participate in the launch of a proposed educational toy store chain (partly on principle) presaged our ultimate closure.

Page 153. "Tom Sawyer attending his own funeral"
"First one and then another pair of eyes followed the minister's, and then almost with one impulse the congregation rose and stared while the three dead boys came marching up the aisle, Tom in the lead, Joe next, and Huck, a ruin of drooping rags, sneaking sheepishly in the rear! They had been hid in the unused gallery listening to their own funeral sermon!" Mark Twain, *The Adventures of Tom Sawyer* (1876).

Page 153. "finding he'd been listed as dead"
"People with whom I had been on the worst terms during my life wrote the most enthusiastic condolences to my mother: 'Gosh' Parry, my horrible house-master, for instance." The *Times* subsequently printed a retraction: "Captain Robert Graves, Royal Welch Fusiliers, officially reported died of wounds, wishes to inform his friends that he is recovering from his wounds at Queen Alexandra's Hospital, Highgate, N." Robert Graves, *Goodbye To All That*, Updated Edition ([1929] New York: Random House, 1957), 226–227.

Page 155. "big-name autographing"
Hillary Clinton, *It Takes A Village and Other Lessons Children Teach Us* (New York: Simon & Schuster, 1996).

EIGHTH RANT: WHAT'S SELLING

Page 158. "exponential power laws"
"In the ecological and economic domains where some of the obvious applications lie . . . power laws are well known from observation, particularly ones governing the distribution of resources. The famous empirical law of wage distribution in a market economy, discovered in the nine-

teenth century by the Italian economist Vilfredo Pareto, approximates a power law for the higher incomes." Murray Gell-Mann, *The Quark and the Jaguar* (New York: W. H. Freeman, 1997), 319.

While I'm attracted to Gell-Mann's explanation of power laws in the context of what he calls complex adaptive systems—since in his schema bookstores clearly qualify as complex adaptive systems—a different explanation by Albert-László Barabási, in *Linked*, his book about the science of networks, makes easier reading: "Pareto's Law or Principle, known also as the 80/20 rule, has been turned into the Murphy's Law of management: 80 percent of profits are produced by only 20 percent of the employees, 80 percent of customer service problems are created by only 20 percent of consumers, 80 percent of decisions are made during 20 percent of meeting time, and so on." A few pages later Barabási continues, "Every time an 80/20 rule truly applies, you can bet that there is a power law behind it. Power laws formulate in mathematical terms the notion that a few large events carry most of the action. Power laws rarely emerge in systems completely dominated by a roll of the dice. Physicists have learned that most often they signal a transition from disorder to order. . . . Power laws are at the heart of some of the most stunning conceptual advances in the second half of the twentieth century, emerging in fields like chaos, fractals, and phase transitions." Albert-László Barabási, *Linked: The New Science of Networks* (Cambridge, MA: Perseus, 2002), 66, 72.

Page 159. "100 of the more than 45,000 new titles"
David D. Kirkpatrick, "Barnes & Noble's Jekyll and Hyde," *New York Magazine*, July 19, 1999.

Page 159. "rows of bookcases"
The wallpaper analogy is widely invoked. For instance: "What do you get if you double the sales space in a low-growth industry? Basically: wallpaper . . . books that make stores look full and rich but that can't possibly sell. And then, when the books begin to get dusty, they're returned and, inevitably, replaced with newer, fresher titles that will also, in turn, get dusty and turn into returns. . . . The irony is that some (many?) of the publishers who are suddenly on the receiving end of this first wave of returns helped to finance the super-chains' expansion with new-branch store discounts, sweetheart deals and very-extended credit terms." Carol Seajay, "Returns: Too Much Wallpaper on a No-Growth Industry," *Feminist Bookstore News*, November/December, 1996. Quoted in "Books as wallpaper? An Explanation for Returns," *Publishers Weekly*, November

11, 1996.

Page 161. "'each person should have the opportunity'"
Leonard B. Meyer, "The Aesthetics of Stability," *Music, The Arts, and Ideas* (Chicago: University of Chicago Press, 1967), 178. More succinctly: "The great Zen Master Yang-shan said, 'In my shop I handle all kinds of merchandise. If someone comes looking for rat shit, I'll sell him rat shit. If someone comes looking for gold, I'll sell him pure gold.'" "Notes," *Bhagavad Gita*, trans. Stephen Mitchell (New York: Harmony, 2000), 191. This I gather is a gloss on Mahayana Buddhism's key doctrine of Expedient Means: "Numberless thousands of myriads of millions of kinds of living beings come before the Buddha and hear the Dharma [law]. The Thus Come One [Buddha] at this time observes these beings, their keen-ness or dullness, their exertion or laxity, and in accord with what they can bear, preaches the Dharma to them in an incalculable variety of modes, each causing them to rejoice and enabling them speedily to gain good advantage." *Scripture of the Lotus Blossom of the Fine Dharma (The Lotus Sutra)*, translated from the Chinese of Kumarajiva by Leon Hurwitz ([circa 350–410 A.D.] New York: Columbia University Press, 1976), 102.

CHAPTER 8: DEBTORS' PRISON

Page 169. "junk that sold when overpriced"
"A commodity appears, at first sight, a very trivial thing and easily under-stood. Its analysis shows that in reality it is a very queer thing, abounding in metaphysical subtleties and theological niceties. So far as it is a value in use, there is nothing mysterious about it. . . . The form of wood is altered by making a table out of it; nevertheless, this table remains wood, an ordi-nary material thing. As soon as it steps forth as commodity, however, it is transformed into a material immaterial thing. It not only stands with its feet on the ground, but, in the face of all other commodities, it stands on its head, and out of its wooden brain it evolves notions more whimsically than if it had suddenly begun to dance." Karl Marx, *Capital*, vol. 1, trans. Samuel Moore and Edward Aveline ([1887] New York: International Pub-lishers, 1967), 76. Cited in Walter Benjamin, *The Arcades Project* (Cambridge, MA: Harvard University Press, 1999), 196–7.

Page 170. "touristy toy store"
Daniel Harris on the hypocrisy of people like me: "The typical objection to consumerism is highly moralistic, based on . . . the conviction that the materialism of the marketplace detracts from our spiritual and intellec-

tual well-being, that shopping is a vicious pastime for the simple-minded, and that politically responsible people take pleasure only in books and ideas and eschew narcissistic luxuries that inevitably seduce the righteous from the straight-and-narrow." Daniel Harris, *Cute, Quaint, Hungry and Romantic: The Aesthetics of Consumerism* (New York: Basic Books, 2000), xv–xvi.

Page 175. "'I have David Schlessinger on the line'"
I've put many of David's comments in quotation marks, but of course I'm reconstructing this conversation from memory as best I can.

Page 178. "'make money selling more sidelines'"
On the Christian Booksellers Association's identity crisis: "Many publishers will not be happy to lose the word book from the association's name, but several admitted that the proposed change reflects the reality that books (apart from Bibles) now account for only 28% of sales in CBA member stores." Phyllis Tickle and Lynn Garrett, "1995 CBA Show at Denver a Mix of Functions, Identities: for Christian 'Booksellers,' Books are Minor," *Publishers Weekly*, July 31, 1995.

NINTH RANT: PUBLISH, PERISH

Page 193. "'contribute something worthwhile to mankind'"
Herbert S. Bailey Jr., *The Art and Science of Book Publishing* (New York: Harper & Row, 1970), 195.

Page 193. "paying exorbitant tax"
"In January 1979, the U.S. Supreme Court ruled—in a case brought by the Thor Power Tool Company against the Internal Revenue Service—that, contrary to what the plaintiff claimed, warehouse stocks of tools could not be depreciated for tax purposes unless they had left warehouse inventory. . . . Soon thereafter, the Internal Revenue Service ruled that this decision . . . was binding on . . . the publishing industry. To the I.R.S., books are products just like tools, toilet paper, or detergents. . . . Now it is no longer economically feasible to maintain stock on many titles and sell them gradually through backlist orders, and now a house that formerly kept titles in print may decide to remainder one, or to destroy all copies of it entirely, rather than to bear the cost of maintaining it in print." Lewis A. Coser, Charles Kadushin, and Walter W. Powell, *Books: The Culture and Commerce of Publishing* (New York: Basic Books, 1982) 370–1.

Page 194. "wholesaler MBS Textbook"
Jim Milliot and John Baker, "McGraw Hill Charges Huge Sales of Books Aimed for Destruction," *Publishers Weekly*, June 19, 1995. I'm not suggesting Len Riggio should be held accountable for all alleged peccadilloes possibly perpetrated by his ambitious managers.

Page 195. "efficient remainder dealer"
Remainders are a terrific business opportunity. Attend the autumn Chicago International Remainder and Overstock Book Exhibition to learn the ropes: CIROBE, 1501 East 57th Street, Chicago, IL, 60637. www.cirobe.com.

CHAPTER 9: PAYING THE PRICE

Page 201. "new American Girl books"
Connie Porter, *Meet Addy: An American Girl* (Appleton, WI: American Girl, 1994).

Page 203. "'People want *that* ending'"
The Nora Ephron film *You've Got Mail* contains several subversive subtexts, the most significant of which is that the strong-minded children's bookseller, in marrying the non-literary chain-store owner, effectively obtains power and influence over the superstore (in any sequel: i.e., behind every great man there is a great woman).

While chain-superstore owner Joe Fox (presumably modeled after Barnes & Noble's Steve Riggio, and played in the movie by actor Tom Hanks) can only draw on his lunk-headed *Godfather*-movie ideas of competition (his oft-repeated phrase "to the mattresses" means "man the barricades and conduct sneak attacks"), the independent bookseller Kathleen Kelly (played by Meg Ryan) deploys her weakness to co-opt her attacker. This power of the weak message echoes a similar theme in Jane Austen's *Pride and Prejudice* (1813), the novel from which substantial elements in *You've Got Mail* derive, and not incidentally Kathleen Kelly's favorite book, which she insists Joe Fox read.

Jane Austen promoted the Wollstonecraftian heroine in a softened form: the woman who obtains power via a male intermediary. "[Austen's] ironic narrative subjects systems of authority to damaging skepticism; she celebrates intellect, feeling and moral sense in her heroines and ridicules their absence in others. With concerns close to Mary Wollstonecraft's, she adopts a conservative approach to accommodating women's aspirations to existing social structures." Virginia Blain, Isobel Grundy, and Patricia Clements, "Jane Austen," *The Feminist Companion to Literature in English: Women Writers from the Middle Ages to the Present* (New Haven, CT: Yale University Press, 1990), 40.

Compare, in particular, *Pride and Prejudice*'s Elizabeth Bennet, fantasizing about becoming the mistress of Mr. Darcy's estate Pemberley while on a tourist visit, and finding herself unexpectedly face to face with Darcy himself—this during the very period when the two are feuding—with *You've Got Mail*'s Kathleen Kelly, irrepressibly (if tearfully) hand-selling Noel Streatfeild *Shoes* books during a foray into Joe Fox's superstore, at a moment she should be capable only of anger since he's just put her own store out of business—Joe Fox then unexpectedly appearing to witness her salesmanship among his customers (presumably the character Kathleen Kelly, in visiting Joe Fox's store, is subconsciously modeling her actions on those of her own fictional favorite, Elizabeth Bennet). Both characters— Elizabeth Bennet and Kathleen Kelly—will go on to win covert authority over their future husbands' holdings, post-nuptials.

As a key additional subtext—perhaps unintended by auteur Ephron—consider Virginia Woolf's analysis, in the feminist classic *A Room of One's Own* (London: The Hogarth Press, 1929), of Jane Austen's artistic situation. Woolf suggests Jane Austen, writing without privacy in the family sitting room—implicitly operating under analogous ideological scrutiny—placed her social commentary between the lines. Similarly, Nora Ephron, a published author with books for sale at chain superstores, *encodes* her message about chain stores' impact on individuality and expression. (If authors' voices weren't stifled for fear of being banned from chain bookstore shelves, they'd come right out and shout— together now—"Screw the chains!")

As it stands, thanks to Nora Ephron's clever delivery of sexy subtext, *You've Got Mail*—a staple of American culture whose title is the same as America Online's ubiquitous corporate slogan—has helped maintain the romantic allure of independent bookselling, to the detriment of those big corporations that would prefer the public forget what it is excellent indies offer: outstanding booksellers in residence.

Page 203. "compact book with a yellow cover"
Esmé Codell, *Educating Esmé* (Chapel Hill, NC: Algonquin Press of Chapel Hill, 1998). In a subsequent book, Esmé dubs me her *Boss of Storytelling:* "A visceral enthusiasm permeated all his interactions with children, and in this way he was a great inspiration to me, and to many families for whom he modeled his effervescent technique. He taught me

that when you are going to give a performance to children, give it up and give it all!" Esmé Codell, *How to Get Your Child to Love Reading, For Ravenous and Reluctant Readers Alike: Activities, Ideas and Inspiration for Exploring Everything in the World Through Books* (Chapel Hill, NC: Algonquin Press, 2003), 346.

I owe my own improvisation skills to Victor Podagrosi of Child's Play Touring Theatre; Josephine Forsberg of The Players Workshop of Second City; Alan Silva ("Why would anyone ever want to do anything less than PER-FECT?") of The Institute for Advanced Cultural Perception; Douglass Ewart and Mwata Bowdoin ("What do you do if only you show up? You HIT!") of the Association for the Advancement of Creative Musicians; and Ned Corman, founder of The Commission Project and longtime jazz-band leader at Penfield High School ("If you're gonna make a mistake, make it LOUD!").

Page 205. "Mutual irritation compounded"
As an independent businessperson I accept responsibility for the deterioration of my company's relationship with my client, Chicago Children's Museum. For the duration of our contract I made no negative public statements; when asked for my opinions of the museum I was complimentary. For example: "The Chicago Children's Museum is a marvelous success story. . . . I'm their front doorstep and am often providing information about the museum, so I feel like I'm a vital part of the museum's activities." Karen Schwartz, "Museum Store Owner," *The Chicago Tribune,* July 11, 1999.

Page 205. "Hicks's new company Event Network"
For information about Tom Hicks see "Thomas O. Hicks," *UT Watch,* accessed January 8, 2011, www.utwatch.org/utimco/hicks.html.

Event Network's website is at www.eventnetwork.us. Event Network has handled the traveling stores for Clear Channel's shows *Treasures of the Vatican* and *Titanic,* while operating full-time stores at many museums that regularly hosted Clear Channel exhibits.

"Clear Channel . . . believes much of its future growth and profit in entertainment lies . . . within the hallowed walls of America's science and history centers, museums and art galleries. In almost every case, these institutions are subsidized by taxpayers. . . . 'Whether it's Madonna, or a Broadway show, or treasures from the Vatican,' says Adam Phillips, Clear Channel Entertainment's executive vice president for corporate development, 'it's all product to us.'" Chris Jones, "The Corporate Seduction of Museums: Blockbusters Can Be the Salvation for Exhibitors, and Media Giant Clear Channel is Eager to Provide Them—for a Price," *The Chicago Tribune,* February 16, 2003.

Page 206. "Oaxacan wood carving exhibit"
A great source is Shepard Barbash and Vicki Ragan, *Oaxacan Wood Carving: The Magic in the Trees* (San Francisco: Chronicle Books, 1993).

Page 208. "attracted grants"
Our National Endowment for the Arts grants were for the 2003, 2004 and 2005 fiscal years. For instance: "Child's Play Touring Theatre, Chicago, IL. CATEGORY: Creativity. FIELD/DISCIPLINE: Theater. $12,000 to support the development of a new program called Writing Our World (WOW!). Using stories and poems written by children and collected by Child's Play's global writing exchange, the WOW! Show will be presented to young audiences around the country." National Endowment for the Arts, www.nea.gov/grants/recent/03grants/states1/IL.html. Also: www.cptt.org/productions/repertory/wow/index.html.

Page 208. "fundraising campaign"
PovertyFighters.com hosted seven click-drives between 2002 and 2007.

Page 208. "We didn't want a legal fight"
Deciding to walk away from our contract at enormous cost was terribly confusing. The museum felt it had specific grounds to terminate: we'd been paying late for years (compensating for this with thousands of dollars in interest fees, however). We responded with our own charges. Nevertheless, we felt the core issue was whether the board had an unwritten, extracontractual right to control the trajectory of the museum they'd created. We fundamentally agreed that we were there to serve them: they'd trusted us because of our prior reputation. This is why we didn't take them up on their offer (I was reminded that their attorneys served *pro bono*) to go to court.

Page 209. "a new museum"
"Tucked in the hills of western Massachusetts, at Amherst, the museum has quickly become a travel destination for families and school groups who want to look at Carle's original collages as well as rotating exhibits of other artists' work. After presenting children with one popular book after another, Eric Carle gave all of the children of the United States and the world another unique gift—our first permanent American museum to house original picture-book art." Anita Silvey, *100 Best Books for Children* (Boston: Houghton Mifflin, 2004), 7. Eric Carle Museum of Picture Book Art, 125 West Bay Road, Amherst, MA 01002, www.carlemuseum.org.

Page 209. "Eric had visited The Children's Bookstore"
Eric Carle, *Animals, Animals* (New York: Putnam, 1993).

TENTH RANT: SELLING HIGH

Page 211. "fifteenth-century-style title"
"The style of the barker inviting customers to his booth did not differ from that of the hawker of chapbooks, and even the long titles of these books were usually composed in the form of popular advertisements." Mikhail Bakhtin, "The Language of the Marketplace," *Rabelais and His World,* Translated by Hélène Iswolsky ([1968] Bloomington, IN: University of Indiana Press, 1984), 153, 156.

Page 211. *"for Whom a Book Is Born"*
Optimistic overproduction is a tradition. Harvard librarian George Parker Winship reports that many fifteenth-century printers "worked themselves straight into bankruptcy by printing numerous editions of the literary classics"; historian Fernand Braudel reports that "one calculation puts the total of incunabula (books printed before 1500) at 20 million. Europe had perhaps 70 million inhabitants at the time." David Fromkin points out that Gutenberg himself "lived a troubled life of debts, litigation, and failed partnerships. A creditor . . . ruined him financially and took control of the type for Gutenberg's two masterpieces, a Bible and a Psalter." George Parker Winship, *Gutenberg to Plantin: An Outline of the Early History of Printing* (Cambridge, MA: Harvard University Press, 1926). Quoted in John T. Winterich, *A Primer of Book Collecting* (New York: Greenberg, 1926), 28; Fernand Braudel, *The Structures of Everyday Life, Civilization & Capitalism, 15th–18th Century,* vol. 1 (New York: Harper & Row, 1981), 400; David Fromkin, *The Way of the World: From the Dawn of Civilizations to the Eve of the Twenty-First Century* (New York: Random House, 1998), 151.

Page 212. "an outright, not a returnable basis"
Carl Kroch is quoted in Lewis A. Coser, Charles Kadushin, and Walter W. Powell, *Books: The Culture and Commerce of Publishing* (New York: Basic Books, 1982), 359.

Page 213. "application of mind to nature"
Ralph Waldo Emerson, "Wealth," *Conduct of Life* (Boston: Houghton Mifflin, 1860), 72–73.

Page 214. "asserted every renter's right to repair and deduct"
"The Tenant's Bill of Rights. A tenant has the right to: A clean, safe place to live; Heat in the wintertime; Hot and cold running water; Drains that work; Windows that work; Screens and storm windows; A working toilet; A front and back door that lock; Roofs, ceilings and walls that don't leak; Privacy and protection from unreasonable intrusion and harassment from the landlord; Repairs made quickly and properly; Roach-free, rat-free, and mouse-free living; A structurally sound building; A building with smoke detectors, fire extinguishers and fire escapes; The right to complain about violations of your rights without retaliation; The right to remain in your apartment until you choose to move out; The right to move out when necessity arises, for any number of legitimate reasons; A lease which guarantees these rights in writing; The right to enforce these rights by rent withholding, tenant actions and in a court of law; The right not to have your property seized, not to be locked out, evicted or refused a lease renewal without probable cause and due process of law; and, The right to recover damages because of violations of your rights." Ed Sacks, *Chicago Tenants' Handbook: The Tenants' Rights Bible*, 2nd ed., Revised (Chicago: Pro Se Press, 1992), iii. Also: Ed Sacks, *Savvy Renter's Kit*, 2nd ed. (Chicago: Dearborn Trade, 1998).

CHAPTER 10: GIVEBACK TIME

Page 217. "a just-released book"
Eric Carle, *Slowly, Slowly, Slowly Said the Sloth* (New York: Penguin, 2002).

Page 218. "titles I should stock in his new museum store"
Carolyn Lanchner et al., *Fernand Leger* (New York: Museum of Modern Art, 2002).

Page 218. "pointing to images"
"[Painter] Franz Marc wrote: 'Have we not learned from a thousand years of experience that things cease to speak the more we hold up to them the visual mirror of their appearance? Appearance is eternally flat. . . .' For Marc, the goal of art was 'to reveal unearthly life dwelling behind everything, to break the mirror of life so that we may look being in the face.'" Aniela Jaffé, "Symbolism in the Visual Arts," *Man and his Symbols*, Conceived and Edited by C. J. Jung (Garden City, NY: Doubleday, 1964), 262.

Page 218. "that had informed books he'd created"

Carle on his childhood mentor: *"EC [Eric Carle]:* Herr Krauss . . . had hung out and studied with the German Expressionists, whose art the Nazis condemned as 'degenerate,' and was forbidden to be shown or exhibited. . . . He asked me one day to come to his house, where he showed me reproductions of Expressionist and abstract paintings. That was when he pointed out the loose and sketchy quality of my own work, and when I heard him call the Nazis 'charlatans' and 'Schweine,' which was utterly amazing—a very dangerous thing for him to do. *LSM [Interviewer Leonard S. Marcus]:* Would you say he risked his life by inviting you over? *EC:* I certainly think so. As a Socialist and an Expressionist, he already had two strikes against him. If I had turned him in, something I didn't even think of, he would have been interviewed by some horrible official person, who would have brought out his past, his mistakes, and next thing you know he might have been sent to a concentration camp." Leonard S. Marcus, "Eric Carle: Born June 25, 1929, Syracuse, New York," *Ways of Telling: Conversations on the Art of the Picture Book* (New York: Penguin, 2002), 40–41.

N.B. Eric Carle's family had returned from the United States to their native Germany in 1935, when Eric—born a citizen of the US—was six years old.

Page 218. "On the wall by his desk"
Leonardo da Vinci, *Notebooks* (ca. 1510–1514), W19013v.

Page 220. "'What do you see? What makes you say that?'"
Visual Thinking Strategies are taught by the organization Visual Understanding in Education, 119 West 23rd Street, Suite 905, New York, NY, 10011, www.vue.org.

Page 223. "I'd toured schools"
Norton Juster, *The Phantom Tollbooth* (New York: Random House, 1961).

CHAPTER 11: AMAZON ATTACK

Page 225. "'Sometimes resistance caused riots.'"
Eric Laursen and Seth Tobocman, *Understanding The Crash* (New York: Soft Skull Press, 2010), 101.

Page 226. "Against the odds, since 1999"
Karen Schechner, "Bluestockings: Books, Events, and Activism on New York's Lower East Side," *Bookselling This Week*, July 22, 2010, http://news.bookweb.org/news/bluestockings-books-events-and-activism-

nycs-lower-east-side.

Page 226. "the British destroyed his bookstore"
For instance see Anita Silvey and Wendell Minor, *Henry Knox: Bookseller, Soldier, Patriot* (Boston: Clarion Books, 2010), a delightful picture book.

Page 228. "Jeff Bezos said this"
Chris Anderson, editor of *Wired Magazine* and author of *The Long Tail*—which is an energetically pro-Amazon book—had one of his central assertions about Amazon's miraculous business model challenged by Amazon.com founder Jeff Bezos in a Bezos comment to an Anderson blogpost. I found this first-hand reporting by Bezos astonishing. Not as astonishing is that within a year the Bezos comment had been deleted, and the Anderson blogpost had been completely rewritten. Below is the link to the rewritten blogpost. While Bezos's comment has been eliminated some of the comment's content is now included in the body of the rewritten blogpost: ". . . I've now spoken to Jeff Bezos (and others) about this. He doesn't have a hard figure for the percentage of sales of products not available offline, but reckons that it's closer to 25–30%." Chris Anderson, "Objection #1," *The Long Tail: Chris Anderson's blog* (blog), October 10, 2004, http://longtail.typepad.com/the_long_tail/ 2004/10/objection_1.html.

So, Jeff Bezos says that sales of products *only available online* are close to 25–30 percent of total Amazon sales, meaning that 70–75 percent of Amazon sales are of items *already available in stores;* a very small portion of Amazon's many millions of otherwise mostly slow-selling items.

Page 229. "'Americans are buying more of fewer titles'"
"At the Book Standard's Summit 2005, held on Thursday in New York City . . . one of the most-repeated statistics was mentioned early in the program by Jim King, senior v-p and general manager of Nielsen BookScan, who noted that 93% of all ISBNs of books whose sales were tracked by the company during 2004 sold less than 1,000 units. . . . Some 1.15 million ISBNs (often representing several editions of one book) accounted for 13% of all sales during 2004, and the remaining 7% of ISBNs accounted for 87% of sales, prompting King to suggest that in 2004 that the old 80/20 rule of 80% of sales coming from 20% of titles had become a 90/10 rule." "Change: Book Standard Summit, Part 1," *Shelf-Awareness.com* (September 26, 2005), http://www.shelf-awareness.com/issue.html?issue=58.

"[The] apparent anomaly of greater choice resulting in a narrower selection finds a corollary in Amazon's use of metrics to recommend titles based on previous purchases. The algorithms at work here are highly sophisticated and are widely credited with expanding consumer choice. Yet such metric-based systems can simultaneously increase the variety of books purchased by individual customers while decreasing the overall variety of books bought by everyone. This is because, as blogger Whimsley [AKA Tom Slee, author of *No One Makes You Shop At Wal-Mart*] explains, 'In Internet World the customers see further, but they are all looking out from the same tall hilltop. In Offline World individual customers are standing on different, lower hilltops. They may not see as far individually, but more of the ground is visible to someone.'" Colin Robinson, "The Trouble With Amazon," *The Nation*, August 2, 2010, http://www.thenation.com/article/37484/trouble-amazon; Tom Slee, *No One Makes You Shop At Wal-Mart*, (Toronto: Between The Lines, 2006).

Page 230. A more generous assessment:
"Seth Tobocman's *Understanding the Crash* produced with Eric Laursen, a contributor to the *Nation*, and Jessica Wehrle, homes in on the late-2008 recession that still defines this country's economy. Anything but optimistic, it's appropriately rendered in black and white and . . . represents a sharp history lesson. Tobocman's illustrations are pointed, large, and stark, evocative of propaganda posters of the '50s. He focuses on the collapse of neighborhoods in his native Cleveland and in Miami; he blames the former on subprime mortgages, the latter on the speculative stock market and the deregulation craze Ronald Reagan launched. This sobering, dramatic book effectively swirls lefty economics, history, and politics to attack the lack of scaffolding in George W. Bush's vaunted and failed 'ownership society.'" Carlo Wolff, "Drawing Attention: A Grab Bag of Graphic Novels Embraces the Sensual, Political, Personal, and Fantastical," *Boston Globe*, December 26, 2010, http://www.boston.com/ae/books/articles/2010/12/26/graphic_novels_that_embrace_the_sensual_political_and_fantastical.

Page 230. Citation for critics:
"WRITER: I'm a writer. READER: In my opinion you're shit! THE WRITER stands for a few minutes, shaken by this new idea, and falls down in a dead faint. He is carried out." Daniil Kharms, "Four Illustrations of How a New Idea Disconcerts a Man Unprepared for It," *Incidences*, ed. and trans. Neil Cornwell (London: Serpent's Tail, 1993), 63.

Page 230. "a division of Reed Elsevier Inc."
Publishers Weekly was brought out by its management in 2010 and is no

longer part of Reed Elsevier.

Page 231. Creative destruction.
For an excellent history of Amazon's business strategy, try:
Dan Gallagher, "Amazon's Bezos is Anything but an Open Book; He's Made a Lucrative Career of Bewildering Investors, Consumers," *MarketWatch.com*, December 7, 2010, http://www.marketwatch.com/story/jeff-bezos-is-anything-but-an-open-book-2010-12-08.

A countervailing analysis, focusing on the damage Amazon has done to readers, authors, and publishers, can be found in Colin Robinson, "The Trouble With Amazon," *The Nation*, August 2, 2010.

Page 233. "Friends of Libraries Groups launched used bookstores"
Links to resources for Friends groups considering whether to open a year-round bookstore: "Idea Sharing: Friends Bookstores," *Association of Library Trustees, Advocates, Friends and Foundations*, http://www.ala.org/ala/mgrps/divs/altaff/friends/ideasharing/book-stores/index.cfm.

Page 233. "innovators like More Than Words"
This is one of the most important breakthroughs in bookstore conceptualization: a staffing structure that brings in revenue via foundation and government subsidy, instead of paying it out as payroll. www.mtwyouth.org.

Page 233. "money-losing—because heavily discounted—new-book sales"
On Amazon's internal numbers, independent analyst Morris Rosenthal has for many years been the best source. Here's one of his blogposts on this subject: "Amazon Profit Driven By MarketPlace Sellers?," *Self-Publishing 2.0*, February 1, 2010, http://www.fonerbooks.com/2010/02/amazon-profit-driven-by-marketplace.html.

Page 233. "achieved a key target"
General Merchandise growth rates on Amazon.com are much faster than media growth rates, a trend that analysts forecast will continue. For instance, "Lately, Wal-Mart and Amazon have been encroaching on each other's turf. Amazon has bolstered its general merchandise selection to the point where these sales now surpass its sales of books and music." Jeffrey Grau, "How the Davids of the E-Commerce World Can Beat the Goliaths," *Emarketer.com*, October 19, 2009), http://www.emarketer.com/blog/index.php/how-the-davids-of-the-e-commerce-world-can-beat-the-goliaths/.

Page 234. "Amazon's market share has certainly increased steadily"
"Amazon is now the biggest book retailer, both in North America and overseas, Barnes & Noble saw sales drop around 5% on the year, and Borders is on its last legs." Morris Rosenthal, "Book Sales Statistics: Amazon, Barnes & Noble and Borders Sales Numbers Annual Update," *Fonerbooks.com*, http://www.fonerbooks.com/booksale.htm. The charts and graphs on this website are terrific.

Page 234. "stuck at $25 billion annually"
"The Association of American Publishers (AAP) has today released its annual estimate of total book sales in the United States. The report, which uses data from the Bureau of the Census as well as sales data from eighty-six publishers inclusive of all major book publishing media market holders, estimates that U.S. publishers had net sales of $23.9 billion in 2009, down from $24.3 billion in 2008, representing a 1.8% decrease. In the last seven years the industry had a compound annual growth rate (CAGR) of 1.1%." Association of American Publishers, "AAP Reports Book Sales Estimated at $23.9 Billion in 2009," *Industry Statistics 2009*, April 7, 2010, http://www.publishers.org/main/IndustryStats/indStats_02.htm.

Page 234. "informal network of collective bookstores"
See for instance, "Listing infoshops by region," *Infoshop Network*, http://www.infoshopnetwork.org/infoshops/regional.

Page 236. "a history of The Wooden Shoe"
A shorter version is available online: "Wooden Shoe is an all-volunteer democratic collective, run by consensus. It has existed for 32 years, a long stretch for any business let alone a non-hierarchical business whose goal is not profit but a kind of anti-profit. It seeks to overturn capitalism and the state by using its weaknesses against it, through education and agitation, similar to how the Huns used the roads that Rome built to sweep into Italy and bring the Roman Empire to its end." James Generic, "An Abridged History of the Collective and the Store," *Wooden Shoe Books*, http://www.woodenshoebooks.com/history.html.

Page 236. "Plowshares anti-nuclear action"
"Ko-Yin and Sicken commemorated the 53rd anniversary of the atomic bombing of Hiroshima, Japan, last August 6 by using sledgehammers to symbolically disarm an active U.S. Air Force Minuteman III nuclear missile silo in northeast Colorado." "Minuteman III Plowshares Sentenced,"

Nuclearresister.org, http://nuclearresister.org/old/nr116/nr116minuteman .html.

Page 237. "outreach program"
"A day devoted to dialogue, debate and discussion of the issues that face our nation and world. . . . All events are free and open to the public." "Day of Dialogue VIII: Public Issues in a Global World," *Hofstra University Center for Civic Engagement,* October 27, 2010, http://www.hofstra.edu/Academics/Colleges/HCLAS/CCE/cce_events_dayofdialogueVIII.html.

AFTERWORD: THE RIGHT TO THINK AT ALL

Page 242. "Schwartz's has since closed"
The silver lining was that several branch managers reopened former Schwartz locations as stand-alone bookstores. See for instance Geeta Sharma Jensen, "Harry W. Schwartz Bookshops to Close," *Milwaukee Journal Sentinel,* January 19, 2009, http://www.jsonline.com/entertainment/arts/37807069.html.

APPENDIX: SHOWCASING YOUR STORE

Page 258. "Jesse Jackson is scheduled"
Neither Dukakis nor Jackson ultimately participated.

Page 261. "currently running"
We did not entirely complete the off-site workshop series at the housing project.

ACKNOWLEDGMENTS

Page 267. "'When a man writes to the world'"
John Milton, *Areopagitica* (1644).

Page 267. "a thousand manuscript pages"
Stefan Zweig, *The World of Yesterday* (Lincoln, NE: University of Nebraska Press, 1964), 320.

Page 268. "'by mending'"
Laura (Riding) Jackson, "Autobiography of the Present," *The Poems of Laura Riding* (New York: Persea Books, 1980), 173.

BIBLIOGRAPHY

PERIODICALS & WEBSITES

American Booksellers Association "ABA Sales Tax Initiative."
BookWeb. http://www.bookweb.org/advocacy/salestax.html.

American Booksellers Association. "Winter Institute." *BookWeb.*
http://www.bookweb.org/events/institute.html.

Anderson, Chris. "Objection #1." *The Long Tail: Chris Anderson's blog*,
October 10, 2004. http://longtail.typepad.com/the_long_tail/
2004/10/objection_1.html.

The Andersonville Study of Retail Economics.
http://www.andersonvillestudy.com/.

Association of American Publishers. "AAP Reports Book Sales Estimated at $23.9 Billion in 2009." *Industry Statistics 2009.* Last
modified April 7, 2010. http://www.publishers.org/main/
IndustryStats/indStats_02.htm.

Baker, John and Jim Milliot. "McGraw Hill Charges Huge Sales of
Books Aimed for Destruction." *Publishers Weekly*, June 19, 1995.

Bekken, Jon. "Feeding the Dinosaurs: Economic Concentration in the
Retail Book Industry." *Publishing Research Quarterly* (1997):
Volume 13, Number 4, 3–26.

Belkin, Lisa. "Discounter Purchases B. Dalton: Barnes & Noble Adds
779 Units To Book Realm." *New York Times*, November 27, 1986.

Berger, David and Peterson, Richard A. "Cycles in Symbol Production:
The Case of Popular Music." *American Sociological Review*, no. 40
(April 1975).

Blades, John. "Staying Alive: The Children's Bookstore on Lincoln
Avenue Has Shut Down, Possibly for Good. But Independent Book
Sellers Say They're Not an Endangered Species, Even if Superstores
Rule the Literary Seas." *The Chicago Tribune*, March 20, 1996.

Bolle, Sonja. "Chicago's Children's Bookstore: Imaginative Owners
Combine Retail and Theatrical Talents in an Award-winning Business." *Publishers Weekly*, February 26, 1988.

Cleaver, Joanne. "3 R's: Reading, 'Riting, Raising Funds." *Crain's Chicago Business*, September 11, 1995.

Cleaver, Joanne. "Expanded Kids' Museum on Learning Curve; Copes with Lagging Contributions from Public." *Crain's Chicago Business*, November 11, 1995.

Coffey, Michael and John Mutter. "Many Unhappy Returns: A Poor Holiday Season, Wholesalers Cleaning House and Cost-conscious Buyers are Haunting Distributors and Small Presses." *Publishers Weekly*, July 17, 1996.

Cox, Meg. "Risky Plot: Barnes & Noble's Boss Has Big Growth Plans That Booksellers Fear." *Wall Street Journal*, September 11, 1992.

Davis, Garrick. "Literary Reading in Dramatic Decline, According to National Endowment for the Arts Survey." *National Endowment for the Arts*, July 8, 2004.
www.nea.gov/news/news04/ReadingAtRisk.html.

Ehrenfeld, Tom. "Bookstore Owner Refuses to Grow, Pays Price: A Look at Why a Legendary, Community-Based Bookstore Failed After Years of Success." *Inc. Magazine*, October, 1996.

French, Kristen. "Barnes & Noble Flexing Publishing Muscle." *The Street*, February 16, 2002. http://www.thestreet.com/markets/kristenfrench/10009418.html.

Furman, Phyllis. "Profits, but Little Respect: Despite Stellar Rise, Barnes & Noble Exec Remains Outsider." *Crain's New York Business*, February 26, 1996.

Gallagher, Dan, "Amazon's Bezos is Anything but an Open Book; He's Made a Lucrative Career of Bewildering Investors, Consumers." *MarketWatch*, December 7, 2010. http://www.marketwatch.com/story/jeff-bezos-is-anything-but-an-open-book-2010-12-08.

Generic, James. "An Abridged History of the Collective and the Store." *Wooden Shoe Books*. http://www.woodenshoebooks.com/history.html.

Goodman, Jillian. "Indie Bookstores Rising—An Inside Look at Greenlight Book's Monthly Ledgers." *New York Magazine*, August 1, 2010.

Grau, Jeffrey, "How the Davids of the E-Commerce World Can Beat the Goliaths." *eMarketer* (blog), October 19, 2009.
http://www.emarketer.com/blog/index.php/how-the-davids-of-the-e-commerce-world-can-beat-the-goliaths/.

Hoffmann, Eli. "Barnes and Noble: It's All in the Books." *Barron's Magazine*, October 22, 2006. http://seekingalpha.com/article/18951-barnes-and-noble-it-s-all-in-the-books.

Howorth, Richard. "Independent Bookselling & *True* Market Expansion." *BookWeb*, January 1999. http://web.archive.org/web/19990822110434/http:/www.bookweb.org/news/btw/1932.html.

Independent Booksellers of New York City. http://ibnyc.wordpress.com.

Indiebound. http://www.indiebound.org/.

Jensen, Geeta Sharma. "Harry W. Schwartz Bookshops to Close." *Milwaukee Journal Sentinel*, January 19, 2009.

Jones, Chris. "The Corporate Seduction of Museums: Blockbusters Can Be the Salvation for Exhibitors, and Media Giant Clear Channel is Eager to Provide Them—for a Price." *The Chicago Tribune*, February 16, 2003.

Katie. "Sedition Books Burns." *Houston Indymedia*, February 26, 2007. http://houston.indymedia.org/news/2007/02/56533.php.

Kirkpatrick, David D. "Barnes & Noble's Jekyll and Hyde." *New York Magazine*, July 19, 1999.

Kuralt, Wallace H. "Allegations and Proposed Reform by Wallace H. Kuralt, Owner of the Famous, 40-Year Old, But Now-Failed Bookstore Chain." *Lawmall.com*, March 14, 2002. www.lawmall.com/rpa/rpa_whk1.html.

Laties, Andrew. "Showcasing Your Store: A Children's Bookseller With an In-store Theater Company Shares His Experience With Creating Lively Events That Attract Both the Public and the Media." *American Bookseller*, February/March 1988.

Malcolm, Andrew. "Chicago's Largest Bookstore Chain Is Being Turned Over to Employees." *New York Times*, June 22, 1986.

Milliot, Jim and John Mutter. "Paper Crunch Presages Higher Book Prices." *Publishers Weekly*, May 1, 1995.

"Minuteman III Plowshares Sentenced." *Nuclearresister.org*. http://nuclearresister.org/old/nr116/nr116minuteman.html.

Mutter, John. "Change: Book Standard Summit, Part 1." *Shelf Awareness*, September 26, 2005. http://www.shelf-awareness.com/issue.html?issue=58.

Mutter, John and Maureen O'Brien. "ABA Sues Five Publishers." *Publishers Weekly ABA Show Daily*, May 28, 1994.

Nieva, Richard. "State Siezes Vox Pop, but not its Spirit." *Brooklyn Ink*, October 7, 2010. http://thebrooklynink.com/2010/10/07/15254-state-seizes-vox-pop-but-not-its-spirit.

Robinson, Colin. "The Trouble With Amazon." *The Nation*, August 2, 2010.

Roeper, Richard. "Bookstore's Owners Have Way With Words." *Chicago Sun-Times*, January 18, 1996.

Rosen, Judith. "Converting Mindshare to Market Share: Survey points to ways indies can win over customers." *Publishers Weekly*, June 21, 2010.

Rosenthal, Morris. "Amazon Profit Driven By MarketPlace Sellers?" *Self-Publishing 2.0*, February 1, 2010. http://www.fonerbooks.com/2010/02/amazon-profit-driven-by-marketplace.html.

Rosenthal, Morris. "Book Sales Statistics: Amazon, Barnes & Noble and Borders Sales Numbers Annual Update." *Foner Books*, 2010. http://www.fonerbooks.com/booksale.htm.

Rubinstein, Dana. "What You're Looking For: Fort Greene Retail Survey Shows Big Needs." *Brooklyn Paper*, March 22, 2008.

Schechner, Karen. "Bluestockings: Books, Events, and Activism on New York's Lower East Side." *Bookselling This Week*, July 22, 2010. http://news.bookweb.org/ news/bluestockings-books-events-and-activism-nycs-lower-east-side.

Schwartz, Karen. "Museum Store Owner." *The Chicago Tribune*, July 11, 1999.

Schwartz, Nomi. "St. Mark's Bookshop—An Award-Winning Environment for Discriminating Readers." *BookWeb*, July 24, 2003. http://news.bookweb.org/news/st-marks-bookshop-award-winning-environment-discriminating-readers.

Scroop, Daniel. "The Anti-chain Store Movement and the Politics of Consumption." *American Quarterly* 60, no. 4 (2008): 925-949.

Seajay, Carol. "Returns: Too Much Wallpaper on a No-Growth Industry." *Feminist Bookstore News*, November/December, 1996.

Shelby, Joyce. "Plan for Independent Store Nets Prize." *New York Daily News*, January 28, 2008.

Shonwald, Josh. "After 40 Years, Seminary Co-op's Inventory continues to lure." *University of Chicago Chronicle*, October 4, 2001. http://chronicle.uchicago.edu/011004/bookstore.shtml.

Stockton-Bagnulo, Jessica. *Written Nerd* (blog). http://www.writtennerd.blogspot.com/.

Stone, Brad. "Amazon Erases Orwell Books From Kindle." *New York Times*, July 17, 2009. http://www.nytimes.com/2009/07/18/technology/companies/18amazon.html.

Trachtenberg, Jeffrey. "An Industry Gone Mad." *Wall Street Journal*, June 3, 2005.

White, Ed. "Kids Would Run the Oval Office Differently." *Associated Press*, November 7, 1988.

World War 3 Illustrated. http://www.worldwar3illustrated.org/.

Wolff, Carlo. "Drawing Attention: A Grab Bag of Graphic Novels
Embraces the Sensual, Political, Personal, and Fantastical." *Boston
Globe,* December 26, 2010. http://www.boston.com/ae/books/arti-
cles/2010/12/26/graphic_novels_that_embrace_the_sensual_politic
al_and_fantastical.

BOOKS, MUSIC, VIDEO

A Guide For Volunteer Board & Committee Members. New York: American Booksellers Association, 1985.

Alinksy, Saul. *Reveille for Radicals.* 2nd ed. New York: Vintage, 1969.

Andis, Kitrell. *Bookstore.* Indianapolis, IN: GeekSpeak Unique Press,
1996.

Attali, Jacques. *Noise.* Translated by Brian Massumi. Minneapolis, MN:
University of Minnesota Press, 1985.

Ayers, Bill. *Fugitive Days.* Boston: Beacon Press, 2001.

Bailey Jr., Herbert S. *The Art and Science of Book Publishing.* New
York: Harper & Row, 1970.

Barabási, Albert-László. *Linked: The New Science of Networks.* Cambridge, MA: Perseus, 2002.

Barnet, Richard J., and Cavanagh, John. *Global Dreams: Imperial Corporations and the New World Order.* New York, Simon & Schuster,
1994.

Birkerts, Sven. *The Gutenberg Elegies: The Fate of Reading in an Electronic Age.* Boston: Faber & Faber, 1994.

Braudel, Fernand. *The Structures of Everyday Life, Civilization & Capitalism, 15th–18th Century.* Vol. 1. New York: Harper & Row, 1981.

Braudel, Fernand. *The Wheels of Commerce: Civilization & Capitalism
15th–18th Century.* Vol. 2. New York: Harper & Row, 1982.

Brecht, Berthold. *Galileo.* New York: Grove Press, 1994.

Brent, Stuart. *Seven Stairs: An Adventure of the Heart.* New York: Simon
& Schuster, 1989.

Camus, Albert. *The Rebel: An Essay on Man in Revolt.* Translated by
Anthony Bower. New York: Alfred A. Knopf, 1956.

Caravette Productions. *The Art of Selling Children's Books.* Tarrytown,
NY: American Booksellers Association, 1992. Videocassette (VHS).

Codell, Esmé. *Educating Esmé.* Chapel Hill, NC: Algonquin Press of
Chapel Hill, 1998.

Codell, Esmé. *How to Get Your Child to Love Reading, For Ravenous
and Reluctant Readers Alike: Activities, Ideas and Inspiration for*

Exploring Everything in the World Through Books. Chapel Hill, NC: Algonquin Press, 2003.

Cody, Pat, and Fred Cody. *Cody's Books: The Life and Times of a Berkeley Bookstore, 1956 to 1977.* San Francisco: Chronicle Books, 1992.

Coser, Lewis A., Charles Kadushin, and Walter W. Powell. *Books: The Culture and Commerce of Publishing.* New York: Basic Books, 1982.

Dickinson, Emily. Edited by Thomas H. Johnson. *The Complete Poems of Emily Dickinson.* Boston: Back Bay Books, 1976.

Donkin, Ellen. *Getting into the Act: Women Playwrights in London, 1776–1829.* London: Routledge, 1995.

Emerson, Ralph Waldo. *Conduct of Life.* Boston: Houghton Mifflin, 1860.

Freire, Paolo. *Pedagogy of the Oppressed.* Translated by Ramos, Myra Bergman. New York: Seabury, 1970.

Gell-Mann, Murray. *The Quark and the Jaguar.* New York: W. H. Freeman, 1997.

Godin, Seth. *Permission Marketing: Turning Strangers into Friends and Friends into Customers.* New York: Simon & Schuster, 1999.

Haight, Anne Lyon. *Banned Books, 387 B.C. to 1978 A.D.* 4th ed., updated and Enlarged by Chandler B. Grannis. New York: Bowker, 1978.

Hale, Robert, ed. *A Manual of Bookselling,* 4th ed. New York: Harmony Books, 1987.

Harris, Daniel. *Cute, Quaint, Hungry and Romantic: The Aesthetics of Consumerism.* New York: Basic Books, 2000.

Heilbroner, Robert and Aaron Singer. *The Economic Transformation of America, 1600 to the Present.* 4th ed. Fort Worth TX: Harcourt Brace College, 1999.

Ives, Charles. *Essays Before a Sonata.* New York: Knickerbocker Press, 1920.

Kim, Amy Jo. *Community Building on the Web: Secret Strategies for Successful Online Communities.* Berkeley, CA: Peachpit Press, 2000.

Laursen, Eric, Seth Tobocman, and Jessica Wehrle. *Understanding The Crash.* New York: Soft Skull Press, 2010.

Leonard, Eliot. *Operating a Bookstore: Practical Details for Improving Profit.* Tarrytown, NY: Booksellers House, 1992.

Litowinsky, Olga. *It's a Bunny-Eat-Bunny World: A Writer's Guide to Surviving and Thriving in Today's Competitive Children's Book Market.* New York: Walker, 2001.

Marcus, Leonard S. *Ways of Telling: Conversations on the Art of the Picture Book*. New York: Penguin, 2002.

Matthews, Jack. *Collecting Rare Books for Pleasure & Profit*. Athens, OH: Ohio University Press, 1981.

Medawar, P. B. *The Uniqueness of the Individual*. London: Methuen, 1957.

Meyer, Leonard B. *Music, The Arts, and Ideas*. Chicago: University of Chicago Press, 1967.

Milton, John. *Areopagitica*. 1644.

Naisbitt, John, Nana Naisbitt, and Douglas Philips. *High Tech /High Touch*. New York: Broadway Books, 1999.

Paradise Printed & Bound: Book Arts in Northampton & Beyond. Northampton, MA: 350th Anniversary Committee, 2003.

Plotnik, Arthur. *The Elements of Editing*. New York: Macmillan, 1982.

Reiss, Alvin. *Cash In!: Funding and Promoting the Arts*. Backinprint.com, 2000.

Russell, John. *An Alternative Art*. New York: Museum of Modern Art, 1975.

Schwartz, Evan I. *Digital Darwinism*. New York: Random House, 1999.

Schwartz, Harry W. *Fifty Years in My Bookstore: Or a Life With Books*. Tarrytown, NY: Booksellers Publishing, 1991.

Schwitters, Kurt. *Pppppp: Kurt Schwitters Poems, Performance, Pieces, Proses, Plays, Poetics*. Translated by Jerome Rothenberg, and Pierre Joris. Philadelphia, PA: Temple University Press, 1994.

Scripture of the Lotus Blossom of the Fine Dharma (The Lotus Sutra). Translated from the Chinese of Kumarajiva by Leon Hurwitz. New York: Columbia University Press, 1976.

Seybold, Patricia B., with Ronnie T. Marshak. *Customers.com: How to Create a Profitable Business Strategy for the Internet and Beyond*. New York: Random House, 1998.

Silvey, Anita. *100 Best Books for Children*. Boston: Houghton Mifflin, 2004.

Silvey, Anita. Illustrated by Wendell Minor. *Henry Knox: Bookseller, Soldier, Patriot*. Boston: Houghton Mifflin, 2010.

Sinclair, Upton. *The Jungle*. 1906.

Slee, Tom. *No One Makes You Shop At Wal-Mart*. Toronto: Between The Lines, 2006.

Spolin, Viola. *Improvisation for the Theater*. Evanston, IL: Northwestern University Press, 1963.

Sutherland, Zena. *Children and Books*. 9th ed. New York: Addison Wesley Longman, 1997.

Tagore, Rabindranath. *Sadhana*. New York: Macmillan, 1913.

Tobocman, Seth. *You Don't Have To Fuck People Over To Survive*. Oakland: AK Press, 2009.

Warrior of Zen: The Diamond-hard Wisdom Mind of Suzuki Shosan. Translated by Arthur Braverman. New York: Kodansha America, 1994.

Wimsatt, William Upski. *No More Prisons*. New York: Soft Skull Press, 1999.

Winship, George Parker. *Gutenberg to Plantin: An Outline of the Early History of Printing*. Cambridge, MA: Harvard University Press, 1926.

Woolf, Virginia. *A Room of One's Own*. London: The Hogarth Press, 1929.

Zweig, Stefan. *The World of Yesterday*. Lincoln, NE: University of Nebraska Press, 1964.

INDEX

ANDREW LATIES cofounded The Children's Bookstore, Children's Bookfair Company, The Children's Museum Store, PovertyFighters, The Eric Carle Museum Bookshop, and Vox Pop. He shared the 1987 Women's National Book Association Pannell Award for bringing children and books together.

EDWARD MORROW is the cofounder and proprietor of Northshire Bookstore in Manchester Center, Vermont.

BILL AYERS is a distinguished professor at University of Illinois, founder of Small Schools Workshop and Center for Youth and Society, and author of fifteen books on teaching and children's rights.

ABOUT SEVEN STORIES PRESS

Seven Stories Press is an independent book publisher based in New York City. We publish works of the imagination by such writers as Nelson Algren, Russell Banks, Octavia E. Butler, Ani DiFranco, Assia Djebar, Ariel Dorfman, Coco Fusco, Barry Gifford, Hwang Sok-yong, Lee Stringer, and Kurt Vonnegut, to name a few, together with political titles by voices of conscience, including the Boston Women's Health Collective, Noam Chomsky, Angela Y. Davis, Human Rights Watch, Derrick Jensen, Ralph Nader, Loretta Napoleoni, Gary Null, Project Censored, Barbara Seaman, Alice Walker, Gary Webb, and Howard Zinn, among many others. Seven Stories Press believes publishers have a special responsibility to defend free speech and human rights, and to celebrate the gifts of the human imagination, wherever we can. For additional information, visit www.sevenstories.com.